TRAVELLER'S TALES

BOOK ONE

INNOCENT YOUTH TO SOBER MATURITY

Mirador Publishing,
10 Greenbrook Terrace
Taunton
Somerset
UK
TA1 1UT

To Paul and Jane
Come and travel the world with me!

Rosemary

TRAVELLER'S TALES

BOOK ONE

INNOCENT YOUTH TO SOBER MATURITY

ROSEMARY LEE

Contents

Introduction	7
Becoming a Traveller	9
The World is my Oyster!	13
Siberia and Mongolia 1977	13
Nepal – Everest Base Camp 1979	21
Ecuador – Galapagos and Upper Amazon 1980	29
Nepal – Annapurna Circuit 1983	35
Thailand 1983	43
New Zealand 1983	51
Australia 1984	57
Albania 1985	67
Syria and Jordan 1986	77
China 1986	87
Turkey 1988	97
Morocco 1989	109
North America – the West 1990	119
North America – the East 1990	135
Yemen 1992	151
North America – Yukon and Alaska 1993	175
Oman 1998	195
Peru 1999	213

Introduction

LET'S GET THIS STRAIGHT. I am not an explorer nor an adventurer. I am not a latter-day Freya Stark, who crossed the deserts of Arabia by camel in the 1930's. Nor am I a journalist, who uses the might of a TV company to launch themselves into some of the most dangerous corners of the world. I am just a holidaymaker, who enjoys visiting unusual places. I (almost always) allow a tour operator to make all my travel arrangements for me and allow local guides to take me to the places they think I should see. Any one of you could do the same.

Yet, once in these unusual destinations, I try to get away from my tour group whenever possible; to discover hidden corners, and people who can help me to understand the country I am visiting. And I keep detailed diaries to record my thoughts and impressions as I travel, so that at any time in the future I can transport myself back into the scene in a way which no amount of photographs could do. I want to share some of those images with you, using extracts from my diaries, and perhaps help you to travel with me to some amazing parts of the world.

Becoming a Traveller

AS A CHILD IN THE 1950's and 60's there were no foreign holidays, unless you count crossing the border from England to Wales, so my first forays beyond these shores came with a school exchange visit to Germany, and later a term at a German university. That was already a bit of an adventure, since a postal strike meant that I could not arrange any accommodation before I arrived. Then a devaluation of the pound meant that funds which should have financed my studies were dramatically reduced – I will not forget my emergency job cleaning in Woolworths, which included removing an entire fish wrapped in newspaper, from the public toilets.

Serious travelling started in 1975 when, as an inexperienced 21-year-old, I was employed to escort 50+ passengers at a time on European coach tours, a job which turned into a career spanning 25 years. In those early years much of the work involved 'flying by the seat of your pants': there were no satnavs to help find hotels (my first visit to Paris required a police escort through Bastille Day crowds to our hotel); there were no computers to research destinations or find useful phone numbers; there were no mobile phones to contact a driver to ask him to bring our coach to pick us up after sightseeing ... and of course, en suite facilities in hotels were still a distant dream. Yet it is from these early tours that I derive most of the stories which impress friends at parties. The tale of the suitcase which fell from the cargo nets swinging our tour's baggage ashore at Ostend (in the era before roll-on/roll-off ferries) ... the eastern passenger travelling without the correct visas, being transported across a border in the coach baggage locker ... the

Israeli family booked out by the hotel into an 'annexe' which turned out to be a brothel, who brought their complaint to me accompanied by the waving of a large knife ... arriving late at the Czechoslovak border after a coach breakdown, to find the official guide had departed, taking with her the name and address of the hotel where we were to stay ... the journey along a Yugoslav coast recently ripped apart by earthquake, to catch the only remaining (hopelessly overloaded) ferry to Italy.

In 1980 I moved to a different company offering higher quality tours, though there were still tense moments: travelling through former Yugoslavia during civil war in Kosovo meant we had to experiment with different routes to avoid the risk of kidnap ... a tour when we had to call at every fuel station along the way trying to beg a few more litres of diesel during a tanker strike ... Hungarian police who stopped us, insisting we had been speeding and demanding a fine/bribe to be paid in local currency, which we did not yet possess ... in Rome, I was faced with a passenger revolt when the Pope declared a special holiday precisely on the days when we were there, so we could visit none of the sights everyone had travelled so far to see ... and there was a tragic moment when one of my passengers died of a heart attack on board the coach. I will not forget the American lady having a panic attack, screaming that her handbag had been stolen from her room during breakfast, though she had actually been looking in the room next door ... nor the lady passengers who needed a demonstration of how to use a French toilet basin before they could relieve themselves ... nor the huge New Zealand farmer who had never left his South Island home before, who swilled Viennese 'heurige' (new) wine as if it were his customary lager beer – the only way we could get him back to the coach was to seize his waist and dance him back along the street of the wine village to the parking place.

European coach tours are far from being 'off-the-beaten-track' expeditions, but seeing the same places repeatedly at different times of year, combined with friendships developed with local guides and hotel staff, meant that I was given a unique insight into the varied lifestyles of each country ... and the chance to open the eyes of my passengers to understand the places they were seeing. Much of Western European tourism was already heavily developed, though tourism behind the Iron Curtain presented far more challenges. Crossing into East Germany (properly called the German

Democratic Republic) was a sobering experience involving strict unsmiling passport checks … mirrors on wheels pushed under the coach to check for potential refugees … hours of queues at borders. However it allowed me to finally meet an East German penfriend face to face, and then to make an annual private visit to her home, experiencing for myself the gradual relaxation of restrictions until finally the Iron Curtain was ripped open by the collapse of Communism in 1990.

My career as a tour manager established a pattern of constant work in the European summer followed by a long winter break – my travels to unusual destinations could begin.

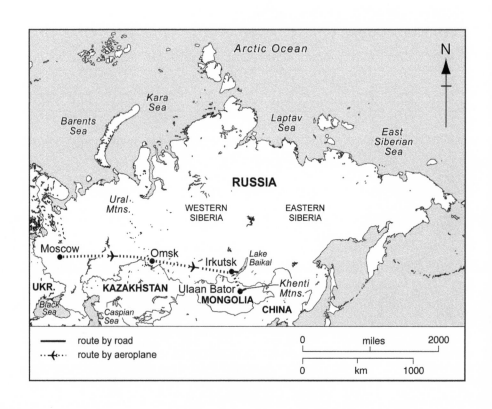

The World is my Oyster!
Siberia and Mongolia (December/ January 1977/ 78)

IN THE WINTER OF 1977, I booked on a short tour to Siberia and Mongolia, while both countries were still locked deep under Communist control. Our aim was to celebrate the New Year amid snow and ice – in fact, though there was plenty of deep snow in Moscow, it was too cold for much snow in Siberia where the temperatures ranged from -25° to -35°C.

Even the Aeroflot flight via Moscow was an experience in the 'care' of a sour-faced flight attendant who reluctantly issued plastic cutlery to eat our lunch of pickled vegetables, then officiously counted it all back in when we had finished. In Moscow, we were transferred from the international to the domestic airport (Dormodievo) where we had a glimpse of life outside the 'tourist bubble' – crowds of silent, resigned-looking Russians were being refused entry to the restaurant (while our briskly efficient British escort swept us past the officious doorman) and as for the toilet ...

"We are guided to it by the aroma emanating from the door. The cubicles are enclosed only by half-doors which can be neither shut nor locked. Once inside you mount a step and balance on the narrow rim of a porcelain basin, all the while trying both to hold the door shut and your trousers up ... meanwhile looking over the half-door at the impatient ladies waiting outside."

En route to Siberia we had a refuelling stop in the middle of the night at Omsk, supposedly just time to disembark and drink a cup of tea, but then a tannoy announced a 2-hour delay. Our escort had clearly experienced Russian delays before because she immediately organised accommodation for us in a nearby run-down barrack building – 6 hours later we returned to the airport to find other tourists had been bedded down overnight on the concrete floors. The return domestic flights were luckily not delayed, though they were notable for the standard of flying:

"We had become used to the Russian habit of going down once to find the airport before returning to cruising altitude to start the official descent, but on this flight, especially at Omsk, I think the tea-boy is flying – we go up and down, our stomachs churning, four times in all ... and when we finally reach Moscow, he waggles his wings a few times and then takes a vertical dive to the tarmac, landing so hard I expect him to lose his wheels."

Finally we reached Irkutsk, fascinated to see life-size statues by the roadside, carved exclusively from frozen snow. Our Intourist guide took us first to see two elegant 16th century churches standing side by side, both transformed into museums, though the next visit was to the town's only operational place of worship – the Church of the Revelation. The guide was keen to show us the graveyard outside, where some of the Octobrists (forerunners of the Communists who toppled the Tsar) were buried – and he was far from pleased when we showed an interest in the Orthodox service going on inside (even though it was attended only by a few elderly ladies). We were hurried away, past the few remaining original wooden houses to have survived the ravages of time and fire, to the River Angara – frozen solid and steaming so hard in the watery sunshine that we could not even see the far bank. Later in the day I had time on my own to look around shops crowded with housewives shopping on their way home from work ...

"... though to my eyes, there seems to be nothing worth buying. In one grocer's there are mounds of smoked Baikal fish, tins of sardines and vodka – nothing else."

In the middle of the day, we headed out of town through the vast forests of the taiga, stopping to visit a tiny village of traditional wooden houses with double, or even triple, walls to insulate them and preserve the heat from their wood-burning stoves. Our destination was Lake Baikal, though sadly the sunshine disappeared before we reached it and our only view of its waters was through a thick veil of heavy snowfall. The museum on its shores not only kept us warm, but plied us with information : Lake Baikal is the deepest lake in the world (up to 1620m deep, so it does not freeze in winter), fed by

500 rivers and streams but with only one exit – the River Angara ... because of this lack of exits, the inflowing water sinks straight to the bottom, rising so gradually that it remains in the lake for at least 400 years ... living in the waters are 1200 different species, up to 1000 being unique (including the Baikal seal, the only fresh-water seal in the world, and strange goggle-eyed fish which I later saw on sale in the shops of Irkutsk).

An evening visit to the local circus rounded off our visit to Siberia, a well-polished performance including a grand finale when a magician, under cover of darkness, transformed the arena into a waving field of corn. I tried to take a flash photo – bringing two ferocious female officials rushing to our section of the audience. Fortunately, I had already put away my camera and could feign innocence.

Before leaving for Mongolia, we were invited to take a ride in a traditional troika in the depths of the taiga forests – a traditional Russian winter treat, skimming over the snow in a horse-drawn sleigh, as if we were in the film Dr Zhivago:

"A van sits by the side of the forest track, blaring loud Cossack-style music while a group of men and women struggle into all the clothing they possess, before lighting a silver samovar by pushing a blazing stick inside. Distant jingling sounds from the trees herald the approach of four troikas, the horses decked with ribbons and steaming, their black coats covered with hoar frost."

I scored the fastest troika of all, my driver constantly looking behind him in delight as the others vanished from view.

The flight in Mongolian Airlines' finest aircraft (the only one with two propellers instead of one) was ... interesting! We were squashed into the plane along with huge sacks of mail which threatened to fall on to us as the plane lurched into the air. The pilot tried repeatedly to get his landing wheels up after take-off, but eventually gave up and we flew all the way with them down, struggling to gain enough height to cross the mountains. Our confidence in the plane, already weak, was dealt another blow when we discovered we could see through small holes in the floor to the ground below! However, it was an exciting flight ... flying over our troikas, then over Lake Baikal – a huge expanse of water beneath towering cliffs ... then tantalising glimpses of range upon range of mountains before descending over rolling plains dotted with settlements of yurts and their animals. Finally, we admired the wrecked planes all around the tiny airstrip which formed Mongolia's premier airport, as we taxied to a halt beside a charming oriental-style control tower, our disembarkation delayed until we had been closely inspected by a white-coated medical attendant.

Our accommodation was the best of the two hotels reserved for foreigners (imaginatively named Ulaan Bator One), where I was given a massive suite with bedroom, shower and (faulty!) WC, plus a vast salon equipped with TV and radio. Unfortunately, it was impossible to turn off the radio, and whenever I turned the volume down, the maid turned it up again. In the 1970's the Mongolian capital Ulaan Bator was a small city, but our driver and guide valiantly tried to give us our money's-worth of sightseeing, driving back and forth to make the city seem larger. We passed hospitals numbered 1-10, power stations 1-5 and housing districts 1-20 – containing basic blocks of flats built mainly by Soviet or Chinese authorities, each trying to win influence over the Mongolians. The town centre was constructed in impressive (pink) neoclassical style, while the suburbs were composed of fenced yurt settlements (packed away for nomadic wanderings in the summer) – though our guide did all he could to distract us from noticing these 'primitive' dwellings. In the city museum we were proudly shown an excellent display on the history of Mongolia, reputed to be the oldest inhabited place in the world – including a model of a mobile yurt used by Genghis Khan, and the skeleton of a 5m-tall dinosaur found in the Gobi Desert in 1924. We were unable to enter the Bogdo temple museum, though ...

"... even the outside is worth seeing with its intricate carving and elaborate paintings. Interesting too is the juxtaposition of traditional Mongolian architecture with the featureless modern blocks of flats behind – although the country is taking steps to preserve its artistic inheritance, it seems to be making no effort to continue it."

However, we were able to enter Gandan Monastery, the only working Buddhist centre left in the country after religion was officially banned as 'an oppression of the people'. It comprised a complex of oriental-style buildings within a high wall, the main temple surrounded by prayer wheels (drums with prayers written on pieces of paper pasted on to them). The temple itself seemed very small, full of old and tattered silk banners with glass-fronted cupboards full of gaudy trinkets. In the centre of the room a service was underway, one monk chanting a mantra accompanied by occasional hand claps, seemingly interrupted at times by other monks. We shuffled respectfully around them, along with a few elderly Mongolians:

"Twice during our visit, a monk takes round a large copper kettle filled with very milky tea. As he approaches, each monk fishes into the depths of his voluminous (and filthy) robe to produce a little bowl. This filled, they drink the tea, wipe the bowl on their robes and hide it away again, before resuming their chanting. Yet throughout, it seems that they are far more interested in us than in what they are doing, following our progress around the room with curious eyes."

Most fascinating of all were the people, mainly dressed in traditional silk 'del' tunics and felt boots. As a group, we were rarely left alone to try to interact with the locals – though one 'cool' American couple among us, decided that they would break away while the rest of us were sightseeing. They found a few young people desperate to wear Western-style jeans and trainers, and swapped their own clothes for Mongolian outfits and felt boots – fine whilst we were in the dry cold of Mongolia but once we returned to the wet snow of Moscow, the boots disintegrated and this couple flew home barefoot in silk dresses! In a country still unused to tourism, we were equally fascinating to the locals – at this time there were few Westerners in Mongolia, just a few businessmen. 'What is their opinion of this unusual group of visitors', we asked our guide. He responded honestly – apparently, we smell repulsively over-perfumed!

Our brief glimpse of Mongolia culminated with a drive out into the Khentei Mountains, quickly leaving behind the tarmac roads to bump along a hard-frozen dirt track. Often the bridges had collapsed so our driver (a determined and forceful man named Hatan Bator: 'Arrow Hero') simply drove down into the river bed to cross the frozen river. We stopped at a shaman cairn (called an Ovoo) – supposedly this ancient religion (pre-dating Buddhism in Mongolia) had also been wiped out by Communism, but the cairn showed every sign of still growing in size as worshippers added a stone to it each time they passed by.

By now it was New Year's Eve, so we celebrated the start of 1978 as the only guests in a modern (summer) resort hotel nestled amid the mountains, across the river from a small settlement of yurts. Next morning, I set out at dawn for a walk in the Mongolian countryside:

"It is bitterly cold: even wearing all the clothing I have (two layers of woollies, long-johns and trousers, fur coat and fur boots), I can feel the cold attacking me, seizing up my joints and freezing shut my eyes behind my iced-up glasses. At one point I wonder if I will ever manage to get back to the hotel ... but it is worthwhile for the memory of a single Mongolian horseman riding by as the sun rises to bathe the snowy hills in pink and red light."

Our coach was also frozen that morning, despite the thick padded jacket around its engine. Lighting a fire beneath it did not work, so the hotel staff summoned up some local horses to tow it away to be worked on ... perhaps a horse-drawn jump-start?

Back in Ulaan Bator, our tour finished with another circus performance – needing the services of both our guides and the redoubtable Hatan Bator to beat a path for us through the doors. Hordes of local people were trying to force their way through the ticket barrier without paying, grinning from ear to ear as they did it (clearly a local sport), and it required some rough ejection by Hatan Bator to retrieve our well-placed seats from interlopers. Once all the seats were filled, spectators continued to pile in until the aisles were packed, and even the clowns trying to dance in from the wings found their way to the central ring blocked:

"The whole of the first act is made up of performing animals – goat, wolf, badger, raccoon, bear, camel, dog, monkey ... even a giant panda. Apart from the trainer working the monkey, goat and wolf, I feel sickened by these acts because the training has clearly been cruel, and the animals patently hate performing. One bear in particular is a picture of misery and despair. Yet perhaps this is just an indication of the harshness of Mongolian life for both man and beast?"

The whole tour was only one week long, but the memory of this fascinating land remained in my thoughts until I was finally able to return 34 years later.

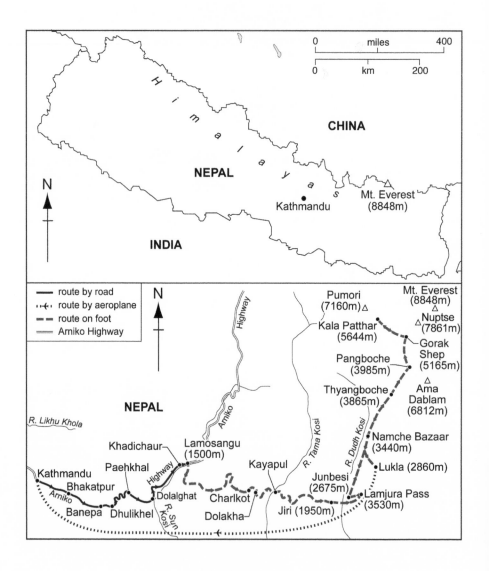

Nepal - Everest Base Camp (February/March 1979)

The trip to Mongolia convinced me that there was no reason I should not follow my travel dreams, so I dared to book a trek in Nepal, a 20-day walk to Everest Base Camp. Full of trepidation, I surveyed the rest of the group at Kathmandu airport – would they be fitness gurus or hulking muscle-bound youths? Fortunately, most were of average fitness – and in those days I was still young and energetic. The trip turned out to be one of the highlights of my life, a treasured memory even now when I can no longer contemplate such strenuous physical exercise. Even the first days in Kathmandu were an eye-opener:

"Narrow streets with no pavements; battered houses with dark openings at ground level for shops. Trolley buses, cars and vans; brilliantly coloured and decorated trucks; unbelievably gaudy bicycle-rickshaws and bicycles – all jostling and hooting their way into the very centre of the road. Crowds of people of all races and classes, walking or pedalling without concern through the melee; children playing and begging; men and women carrying heavy loads in panniers or on a head-band ... or just sitting, squatting, dreaming, washing, chatting."

Group members who had been in Kathmandu before, introduced me to the delights of 'pie shops' – dark and dingy establishments where we sampled super-sweet lemon meringue pie, lowered on a tray into the cafe from the kitchens upstairs via a hole in the ceiling since there were no stairs. The payment was returned upstairs by the same means: a fool-proof security system!

Our first days were spent touring the Kathmandu Valley, including the hilltop Monkey Temple, comprising innumerable Hindu temples, a Buddhist 'stupa' (shrine) and a new Tibetan monastery ...

"... where red-robed monks are praying and chanting from palm-leaf books in the gloom, blowing long horns and banging drums. In the lobby are burning butter-lamps (wicks floating in liquid butter) – giving off the kind of smell you think is bearable, until you find it making your eyes water and your stomach heave!"

Back in Kathmandu we visited the temple of the Living Goddess – a 5-year-old girl, looking just like any other child except for her eyes, which were heavily made up with kohl mascara. When we paid a donation to the temple, she appeared briefly at a window but vanished instantly when she spotted someone trying to take a forbidden photo. There was a special Hindu festival going on during our visit, so the town was crowded with Indian pilgrims, and it seemed that in every quiet corner there were scraggy, wild-eyed Indian mystics, gazing vacantly at the crowds.

Then the trek began, at first learning from our porters, copying their slow, steady pace up a rough stony track, with occasional scenic pauses to catch our breath and admire the view. After a while, we felt confident enough to leave behind the heavily laden porters (carrying up to 30kg each) and stride on beside groves of brilliant red rhododendrons. As the days progressed, our Sherpa guides taught us the 'Sherpa Shuffle' (bend your knees, push out your bottom, take small steps) to relieve the pressure on our knees during descents which sometimes continued for many hundreds of feet. At times the trek was just a pleasant stroll along well-trodden paths above fast-flowing mountain streams; more often it involved precipitously steep ascents or descents on rocky trails, slippery earthen slopes or occasionally high stone stairways – traversing valley after valley, crossing the rivers on bouncing, swaying suspension bridges or precarious logs. In the first few days, we sometimes crossed the route of a new road being built into the mountains – armies of men, women and children using drills to break off chunks of rock from the mountain slopes (one man even guiding the drill bit with his bare hands!), before hammering the rocks into pieces to fill wire cages designed to reinforce the soft roadsides. However, we quickly left all traces of the modern world behind us, following a walking trail from one precipitous valley to another:

"Suddenly we come to the top of a deep valley where a fabulous view opens up. Directly below us is a deep gorge; at the bottom the lusciously green Bokh Kosi River, the sides of its valley thickly forested; at the end of the gorge a ridge of high snow-capped mountains. It is like a fairy-tale route to Paradise, a reminder of the ultimate goal to which all this foot-slogging will eventually bring us."

Our route took us through hillsides inhabited by Indian-looking Tamang people, across high passes into the mountainous home of the mongoloid Sherpa people. Much of the land was terraced for growing rice or wheat (at higher altitudes the crop was barley) and most nights we camped on bare terraces not yet in production, watching shooting stars and twinkling planets in a sky unpolluted by artificial light and carpeted with stars. The nights were cool, but the days filled with burning sunshine – we quickly learned to wash both bodies and clothing in a river at lunchtime, since it was far too cold at night. There were no toilets up here in the mountains, so the first hours walking each day were punctuated by discreet stops behind trees or, above the treeline, trackside boulders.

There were few supplies available in the remote villages we passed, so our porters were carrying most of the food we needed for the trek – fine at first, but as the weeks passed the meals became more and more monotonous and the vegetables (especially the cauliflower, I remember) more and more rotten. Our ever-solicitous Sherpa guides were concerned to hear some complaints about the food, so one afternoon rushed off, after setting up camp, to buy some fresh meat. They purchased a buffalo calf and drove it back to camp, past our tents to the far end of the site to slaughter it. They were so distressed later that night, when some of our group refused to eat the meat, saying 'we can't eat it when we have seen it as a sweet little baby calf'. I was distressed too, but on behalf of our Sherpas – where did our group members think they would find fresh meat? There were no supermarkets up here in the Himalayas! And why would they slaughter the calf elsewhere and then have to carry the meat to camp … why not bring it on its own four feet? Sometimes I despair of our delicate Western ways!

Now the overnight temperatures were dropping further and we even risked a night in a local guesthouse on one especially icy night, laying our sleeping bags on the floor of a single large room – though after contracting fleas (and their incredibly itchy bites) I decided to stick with my tent in future, regardless of the temperature! We crossed Lamjura Pass, at 3500m (11,500ft) our first taste of altitude:

"The Pass goes on and on ... just as I think it must level off, it steepens again. My lungs feel bound by an iron strap, my legs are close to revolution. It's just a question of keeping going, singing (breathlessly!) songs and carols to take my mind off my aching legs, drawing in great gulps of air as the atmosphere thins. In places the path is covered in slippery old snow, in places we pass through stunted rhododendron forest, flattened by the wind. At the top, an abundance of prayer flags, tattered by constant flapping ... then we are descending again, our relieved porters now egging each other on with shouts of 'Piau! Piau!' (let's go!)."

As we climbed further into Sherpa terrain, we began to find every high point crowned with 'mani' walls (stone walls inscribed with prayers) and 'chortens' (small shrines), as well as the fluttering prayer flags of Tibetan-style Buddhism. On one steep path we met the Head Lama of Taksindu Monastery and several of his monks, plodding slowly upwards – after a pause for a chat and photos, he invited us to visit his monastery, exploring prayer halls ringed with low, carpeted benches, their walls painted with colourful dragons and buddhas. Later we also visited Thyangboche Monastery, admiring a collection of ferocious masks used for the annual festival celebrating the triumph of Buddhism over the older religion of Bon, though the main glory of this monastery was its fabulous view along the valley to Everest.

From the first days of the trek, we were drawn onwards by tantalising glimpses far ahead of snow-capped mountain ranges, and after a week the first sight of our ultimate goal – Mount Everest:

"We are following a high-level path above a rushing green river when we round a bend – suddenly ahead of us, the whole skyline is filled with sharp, jagged, snow-capped mountains. For the first time we can see their brown foothills, so for the first time they seem real, rooted in the same earth on which we are standing. There is much debate about which peak is which, but no doubt about Everest itself, tucked in behind the Nuptse Wall, dark and relatively snowless but with its characteristic cloud of spindrift blowing from the peak."

Once we passed the high-level airstrip at Lukla, numbers of tourists suddenly increased – groups of trekkers flown in to save holiday time, now gasping in the altitude-thin air without having spent the weeks acclimatising that we had enjoyed. Sadly, the increase in visitors also brought the bane of tourism: our delightfully located camping sites were littered with cans, old boots, broken bottles and packets ... and behind every large boulder the pollution of innumerable 'calls of nature'. We were following the valley of the Dudh Kosi River, which seemed to channel strong winds blowing down from the Himalayan heights ahead – strong enough to collapse our tents and hurl dirt into our faces and our food. In one place, our enterprising cooks decided that it was impossible to set up their lunch kitchen because of the wind, so they commandeered a local house instead:

"It is a typical Sherpa home – downstairs the cattle chew their cud contentedly in almost total darkness, upstairs is a single long room lined with cupboards and dressers on three walls, with benches beneath open fretwork windows on the fourth. A fire burns in a fireplace in the front wall, the smoke seeping away through a hole in the roof."

Our path brought us to Namche Bazaar, packed with traders for the weekly market and boasting well-stocked shops selling Western food and equipment donated by passing trekkers and mountaineers. From here, it was uphill all the way, plagued by headaches which are the start of altitude sickness (and by the need to pass the vast amounts of water prescribed to ward off the sickness). We reached the poverty-stricken community of Pangboche, a cluster of seasonal shack-like stone houses with wooden slat roofs, surrounded by a few barren potato fields. Here we stopped in a little tea-shop where two monks were reciting prayers for the young man who owned the cafe – he was a high-altitude Everest porter, due to return to the mountain the next week with a Yugoslav expedition, and the prayers were for his safety. A sobering sight to affect our thoughts, as the altitude was affecting our bodies. Yet as our feet grew more leaden and our lungs more constricted, our spirits soared at the sight of massive Himalayan peaks all around us – the ridge of Thamserku at 6623m, the sharp tooth of Kangtega at 6782m, and always ahead of us was Mount Everest (known in Nepal as Sagarmatha), highest in the world at 8848m (29,030ft).

Of course, we were not going to attempt to climb Everest. These days, it seems that almost anyone can reach its summit, if they can pay to be hauled up by Sherpas – an obscenity in my view, to treat such an awesome peak in this way. However, our goal was simply to climb to the top of a small hill called Kala Patthar (not so small actually – its summit is at 5644m/18,550ft) which gives a clear view across to Mount Everest. I started at 5.30am, feeling already like death:

"I am so dizzy I can hardly stand, my head throbs, my legs are weak, my lungs tight. Others pass me by, but I can go no faster. We enter the moraines, up and down from rock to rock – I can hardly move. Should I give up? But others are struggling on, so I stagger a little further to start the agonisingly steep ascent. It gets harder and harder to even put one foot in front of the other. I reach the first shoulder of Kala Patthar ... I can now think of no good reason to continue up this unimpressive hillock when I already have such a good view of Everest. I choose a rock and sit down to admire what I can see, the culmination of all these weeks of walking."

The next day we started our descent to the airstrip at Lukla – walking, running, leaping from rock to rock in celebration at the physical liberation of being able to breathe without gasping, and delight at the growing warmth of the air after the icy cold of high altitude. We flew back to Kathmandu, still dressed in clothing soiled by our exertions and wearing white 'khatas' (ceremonial scarves) – presented to us by our Sherpas in farewell. In the airport, newly arrived tourists fumbled for their cameras to catch their photo of 'genuine trekkers'. Though I did not reach quite such a height as some in my group, I still feel the glow of achievement as I remember my Everest trek.

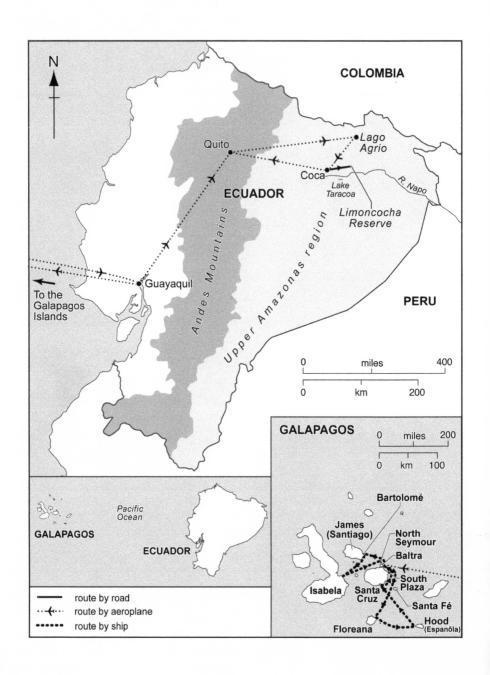

Ecuador - Galapagos and Upper Amazon (January 1980)

KNOWING THAT I HAD BEEN able to meet the challenge of Everest Base Camp inspired me, less than a year later, to realise another seemingly impossible dream – a trip to the distant Galapagos Islands and mysterious Amazon. These were places which I had seen on TV, always as scientific expeditions, but suddenly I found a tour operator offering organised trips for holidaymakers such as myself. How could I miss the opportunity? Only when I arrived in Ecuador did I realise that this was a 'tailor-made' tour and that I would be travelling alone. However, my diaries record no loneliness and lots of kindness from strangers in hotels and airports – another potential barrier to my travels removed. Travel companions are not always necessary, though they do make the journey cheaper!

After a 14-hour flight via Caracas, the first day was spent sightseeing in the steamy heat of Guayaquil on Ecuador's coast, notable not for its buildings but for its people – shoe-shine boys, lottery ticket sellers, men and boys offering car-wash in the road, a white-coated lady offering to take your blood pressure on a street corner. Everywhere I looked there was something new and unexpected to see. I was 'adopted' first by an Ecuadorian naval officer and later by a Dutch businessman, who both undertook to show me the highlights of the city. What an innocent I was in those days, happy to drink beer with strange men and even to get into their cars – but how much my day was enriched by them.

Highlight of the trip was to be a 4-day cruise around the Galapagos Islands, which I hastily extended on-board by another 3 days when I realised that it was possible to visit more islands. We had expert naturalist guides everywhere we went, and my diary is full of careful identifications of the innumerable birds and reptiles which we saw, varying greatly from island to island. We were given a detailed and forceful briefing on how to behave in this unique environment – part of which explained that we must take nothing away from nor bring anything to the islands from outside. Imagine then my distress when I opened my suitcase on board the ship, to find a huge cockroach which had hitched a ride from the hotel room in Guayaquil. I tried to kill it (an impossible task since these insects are so well armoured) and finally captured it and tipped it overboard – hopefully, the islands are not now populated by imported (seagoing) cockroaches!

The very first island (North Seymour) brought home to me just how rich in wildlife these islands are, as we stepped off the rocks where our landing craft had deposited us, on to a marked trail, to find our way blocked by a pair of gulls nesting precisely in the middle of the path. They threatened us with sharp beaks and harsh cries as we stepped carefully over them, forbidden by our guides to set foot outside the official trail, but did not leave their nest. The extended section of my cruise brought me a second time to this island and those gulls were still in place, clearly not feeling any serious threat from the visitors repeatedly stepping over them:

"We pick our way through red lava rocks and succulent cactus to within sight of the blue-footed boobies and their white fluffy chicks. Boobies are performing their ritual courtship, waving their coloured feet and pointing skywards with their long beaks – the air is filled with the honking of the females and whistling of the males as they court, interspersed with frantic shrieks as huge frigate birds swoop threateningly towards the chicks."

On another island (Hood) we met marine iguanas, the males coloured with red and green tints to show their willingness to fight over the smaller black females. They clung to the rocks as the surf broke over them, sneezing out excess salt from their nostrils. On the same island we were lucky to see the last pair of Waved Albatross to leave their breeding grounds, lumbering down the clifftop in an ungainly run, their wedge-shaped faces and bright yellow beaks extended, spreading their 8ft wings as they hurled themselves over the cliffs to soar away for another year at sea. On South Plazas Island we found rare land iguanas, much larger than their marine cousins and yellowish in colour ... and of course we were introduced to the iconic Giant Tortoises, though sadly only in the Darwin Research Centre on Santa Cruz Island, where efforts were being made to breed the different varieties for re-settlement in their original homes.

James Island brought the chance to slip into the sea to swim with fur seals in their grotto, a series of pools linked through lava tunnels where well-worn shelves provided resting places for weary seals. The tide surged through the pools, lifting me up on 4ft waves before dropping me again:

"The musky smell of wet seal pervades the grotto and even the water. One seal surfaces in front of me and sneezes in my face, but they are not really interested in us since we are not agile enough to play with them. Instead they chase each other, leaping and performing backward somersaults, hanging with tail up, touching tail to nose. There is a constant hubbub of hoarse growling and barking, accompanied by threatening eye-rolling as seals try to drive others from the best snoozing spots."

Later, on Bartolome Island, I took a swim with tiny Galapagos penguins in the cold waters of the Humboldt Current, coming all the way from Antarctica, whilst in the much warmer seas on the other side of the island, there were sharks and stingrays – I did not swim there!

The islands themselves, as well as their wildlife, varied considerably in appearance. Floreana was covered in quite luxuriant vegetation (by Galapagos standards) with many different succulents growing as tall as trees, and mangroves beside the shore. Here we walked through dense undergrowth to a lagoon of thick, muddy water exuding a sulphuric smell, home to flocks of flamingoes. Bartolome Island was one of the most recently formed (created 100,000 years ago by volcanic eruption – as were all the islands) and was one of the driest too, so few plants had yet colonised it:

"We land on rough lava rock and walk off over volcanic ash and grit. Only a few wide-spread and long-rooted plants have managed to establish themselves, mainly cactus and grasses, so much of the land is still exposed and shows clearly the lava tunnels and lava 'bombs' (very light and porous rocks thrown from the volcano). We climb into two craters, full of huge pieces of clinker, then plod uphill through thick ash for a spectacular view."

No-one was allowed to stay on the islands overnight, so we had to return to our small (70-berth) cruise ship each evening, but it was not the end of the wildlife spectaculars. One night we were treated to a display of aquatic skill as sealions hunted flying fish by the light of the ship's floodlights:

"They lie in wait in the shadow of the ship, moving silently into pursuit as a flying fish cruises by, gleaming silver in the light. The fish spies danger, beginning to skip at incredible speed over the water with the sealion hot on its heels, swimming underwater with powerful strokes of its front flippers, surfacing for air every 50 yards with a sudden splash. Often the sealion is the victor, snatching a fish with a mighty shake which sends its 'wings' spinning away as the body is gulped down."

The second part of my tour involved a complex journey. Originally, I should have flown from the Galapagos to Quito via Guayaquil, but delays in departure meant that I could not reach Quito before darkness fell. At the time, it was forbidden to fly into Quito after nightfall since the airport was not only threatened by nearby mountains but also by a massive hilltop statue of Christ Redeemer which semi-obstructed the runway approach. So I had another night in Guayaquil, before flying to Quito to catch a 30-seater DC3 prop plane to the oil centre of Lago Agrio, then a 10-seater light plane into the Amazon jungle at Coca, landing on a grassy strip near a river. A pick-up truck bounced me down a rocky track to the riverside, to board a canoe (laden with supplies including someone's new sink unit) with an outboard motor to transport me onwards for an hour to my floating hotel. The intention was to cruise some of the Amazonian headwaters on this Flotel, but some weeks earlier it had run aground so was now used only as accommodation, with sightseeing accomplished by dug-out canoes.

Once again the Flotel's few guests were accompanied by naturalist guides as we were taken on jungle walks, introduced to the huge variety of plant life and trees and the equally huge variety of insects, including a tarantula spider which chose to shelter from a rain shower under the plastic cape of one of my fellow guests. We visited a missionary station at Limoncocha and the stilt houses at Primavera Ranch where we were shown some of the more elusive wildlife like sloth and spider monkey (both caged and unhappy), boa constrictors and anaconda. Most memorable was the walk through the rainforest to Lake Taracoa to board a semi-rotten dug-out canoe tied together for support to another canoe (patched with a piece of corrugated iron) to be paddled out into the lake by 2 young boys for a session of fishing for piranha. As we turned for home ...

"... thunder begins to roll across the sky and heavy rain to fall. We move across the lake, swathed in plastic sheets, helping the boys by paddling ourselves and baling out the leaky canoe with a rusty can. This is a real Amazonian adventure!"

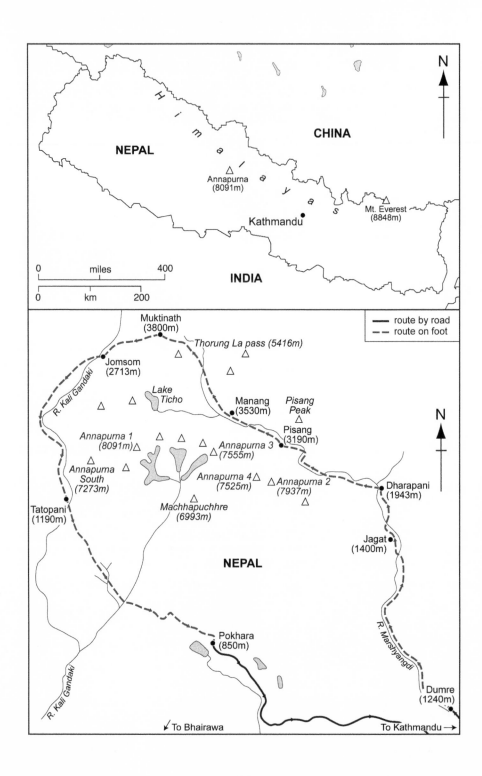

Nepal - Annapurna Circuit (March/ April 1983)

SPRING 1983 SAW ME RETURNING to Nepal for another 3-week trek in the Himalayas, this time a circular trip around the Annapurna Massif. Maybe I was more worldly-wise by now, or perhaps Nepal was busier with tourists, but this time I experienced none of the wide-eyed wonder which characterised the start of my last visit. The exotic sights of Kathmandu were crowded with tour groups and the start of our trek was spoiled by begging children, some begging so hard that they were literally hanging from my arms as I walked – well-meaning tourists had taught them to expect and then to angrily demand 'mitai' (sweets) or 'pin' (pens). Fortunately, within a few days we were out of range of the day-trekkers and the children became a delight, often visiting our camps to chat or learn a few words of English.

Rural Nepal itself seemed to have changed dramatically since my last visit, too, with many signs of development. The paths we followed into the mountains were mostly well-made and sometimes paved with stone; the hillsides often cut into rock or stone stairways; precarious river crossings on logs replaced with modern (monsoon-proof) suspension bridges. The villages usually had a communal tap, instead of having to fetch water from the rivers, and some even had local hydro-power plants providing minimal electric power – at night, some villagers' homes were lit by weak lightbulbs instead of candles. As we walked, we often encountered porters carrying (on their backs) building materials for construction projects higher in the mountains – bamboo poles, lengths of piping, rolls of steel cable, sheets of corrugated iron. The villages along our route also offered frequent simple 'hotels' for tourists, and every possible resting point boasted a tea-house selling Western snacks along with milky Nepalese tea. Tourism was clearly booming and providing funds for the development of the community, as it should. How tragic that the years to come led Nepal into civil war, a royal massacre and then the disastrous earthquake of 2015, all cutting the flow of tourist dollars.

Sadly, there was still desperate need in the villages we visited. Amongst my fellow trekkers was a British doctor, carrying a few essential drugs in case they were needed by us en route, and often villagers came to our camps to ask him for help. One little boy was brought to him after being bitten by a dog several weeks before. The nearest clinic was too far away, so the child had not received any treatment and his leg was seriously infected. I will never forget the look of anguish on our doctor's face as he realised that he had no antibiotics suitable for a child, so could not help. This child was destined to die … from a dog bite.

We started our journey by taking a local bus, westwards on a road which had to be considered a tremendous feat of engineering, achieved by Indian workmen through the difficult terrain of the Himalayan foothills:

"The bus is piled high with our possessions – wicker baskets and stools at the front, our kitbags perched precariously at the back. Inside, we are jammed into narrow seats designed for small Nepalis: we take the front seats while our porters and Sherpa guides are so tightly packed in the back that they can fall asleep and remain upright. By the back door is the conductor with a whistle which he blows to say when his door is closed, and also blows repeatedly to encourage the driver to advance in narrow squeezes – the bus has no wing mirrors! The road is potholed, especially on the sharp bends which send our wheels to the very lip of deep roadside ditches. Children struggle to control cows or goats grazing on the verges, usually in vain – one little girl bursts into tears when she loses sight of the precious cow in her care."

We left the bus at Dumre to start our trek along a dusty dirt road through paddy fields. Occasional open pick-up trucks and closed lorries still bounced past us, laden with passengers instead of goods, though I was glad to be walking instead of riding – especially when I spotted a few anguished European faces jammed inside among crowds of locals.

Gradually we settled into a trekking routine again ... up at dawn to pack our belongings ... eating breakfast while our Sherpas packed the tents and distributed loads to the porters ... striding or strolling off at our own pace, supervised by our Sherpa guides only when there were junctions or especially difficult sections in the path ... hot lunch and a pause for washing in the middle of the day (difficult whenever there was a village nearby – the children arrived almost instantly and all hope of modesty vanished) ... drinking tea in camp while waiting for the porters to arrive (our fast-walking cooks always managed to be last to leave each campsite and first to arrive at the next) ... assisting the Sherpas with putting up tents. Most nights we retired to bed after dinner, but sometimes we found some entertainment:

"As we wait for dinner, we are entertained by an old man playing a 'saronghi' (a simple fiddle) and singing, or rather wailing, a special song about climbing Mount Everest. After dinner we pick our way over a long and very bouncy suspension bridge and up a steep, dusty path to the village above. The houses are lit by a single candle, shadowy figures squat on the floors, talking in the gloom. We sample a glass of 'rakshi' spirit (which tastes like smoke-flavoured water), effective in lubricating a sing-song – including a rendering of Alouette taught to a little village boy by French trekkers."

Our route showed a much more varied picture of Nepalese cultures than the Everest trek, passing through areas settled by many different tribal groups. We began amongst the lowland Pahari people with their sarongs and jewellery-pierced noses, growing rice and wheat, living in simple thatched homes of wood and straw, but soon we climbed into the Himalayan foothills where the Gurung people lived. The climate was more extreme here so the housing was noticeably more solid – two-storey stone buildings, where the livestock could live safely downstairs whilst the family climbed a ladder to the upper rooms. Later we met the Thakali people, a neat, well-organised group with solid, whitewashed stone houses and water-pipes bringing clean water from higher in the mountains to taps and washbasins throughout the village. As we walked higher, the rice paddies were replaced by terraced fields of barley, and we encountered strings of mules carrying the trade goods which were a major source of income to these people:

"At one spot our descent into the valley is delayed as 110 mules and ponies jostle past at high speed with plumes waving on their heads and bells clonking around their necks. It is not wise to dispute the path with a mule, we

learn, since he will either squash you into the rocks or knock you into the abyss, if you are foolish enough to stand on the outer side of the path."

After 4 days we reached the region of the Manangi people, where the predominant faith was Tibetan Buddhism instead of Hinduism. The villages here showed evidence of considerable wealth (from trading) with well-built stone houses, often clinging to steep hillsides, one above the other in a complex communal structure. Village streets were usually paved in stone with central gutters to clear excess water. We were walking towards the Tibetan border, closed to us but still open for local people – we encountered several groups of Tibetan traders and the influence of Tibetan lifestyle was evident all around us:

"The sound of drums draws us into a house temporarily transformed into a 'gompa' (temple), to find a group of monks brought here from Tibet to chant prayers in memorial to people from this village who died in a bus crash a month ago. The drums accompany the prayers, with the noise rising to a crescendo at the end of each prayer in a cacophony of blaring human-bone trumpets, crashing cymbals and the weird wailing of a conch shell."

The insight into different lifestyles was interesting, but what drew me to the trek was the chance to walk again in fantastic mountain scenery – and I was not disappointed. Ascending along the Marshyangdi Valley led us into narrow gorges on paths cut into sheer rock cliffs, beneath cascading waterfalls, and through dense forests of fragrant pine or red-flowering rhododendron studded with vivid white magnolia blossoms. After a week of walking, we were rewarded by our first sight of Annapurna's peaks – the highest is 8000m (26,000ft) but there are also 29 other peaks on the Massif which are over 6000m high:

"We are fascinated by a windswept peak with a huge trail of spindrift, which gradually reveals itself as Annapurna IV as we walk onwards. It looms up massively from our path with a perfectly proportioned hollow to one side, where a glacier nestles, its ice melting into a stream which flows out to meet the Marshyangdi River far below us."

Annapurna is infamous for unstable snow which often results in avalanche, and we frequently heard the roar of slipping snow echoing off the sides of the valley as we walked – one tremendous avalanche was loud enough to wake us in camp one morning.

Now our goal was the Thorung La Pass, at 5400m (17,700ft) the highest altitude I have ever reached on foot. Our group of trekkers was nervous as we approached the pass – though not nearly as tense as our Sherpa guides who had the responsibility of keeping our whole group of tourists and porters safe. Many of the porters were dressed only for the lower altitudes where they lived – they were officially issued with training shoes, socks and snow-goggles, but many had only a thin shirt and shorts to wear, so we raided our packs for spare jumpers and waterproof trousers as a loan or gift to help them through. Even so, we had to stop at intervals on the ascent to assist them over a particularly icy rock or snowy path, especially since many were used only to barefoot walking and became clumsy in their unaccustomed footwear. In one day, we ascended 750m to an overnight 'high camp', pitching our tents amid the whirling flakes of a snowstorm, and next day continued nearly 1200m (4000ft) more to the summit of the Pass. We started in the dark, with our boots half-frozen, walking in a strict crocodile at the pace of the slowest, following the lead of our Sherpa guides along an indistinguishable path amid a jumble of peaks and cols – I cannot imagine how anyone first discovered this Pass!

"For hours we trudge up and down gravelly or rocky slopes, yet the Pass comes no nearer. On some slopes we have to kick steps in the snow, on others the ascent is only a slow plod. The altitude increases ... the walking gets harder ... I am developing symptoms of altitude sickness – headache, nausea and faintness. The whole walk has become an unending trudge. All I can see is the ground beneath my feet and my only thought is to keep those feet moving. In a blurred haze I reach the summit but can admire no view – all I see is a stone cairn, all I feel is a biting wind. I do not even bother with a triumphant photo, but just stumble off down the rocky scree slope to a lower altitude."

I think I was probably at my physical limit at this point, but unlike the Everest trek where I could choose to turn back, there was no choice but to continue – failing to cross this Pass meant that I would miss the second part of the trek.

The far side of the Pass was a complete contrast to the forested landscape we had enjoyed beforehand. The pilgrimage village of Muktinath lay in the rain-shadow of the Massif and was surrounded by barren, arid, brown hills, heavily eroded by the constant strong winds which blew down the Kali Gandaki Valley. We visited the pilgrimage site before continuing our trek – a tiny natural-gas flame which burned in the centre of a running stream. It seemed a very minor miracle to us, yet pilgrims travelled here in their thousands – throughout the last week of our trek, we passed many Nepalis and Indians making their way to the shrine, joined by increasing numbers of Western hikers. Again, the village streets were lined with trekking 'hotels', teashops and even rickety wooden structures housing rudimentary long-drop toilets. In the village of Tatapani came the unexpected luxury of a hot bath, sitting beside the muddy, ice-cold river at a point where bright red, steaming hot water was trickling from a sulphuric-smelling spring – conveniently spaced rocks allowed pools to form where the hot and cold water could mix into a pleasant temperature for washing.

Finally we returned to 'civilisation' at the town of Pokhara, making our last camp beside its tranquil lake – though here, for the first time, our Sherpas insisted on setting a guard on our tents: does 'civilisation' always have to mean that the honesty and hospitality of the mountains has been lost?

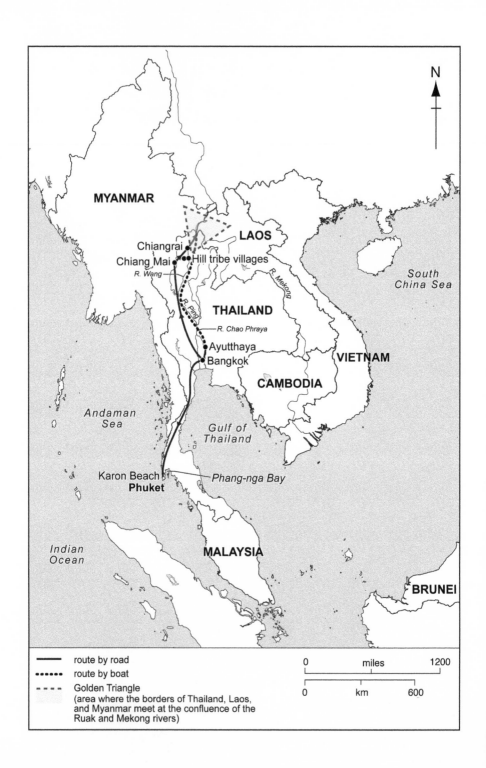

N

MYANMAR

Chiangrai
Chiang Mai
R. Wang
Hill tribe villages

LAOS

R. Ping

R. Mekong

THAILAND

R. Chao Phraya

Ayutthaya
Bangkok

South
China Sea

VIETNAM

CAMBODIA

Andaman
Sea

Gulf of
Thailand

Karon Beach
Phuket

Phang-nga Bay

Indian
Ocean

MALAYSIA

BRUNEI

route by road
route by boat
Golden Triangle
(area where the borders of Thailand, Laos,
and Myanmar meet at the confluence of the
Ruak and Mekong rivers)

0   miles   1200

0   km   600

Thailand (October/ November 1983)

BOOKING FOR A TOUR MANAGER'S congress in Thailand gave me the idea to extend this short trip into a marathon 3-month adventure, starting with a tour which offered a trek into the northern hills of Thailand, though first we were shown the glories of Bangkok. Most imposing was the compound of the Grand Palace, a cluster of buildings in myriad different styles, all restored a few years before my visit so that they sparkled with gold leaf and mosaics of glass and porcelain. At its heart was Thailand's holiest Buddhist shrine, housing the Emerald Buddha – actually made of semi-precious jasper, but dressed in one of three solid gold costumes (varied for the hot season, wet season and cool season) changed at the start of each new season by the king himself. Seeing the statue wearing an off-the-shoulder robe confirmed to me that we were visiting in the wet season (though it needed little confirmation):

"I am treated to a display of monsoon climate. Since arrival, the air has been hot and oppressive, and so steamy that I almost feel I could wring moisture from it. Now the heavy black clouds build up until they explode in a torrential downpour which slows the traffic and pours from the roofs in a series of spouts reminiscent of a Hindu water temple."

The Thai people were devoutly Buddhist, yet had nevertheless not lost their respect for animist spirits: I was fascinated to see that every time a spirit was displaced from its home by the building of a new property, it was provided with an ornate 'spirit house' – like an exotic doll's house perched on a platform outside many of the new buildings in the city.

Many of the citizens of Bangkok lived beside or even on the water, their homes regularly flooded by monsoon-filled rivers. Since many Thais seemed to have few possessions, they simply piled their belongings on to tables and benches in their stilt homes as the floods arrived (every November and December) and waited for the water to subside. Until the 1930s there were few roads in Thailand and transport was only by boat, so to explore the most traditional parts of the city we piled into brightly painted, elegantly slim canoes powered by outboard motors with long propeller shafts – appropriately named 'long-tail boats':

"We pack ourselves in, raise the plastic sheeting along the sides ... and we're off! It feels like being in an open-topped racing car in a rainstorm, with the scenery hurtling past us. The boat reverberates with the vibration of the motor and clouds of spray fly up and over us. The best position is certainly the prow, raised up above the water level as if straining to take flight."

Our ride took us past waterside villages to a floating market (filled with local people and their produce, unlike the touristy Damnoen Saduak market I visited later), where tiny boats jostled against each other, laden with freshly picked fruit and vegetables.

For our last evening in Bangkok, we ate in one of the strangest restaurants I have ever visited – the Seafood Paradise. At first sight it was simply a well-stocked supermarket with mountains of familiar and unfamiliar fruits and vegetables alongside displays of fish with weird names like Bubble Fish and Red Snapper. We collected the raw ingredients for our dinner from the shelves, paid for them (as if in a supermarket), then sat down with our purchases to consult a menu explaining how the food could be cooked – paying the waiter for the cooking process. As we headed home after the meal, it seemed as if the city had been transformed:

"The familiar petrol station near our hotel has been taken over by a large street restaurant where young girls are washing up in large bowls beside the pumps, while customers select their food from brightly lit stalls of fish and vegetables on the forecourt. The 'girlie' bars and massage parlours are also now well-lit and bustling with activity, with attractive Thai girls at the entrances inviting customers to enter. Everywhere people are walking and talking, squatting in groups to chat or play cards, or just to enjoy the balmy evening air."

Next day we boarded a packed public Express coach to drive to the northern city of Chiang Mai, on roads which clearly demonstrated Thailand's ongoing battle with water:

"There are floods everywhere: blocking the road, flooding whole villages. In some places, irrigation channels have become roaring torrents of muddy water, threatening to engulf the road, which now lies just a few inches above the water. Many houses sit marooned amid the floodwaters, yet still the housewives are hanging their washing out to dry on their verandahs. Farmers are wading into their fields, up to their chests in water, sickles in hand as they try to rescue some of the harvest, hanging it on wires across the fields to dry in the sun, threshing their grain in the middle of the road – the only dry place available."

Once in the city, there were more gaudy shrines to visit including the great temple of Doi Suthep, perched at the summit of a steep hill amid thick green forest. Our taxi took us as far as possible, the driver struggling between 1st and 2nd gears, but the last stage was on foot – up the 290 steps of a massive staircase, rising into the clouds where a huge gold-tiled 'chedi' (a shrine containing one of Buddha's bones) loomed from the mist. Chiang Mai was renowned for its skilled craftsmen so sightseeing also took us to workshops producing traditional handicrafts (including woodcarving, lacquerware and silk farming), which I found interesting ... but my thoughts were already focused on our forthcoming 5-day trek.

We set out first along a dirt road with our kitbags in an ox-cart, then turned on to a narrow track (our baggage transferred to the backs of porters) through dense bamboo forest with the path ahead of us mottled with bright red spots spat out by betel-nut chewers. We were often walking through heavy rain showers, wading through fast-flowing streams or scrambling up and down muddy slopes:

"The last fall of rain has made the paths difficult, especially wearing gym shoes (necessary footwear for river crossings). I slither down the steep slopes, hunting for roots in which to wedge my toes, or branches to grasp as I slide by. Once down, we always have to scramble up the next slope, still hunting for grip – as if the ascents are not difficult enough anyway! My trousers are coated with mud from many falls but slowly the path dries out and I can enjoy the beautiful flowers and butterflies dancing in the returning sunshine."

The trek itself was difficult, plagued by mosquitoes and leeches, but the places we visited were fascinating. Every night we stayed in remote villages with different tribes: Lahu, Akha, Red Karen – each with their own customs and costumes. The houses were made of wood and bamboo, raised up on stilts to discourage insects and other livestock from taking up residence (though we often found lizards, beetles and once even a scorpion under our sleeping bags in the morning). The village streets were crowded with children, amusing themselves through the day under the supervision of one or two elderly relatives whilst their parents were working out in the fields. Domestic animals, mainly chickens and pigs, wandered freely between the houses:

"We are made welcome, our visit seen as a status symbol, indicating that the house is good enough for guests. We lay our sleeping bags on the floor of split bamboo covered by woven mats of bamboo leaf; a cooking alcove contains a sandpit on which to lay the fire; heads of corn are drying under the roof. Through the night we hear the squealing of pigs below us, then just before dawn we are woken by cockerels and the sound of women beginning to pound the day's rice."

Most of the tribes were Christian, converted by missionaries who were still amongst the most respected members of the local community, running schools and health clinics as well as simple churches. One lunchtime, however, was spent in a village of the pagan Akha tribe, who lived in terror of spirits in the world around them, building their villages as far from running water as possible to escape the water gods. As a consequence, they found it difficult to stay clean – water carried up from the nearest river was so precious that it was only used for cooking and drinking. Their houses bore carved decorations designed to ward off spirits, and the village entrance was marked by a 'spirit gate' which no demon could pass – we were warned not to touch any part of it, since the penalty was death (our guide told us that even children who unwittingly touched it whilst playing, were put to death). The women wore an ornate headdress hung with silver coins, never removed since it represented a woman's personal wealth and status – female babies wore a cap with just one coin sewn on to it.

Most exciting was an overnight spent in a village belonging to the Chinese KMT group, exiled many years before by the Communist Chinese government and now operating as warlords in these remote jungles, financed by the opium trade (our guide had already paid a fee to be allowed to pass through their region). We were supposed to be reaching a well-organised Lahu village for the night, but our guide had misjudged the distance we would be able to travel in one day:

"We stumble on wearily through the thick undergrowth, following a newly-cleared path with relief until we discover that it leads only to recently planted opium fields. Nervously we struggle back up the side of the ridge again, realising that even our knowledgeable local guide Su-Pot is not sure where we are. There are no maps of this area, and no-one travels here except from village to fields. No wonder the Thai authorities cannot find and eliminate the opium trade."

As night approached, we were told to wait in a forest clearing whilst Su-Pot went down to the KMT village to ask permission to overnight there, granted only after lengthy negotiations. We were accommodated on rickety bamboo beds in a dark, windowless shed, whilst outside the muddy village street swarmed with curious children. Su-Pot told us that this village was a 'breeding station' for the KMT army, sending children to a huge Chinese-language school in nearby Chiangrai town, then on to a military base for training as guards for the opium convoys. Westerners were not usually allowed to see this place, so I felt lucky to have experienced it.

We emerged safely from the forests at the end of our trek, enjoying the facilities of a modern hotel in Chiangrai to return to Western standards of cleanliness. We also visited a Thai massage parlour, normally frequented by men who use the massage as a prelude to further (sexual) activities. The young men in our group certainly did have to pay for 'extras' after their massage session, but the ladies among us were given a thorough scrubbing in a bath followed by kneading, pummelling ... and bone-breaking, muscle-stretching wrestling manoeuvres.

Relaxed and refreshed, we moved on towards the infamous Golden Triangle, where opium once changed hands for vast sums of gold – now it was a major tourist site, and the nearby roadside villages of hill tribes had been transformed into miserable 'photo opportunities' for mainstream tourism. How privileged I felt to have been a guest of tribes who still lived in their traditional way, instead of being exploited in this human zoo.

My trip to Thailand was not over, though for me the highlight had passed.

We continued southwards again by river on converted rice-barges, watching the flooded landscape and floating debris drift by, calling at muddy villages and market towns along the way, passing through increasingly violent rainstorms.

We disembarked at the ancient Thai capital Ayutthaya, sacked and destroyed in the 18th century by the Burmese, who chopped off the heads of Buddha statues to retrieve the gold (the devout Thai people had still not forgiven the Burmese for this sacrilege). We climbed the precariously dilapidated steps of the highest 'stupa' (shrine) to gaze across a vast expanse of neatly preserved brick ruins – only one building seemed to have been restored, and inside it a massive bronze Buddha was being re-lacquered in preparation for re-gilding.

Back in Bangkok, there was just time to visit Dusit Zoo to see the royal white elephants:

"They are passing the time dancing quietly to themselves, swinging their trunks and moving from one foot to another, wearing beatific expressions which belie the sign 'Beware of elephant throwing stones!' hanging from their enclosure."

In Bangkok I left the tour group to take an overnight bus to the far south of the country, arriving in the depressing bus station at Phuket, fortunate to escape quickly as I accepted the offer (from one of a crowd of people touting their facilities) of a half-price stay in a newly-built bungalow development at Karon Beach – with transport included:

"Over a mile of white sand, backed by coconut palms and occupied only by 3 or 4 visitors. The sea is pale turquoise, warm and not too salty; the shore lined with sand dunes held together by fronds of mauve convolvulus, which enclose a tranquil lagoon. Thatched, lattice-walled huts nestle among the trees behind, the only signs of tourism except for my white and green bungalow. This has to be paradise!"

Two days of relaxation awaited me here, including a full day spent cruising in a long-tailed boat around the amazingly precipitous islands of Pang Nga Bay – stars of films ranging from 'The Beach' to James Bond's 'Man with a Golden Gun':

"The sea constantly wears at the limestone islands so that many are mushroom-shaped or protrude over the sea at water-level. We squeeze

through White Grotto, a gap worn right through the rock, to emerge behind a fringe of stalactites. Ahead of us lies Elephant Island, like a great squatting beast, its trunk crumpled before it. Beyond spreads a shining silver sea, dotted with a jumble of islands which fill the horizon."

Refreshed, I returned to Bangkok to join the tour manager's congress – a complete contrast with accommodation in a luxury 5-star hotel, where drinks were served from the bar by a waitress approaching me on her knees! We were feted by the Thai government with banquets and excursions, ushered through the city traffic by a police escort. Yet my heart remained in the simplicity of the hilltribe villages – this type of luxury tourism is not for me.

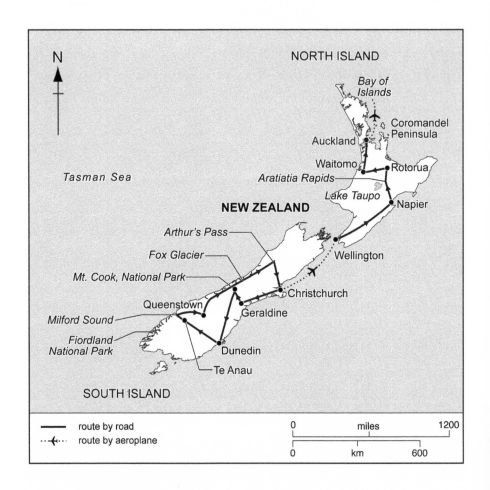

New Zealand (November/ December 1983)

THE NEXT STAGE OF MY 3-month expedition took me to New Zealand, touring first South Island which seemed to me as tranquil as post-war Britain. In Christchurch I was warmly greeted by local people able to recognise that I was a stranger in town … in Geraldine I was the only customer in a large provision store. Everywhere the traffic was light, often composed of cars preserved from the 1950's. Outside the towns, I was struck by the vast numbers of sheep intensively grazing each meadow, and the fact that sheep were given the best pasture (unlike Britain where cattle eat the best grass in the valleys, while sheep wander freely across the hillsides). In uncultivated corners the land was full of wildflowers, especially huge beds of blue, pink or pale-yellow lupins.

Heading southwards we turned into the mountainous heart of the island, taking off for a sightseeing flight over Mount Cook's glaciers:

"At first we see only a mess of dust and rubble pierced by a few lurid green sink holes through to rivers flowing under the ice. Then the rubble clears and below us is a huge, cracked pavement of ice, whitish and gleaming. It turns to pure white as we reach the snow level, dazzling us with its glare. The sides of the valley reveal ridges of bare rock, broken by tumbling icefalls of translucent green and white."

We even landed briefly, though we had not expected this and so were not suitably dressed for a short walk in the powdery snow, in sandals! The southernmost point of our tour was the city of Dunedin, a solid and settled-looking community with houses of stone or brick, unlike the many communities of wooden bungalows we had been seeing elsewhere.

Excitement in the coach rose as we now headed west into Fiordland National Park to visit Milford Sound, following an unsealed dusty road along valleys which soon turned to ravines, between mountain sides which soon turned to precipitous cliffs of barren rock striped with ice-blue glaciers. Suddenly our road reached a dead end, faced by a wall of grey rock – from here we had to continue through the single track 1km-long Homer Tunnel. Private cars were obliged to follow a rota system, half hourly rotation between downward and upward traffic, but our coach was allowed to enter as soon as we arrived, trusting to infrequent passing places in the tunnel to avoid oncoming traffic. Finally we reached the Sound, a flooded valley gouged out by glaciers and filled by the sea. The vertical rock walls acted as a funnel for wind, sometimes magnifying it into a gale which whipped the water into waves, sometimes so still that the water was smooth as a mirror. For our cruise, the water was ruffled but not rough, taking us underneath cascading waterfalls through sheets of spray blown from the cliffs, and past fur seals resting peacefully on rock ledges. The edge of the fjord was covered with boggy grass and moss, dotted with cabbage palms ... but infested with small, biting, black flies which tangled themselves in my hair. Not the best memory of an amazing part of the world!

Near Milford Sound, in Te Anau, we made our first visit to New Zealand's famous glow-worm caves, riding non-motorised punts along the underground river:

"Our guide orders us to silence, then pulls us along the sparsely illuminated tunnel, hand over hand along the ropes. He stops, the lights are doused, the silence intense ... but we are not in utter darkness. The ceilings and walls are spattered with bluish green lights like stars on a moonless night. Glow-worms! Their lights are steady, switching on and off with precision. Our guide turns on a torch to show us inch-long silk threads, sticky traps to which sandflies or mosquitoes, washed into the cave as larvae, are drawn to their deaths by the lights."

Later we visited the more famous and larger Waitomo Caves on North Island, but the magic of my first sight of glow-worms in this cave has left a more lasting impression.

We continued to the higgledy-piggledy community of Queenstown, proudly declaring itself the 'adventure capital of the world'. Our guide presented us with a menu of possible experiences – would I like to go bungy-jumping? Or white-water rafting? I took the tamest option, a jet-boat ride on the fast-flowing Shotover River between cliffs hundreds of feet high:

"Our driver Tim puts the boat into a wide turn to hurl up the first spray, before zooming off into the narrow gorge under the bridge, bouncing harder and harder on the rapids, seemingly on a collision course with the rocks. We swerve clear at the last moment, then Tim yells at us to 'Hang on' before throwing the boat into a 540° turn. When the screaming stops and we have untangled our legs and arms, we are told about the world record achieved here for driving a jet boat up on to dry land, travelling 75ft inland with the boat broken in half and the driver unconscious."

It crossed my mind that New Zealanders have a death-wish!

On alongside the Tasman Sea to the western side of the Mt Cook National Park, this time to see the fast-retreating Fox Glacier. Our coach bumped past the original terminal moraines to the end of the rough track, at the level where the glacier reached in the 1930's, but we were still not in sight of today's glacier. Only when our driver took the coach down into the stony river bed, continuing around a bend in the valley, did we finally see the glacier. The next morning I was blessed with the first clear, sunny day of the trip so far (does it always rain so much in New Zealand?) for a helicopter trip to land on the Fox Glacier, this time properly equipped with rented hobnail boots and a strong spiked stick. Our guide cut steps into the ice for us to walk more safely and even helped us to stride across a crevasse to a point from which we could look out over the entire glacier:

"... a jumbled mass of pinnacles and crevasses, an ice archway dripping its life away in the warm sunshine. Some of the ice is dirtied by dust blown up from the valley, but most is crystalline white or aquamarine blue, so dazzling in the sun that I find it hard to look at it."

The beauty of this area is one of the abiding memories of my time in New Zealand, not just the glacier itself but the thick rainforests which now filled the valley where the glacier once flowed. I took a walk along a bush trail:

"The path is overhung with foliage, cool and peaceful in a golden green light. Bellbirds flute their rich liquid call, other birds whistle and chatter. The trees and rocks are muffled in moss; streamers of lichen and creeper

cling to the branches; dead tree-fern fronds hang down to shroud their parent trunk like a Maori rain-cape."

We crossed Arthur's Pass back to Christchurch to fly on to North Island – much busier and more populated than the south. We toured the bustling streets and gardens of Wellington then drove on through fruit orchards, vineyards and the inevitable sheep pastures to Lake Taupo to see Aratiatia Rapids, an amazing example of how New Zealand was harnessing its natural resources – a fast flowing river hurling itself through a rocky canyon, dammed for the creation of electricity for most of the time, but released for tourists twice a day. At first, we were looking out over no more than a pretty valley with a few quiet pools, until a hooter warned us that the gates were opening, then we watched as a wall of water began to percolate further and further along the canyon, finally filling the entire valley with a boiling white-water stream which churned past our vantage point before disappearing. North Island was where most of the indigenous Maori people live, so we spent time walking (in pouring rain) through the 'thermal reserve' of Whakarewarewa, a reconstructed Maori village amid the bubbling sulphuric pools of Rotorua, where residents were cooking food on pots balanced over steam vents. I left the tour group in Auckland and took a day-excursion by air to the Bay of Islands, cruising by catamaran in and out of thickly wooded islands dotted with isolated holiday homes.

Returning to Auckland I was hosted by Eve (the tour escort who had several times brought clients to join my European tours), who arranged several evening meetings with ex-clients. One of them insisted that I stayed with him for a couple of nights on the Coromandel Peninsula, showing me the remote stony beaches and thick unspoiled native forest where a few of New Zealand's huge ancient trees had survived the onslaught of the timber industry. In fact, throughout my tour of both islands, I was greeted by former clients (warned of my arrival by Eve), standing in the rain outside our hotels, waiting to greet me and give me a box of cakes or biscuits. Such generous hospitality! Along with the beauty of New Zealand's landscapes, this warm-hearted generosity of people I had only met for a few weeks whilst they were touring Europe, sometimes several years previously, is one of my most treasured memories of this 3-month odyssey.

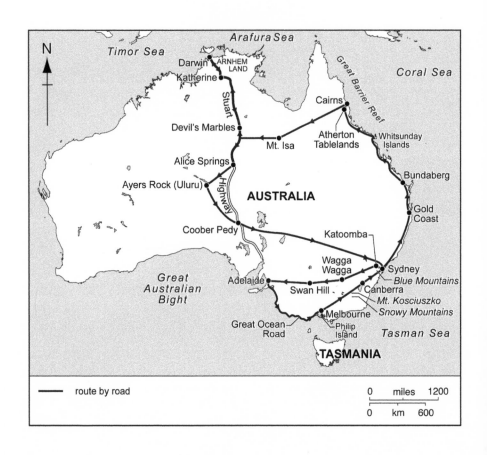

Timor Sea

Arafura Sea

Coral Sea

N

Darwin — ARNHEM LAND

Katherine

Stuart

Cairns

Great Barrier Reef

Devil's Marbles

Mt. Isa

Atherton
Tablelands

Whitsunday
Islands

Alice Springs

Bundaberg

Ayers Rock (Uluru)

Highway

AUSTRALIA

Gold
Coast

Coober Pedy

Katoomba

Great
Australian
Bight

Adelaide

Wagga
Wagga

Swan Hill

Sydney

Blue Mountains

Canberra

Mt. Kosciuszko

Snowy Mountains

Great Ocean
Road

Melbourne

Philip
Island

Tasman Sea

TASMANIA

——— route by road

| 0 | miles | 1200 |
| 0 | km | 600 |

Australia (December 1983/ January 1984)

THE LAST VISIT ON MY grand 3-month journey was Australia, spending a month and a half there altogether, partly driving myself and partly on a coach tour. It all started in Sydney, though I was decidedly underwhelmed by my first sight of the city (my diary describes the historic Rocks district *'as exciting as the back streets of Nottingham'*). A visit to the sparkling Opera House changed my opinion of the city entirely, however: I toured the 4 main halls, each designed in a different way to enhance the sound and visual success of performances, and marvelled at the glorious lobby looking out over the harbour .. and I was lucky enough to acquire tickets to performances of opera and ballet too.

For the first 5 days, I rented a car to explore the south-eastern corner of the country at my own pace. After weeks of organised touring it was a joy to be able to stop the car to look more closely at interesting sights, or to turn off the road to follow an enticing signpost. I headed up into the Blue Mountains, riding the precipitous Scenic Railway at Katoomba (a terrifying ride in a cart which plunged over the cliff-face as carelessly as a waterfall) and the rickety Skyway cable-car which jerked uncertainly across an abyss. Whereas New Zealand had often reminded me of Britain, this was a totally alien environment:

"I leave the car to walk to a suggested viewpoint, following an eroded sandstone path between the burned remains of shrubs. Flies busily investigate me as I pass, and cicadas grate their greetings. Crossing hill after hill, I finally find myself on a protruding rock which falls away hundreds of

feet to the forested Grose Valley below. A wave of sound erupts from the valley – perhaps the song of a million cicadas reverberating from the cliffs? The walls of reddish rock extend as far as I can see in both directions, their lower slopes thick with the 'blue' gum trees which give the mountains their name. This is another world ... I feel totally alone ... everything is different from England. I can recognise not a single bird, plant or insect, not a single sound or smell."

My road took me through the Great Dividing Range into the interior of New South Wales, stopping off at towns whose names were familiar to me from the stories of innumerable Australian passengers on my tours, including Wagga Wagga: every passenger mentioned it, every passenger said it was not worth a visit – they were right! But no-one had mentioned the Jenolan Caves which I discovered only when my road plunged into a natural gash in the rock and a sign indicated that there were caves to visit. I have seen many limestone caves on my travels, but few as impressive as these, with stalactites, stalagmites, water-worn potholes and magnificent 'shawls' of translucent flowstone draped from the roof. The towns in the interior were mainly quiet clusters of verandahed buildings reminiscent of cowboy settlements in western films, whilst the miles between settlements were covered with expanses of arid golden pastureland ('good' sheep country here – totally different from the lush pastures of New Zealand) or vast wheatfields studded with gleaming steel grain silos.

Always on the lookout for mountain scenery, I made my way into the Snowy Mountains. The drive took me through eucalyptus forest alive with parrakeets and cockatoos, past ski villages closed down for the summer, to a point where I could look out at Mount Kosciuszko – no more than a slight rise in a gentle ridge on the horizon, but highest in Australia at 2228m. Much more interesting, heading west beneath a burning sun, was the Pioneer Settlement at Swan Hill, where they had assembled examples of the houses built by the first settlers – often just windowless log cabins with tree trunks as chairs and tables. Those early settlers must have been tough – in another place I discovered a hollow tree which for 2 years was the home of a man and his young family. After days of sweaty, gasping heat, I was relieved to reach the cooler forested hills behind the delightful, friendly city of Adelaide, though it gave me another salutary lesson in the difficulties of living in Australia:

"In the Adelaide Hills I pass through the charming (though rather twee and arty) village of Hahndorf, peaceful as a summer afternoon in the Vienna Woods. But, climbing up into the hills, I am shocked to see the damage caused by the Ash Wednesday fire last year – burned trees are no more than black poles, some just beginning to sprout with fresh greenery; homes and mansions gape at the sky through roofless walls and empty windows. Eucalyptus trees require periodic burning to survive – unlike the European-style homes of modern Australians. As I drive, my car radio crackles with constant firewatch reports from the communities nearby."

Now I turned back towards Melbourne, following the Great Ocean Road past cliffs battered by huge waves, undercut into terraces and overhangs, worn through into natural arches and pillars. It was Christmas Eve, and I was booked into a cheap hotel which had once been a Salvation Army hostel – full of strange characters! Christmas Day lunch was taken in the only restaurant I could find which was actually open, surrounded by other lonely 'singles' – though I had contacted one of my ex-clients and got myself invited for drinks that night. My ex-client tried hard to be welcoming, but I could clearly see that I was an imposition on her Christmas activities, so on Boxing Day I made my own plans, booking on to an excursion to Philip Island to see the tiny Fairy Penguins coming ashore after a day's fishing at sea:

"A ripple of excitement runs through the crowd – the first rafts of bobbing heads can be seen on the sea. The birds allow themselves to be carried inshore by the waves, stand up, decide it is still too light and too dangerous, then scuttle back into the water. Three flotillas come and go for 45 minutes, then finally the most courageous set off in tight formation up the beach, leaving the more fearful dithering behind. The chicks are desperate for food by now, leaving their burrows to look for their parents and wittering plaintively. The parents scuttle past us with heads down and wings out, their customary path enclosed by wire to protect them from us, until they are through the crowds and can disperse into the dunes and bushes to find their young."

The next day I joined a coach camping tour to travel around the parts of the country where I would not feel comfortable driving myself. The first part was mostly disappointing, visiting the capital city of Canberra (still under construction at this time according to a strict design plan, and consequently seeming cold and characterless to me) then passing Sydney again for just a quick stop. For a week we were travelling up the east coast through a string of towns interspersed with agricultural land, changing from cattle pasture and timber forests, to banana and sugarcane plantations as we moved ever northwards into Queensland. Even the renowned Gold Coast did not inspire me, though I laughed at the sight of innumerable surfers chained at the ankle to their boards (in imitation of the ball and chain of their convict ancestors?). Everywhere we went we were followed by grey skies and rain showers – where was the sunshine which I had been promised? By New Year 1984 we had arrived in Bundaberg, famous for sugar, pineapples and especially rum – celebrating in a campsite canteen with an ancient record player and lots of grog!

Finally, we reached Shute Harbour, transferring all our camping gear and baggage via a human chain from coach to launch to sail across to the Whitsunday Islands, surrounded by sparkling turquoise water beneath blue skies and perfect sunshine. At last! Two relaxing days here were full of new experiences for me. There was a first (and last!) attempt at water-skiing, almost drowned by the rush of water as I bounced across the bay on my bottom after failing to stand up straight ... a sightseeing trip by floatplane across the Barrier Reef, taking off and landing in a maelstrom of foaming water hurled backwards across the windows, to gaze down on the brown algae-covered coral reefs and rich blue lagoons of the Reef ... and best of all, an introduction to snorkelling when our plane landed on a lagoon at the outer edge of the Reef – an unforgettable experience which I have never matched in all my later travels:

"As soon as my mask hits the water, I am breathless with awe. Before me is a scene from a Cousteau movie, but I am the only human in this busy world. The side of the reef swells with huge, rounded corals, or sprouts with delicate branches. In places, deep chasms lead tantalisingly into blind canyons of incredible complexity, but in this watery medium I can simply float over towering coral mountains to the next canyon. On over a plateau decorated with every colour and pattern, then I soar like an eagle out into the void again, surrounded by an opaque blue so intense that I feel I must be crushed by it. Fish dart in and out of shelter or drift majestically with the current, so

much at ease in the movement of the sea which buffets me mercilessly towards the jagged coral fingers reaching out for me."

Further north we stopped in the rainforest of the Atherton Tablelands, thick with tangled trees and entwining creepers, adorned with bromeliads and ferns which nestled in the forks of the branches, straining upwards for light and food. We were shown exotic trees like the Curtain Fig Tree (a parasitic climbing fig which deposits its seed on the top of the host tree via bird droppings, then throws down its first roots to the earth, thus gaining strength to strangle and kill its host) and massive Kauri trees, last remnants of the natural hardwood forests which were stripped by early settlers from both Australia and New Zealand, never to be replaced.

Another Barrier Reef experience came as we stopped in Cairns, riding a glass-bottom boat and then snorkelling again around Green Island ... but I was so glad I had already had my first experience of the Reef, because here (in the heart of Reef tourism) the crown-of-thorns starfish had all but wiped out the coral, eating the polyps and leaving only their crumbling limestone shells. Much of the seabed was covered in patches of sand or dead grey coral, flat and featureless with no chasms or cliffs. To compensate the visitors, the authorities were regularly feeding the fish – in this, at least, there was no disappointment:

"In some places the fish swim so thickly that I feel I cannot possibly force my way through them. Swarms of zebra-striped fish; creamy yellow fish swimming so close together that they resemble frogspawn jelly; magnificent and stately rainbow fish shimmering with turquoise; shoals of tiny fluorescent blue sparks. The murky waters are alive with them!"

Turning west, we quickly left behind us the trappings of modern Australia – the road was no longer tarmac but instead just hard-packed red earth; the communities no more than tiny groups of houses, often simple wooden shacks with corrugated iron roofs and huge verandahs; all intensive agriculture was replaced by wide vistas of sparse pastureland dotted with termite mounds, like a vast graveyard. The rainy season seemed to be coming early and heavy showers had been falling over the past days – the roadsides were often flooded, and our driver was careful to keep both coach and trailer away from the verges, for fear of 'bogging'. As the days passed, we were caught more and more often in heavy showers, including one which hit as we stopped for a roadside lunch at a place called 'Dismal Crossing' – what an appropriate name! The rain became ever more persistent as we drove on via the mining centre of Mount Isa, and the police informed us that all roads out of the town were closed by flooding, including the road we had just travelled. Our driver decided to try to continue anyway:

"At Inca Creek we catch up with the blue-overalled policemen and a traffic jam of cars and minibuses not daring to cross the flood, or preparing themselves with sheets of polythene to protect their engines. One car is temporarily stuck in the middle of the creek but gets going again, leaving the road clear for us to plough through, sending great bow waves of water rushing towards dry land. We've made it! ... And so has the car and caravan which tucked itself in tightly behind us, taking advantage of the pathway we carved through the floodwater."

In this way we passed through several more rivers (though the car and caravan had to give up at the next one, parking up for some days until the water-level dropped) and reached the Stuart Highway which runs north to south through the heart of the continent.

We turned north to Katherine, cruising beneath the 200ft high cliffs of Katherine Gorge, seeing our first small crocodiles and tiny rock wallabies, then on to Darwin, the city which hit world headlines in 1974 when it was destroyed by a cyclone – some of the ruins were still preserved in memorial, amongst the reconstructions. We had planned to take an excursion into the aboriginal reserves of Arnhem Land, famous for its buffalo, dingoes and especially birds, but finally the rain defeated us – the road was too deeply flooded for us to progress more than a few miles, so we turned south again. Yet every night our campsites here in the tropics were rich in different forms of wildlife:

"Fruit bats wing slowly and silently overhead in search of food; cicadas strike up their chainsaw chorus to a deafening pitch in the trees overhead. A few parrakeets have a last, loud, garrulous quarrel before settling in for the night. Frogs begin their deep gurgling night-time conversations in the marshes nearby. Mosquitoes lurk out in the darkness around our 'lounge', while black beetles hurl themselves at the fluorescent lights till they fall like hot coals on to our arms and shoulders. Moths and grasshoppers leap frantically from one perch to the next. A 4-inch stick insect delicately lifts one

foot after the other as it assesses the accessibility of the beer in our 'Eskie' fridgeboxes."

Finally, we left the rain behind us as we drove south into the Red Centre of Australia – mile upon mile of wide, flat lands with little to see. Many of our group slept most of the days away, but I was fascinated by the colours: rich red earth, its colour deepened by the rain which had recently fallen; clear blue sky dotted with piles of white cloud which imagination could form into a thousand pictures; flashes of vivid green where the rain had generated new growth on otherwise dry plants. Highlight was a 'bush camp' in a hidden valley amongst the massive boulders of the Devil's Marbles, walking alone by moonlight through spinifex bushes rustling with lizards, toads and snakes (I met one snake in the middle of the path – we both watched each other nervously for a few moments before the snake sprang away into the grass). Then to Alice Springs, meeting at last some aboriginal people living in their traditional nomadic way, and travelling into the nearby mountains to walk between the vibrant 300 metre red cliffs of Standley Chasm. Alice was very much a tourist hotspot, so we were also taken to a camel ranch to ride pure-bred Australian dromedaries – apparently in great demand in Arabia because of their unsullied breeding lines.

Now all our thoughts were on Ayers Rock, at the time still accessible to tourists. In 1984 they were just beginning to demolish the tourist facilities at the very foot of the rock, and to develop a settlement of motels and campsites at Yulara, some miles away. We unfortunately had to camp amid the building sites of Yulara, unshaded by trees or greenery, but we were still able to explore the aboriginal caves around the base of the rock, and even to climb to the top – forbidden now as aboriginal people have reclaimed their rights to this sacred place:

"The rock is steep, so steep that in places I am walking on fingers and toes (if not hands and knees). We are following a chain, implanted into the rock to help climbers, up the remarkably smooth flank of the monolith, across patches where the outer crust is flaking off. The chain ends. Now the rock is worn into potholes, often filled with dark, clear water where freshwater shrimps swim, brought to life by the rain after years of waiting in the dust. Our group strings out as we follow the white dotted line across ridge after ridge of rock, up and down gullies, making our way across the

top of the rock to the summit cairn. To think that it looked flat-topped from below!"

The next day we travelled a short distance to the Olgas, another monolith but eroded into a cluster of huge rocks, for a walk through the Wulpa Gorge:

"At first, we follow a slow-moving stream through trees filled with songbirds, but soon the gorge gets narrower and we must push through bushes which pluck at our shirts with eager fingers. Obstacles litter our path – great slabs of rock which have peeled off and crashed down from above. We scramble under some, over others – one is so high that the lads haul the girls up bodily like sacks of potatoes. Stagnant water now fills the narrow cleft which the gorge has become – we must wedge ourselves between one side and the other, and shuffle along as if climbing a rock chimney, until finally we reach the end of the gorge and can gaze out into the Valley of the Winds."

Australia had one last unique experience to offer us as we tried to continue further south. Though we were no longer plagued by rain showers, the previous rain had created floods so huge that a stretch of the Stuart Highway (not yet a sealed road at this time) was under water. Graders had already been at work scraping new tracks around wet or muddy stretches of the route, but eventually we had to leave the main road (under escort) to follow a railway maintenance track. Even this was blocked at one point by a deep mud-hole, through which our coach was towed by the grader, but finally we reached the railway line itself, an insurmountable barrier for the coach. Our tour company had sourced another smaller vehicle to meet us on the far side of the rails, so we scrambled across the railway carrying our essential baggage, to be transported to a waystation crowded with stranded truck drivers. Here we waited for 2 days, amusing ourselves by chatting to the drivers or paddling in the floodwater, until a ramp was built over the railway for our coach to cross and join us for a marathon journey via the underground mining town of Coober Pedy, back to 'civilisation' and the end of our journey.

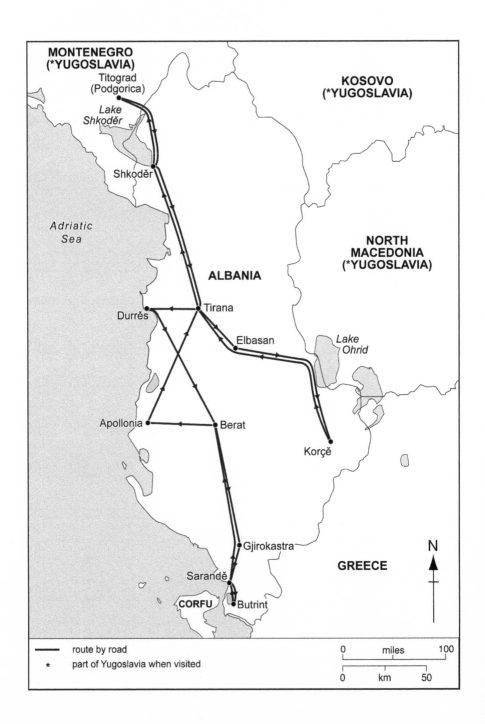

Albania (September 1985)

WHY ALBANIA? THAT WAS THE question my friends were asking when I told them my destination – and to be honest, I was asking myself the same thing! I had tried to do some reading before the trip, and the only guidebook I could find implied that Albania was a drab, colourless land with nothing to see but factories and schools. So why? Perhaps just to put another unusual destination under my belt?

The country was only just opening up after the death, a few months before, of their long-time dictator Enver Hoxha. Tourist facilities were almost non-existent: there were limited hotels... few cafes or restaurants... monotonous food (we ate stuffed peppers and fresh grapes at every lunch for two weeks) ... no international airport (we had to fly into neighbouring Yugoslavia) ... and most problematic of all, no trained guides. We started out under the care of a teacher (Lida) who spoke good English but had no interest in the history or culture of her country – the only information she could provide for us, was the approved 'line' on life in one of the strictest Communist countries in the world (they had broken relations with the Soviet Union in 1961, then even with post-Mao China in 1978, because neither was following the principles of communism strictly enough). She had no interest in learning anything about us, becoming ever more frustrated as we asked the 'wrong' questions or photographed the 'wrong' things, until finally she exploded in rage when we spread out to explore instead of sticking close to her. Halfway through the tour she was replaced by a museum curator who certainly had more of the knowledge we craved, but spoke poor English and only slightly better French.

However, the pleasant surprises began already at the Albanian border. We had been escorted from Titograd (this Yugoslav city only reverted to its ancient name of Podgorica in 1992) by a Yugoslav guide who spent most of the journey warning us that all Albanians were violent troublemakers. So we disembarked with trepidation from our Yugoslav coach at their border control, walking in blazing sunshine with our luggage 100 yards to the Albanian customs post. We were called forward by the Albanian police one by one to show our passports and visas, but then were invited into a cool, shady lounge where we could relax while paperwork and baggage checks were completed:

"The border post feels amazingly hospitable – rugs cover the floor; deep old-fashioned armchairs offer comfortable seating. Outside, border guards eat grapes under a vine-covered trellis. Two Albanian trucks, formalities completed, start up their motors and drive off towards Yugoslavia with a friendly wave to the customs men ... then stillness descends again. Coots paddle peacefully among waterlilies and waving reeds on Lake Skadar, right alongside us, and the air is filled with the sound of cicadas."

This tranquillity continued as we boarded our Albanian coach – the only traffic on the narrow roads was a few trucks, ancient tractors, military vehicles or the occasional 'bendy' bus. Private cars were still banned and people travelled by bicycle, horse or ox-cart, or on foot, though many also asked for a ride from whatever vehicle passed them – we were often gestured to stop (clearly it was normal behaviour that anyone could ask for a lift from any vehicle) though our driver had been instructed that he should not stop, to avoid inappropriate contact between us (dangerous?) foreigners and local people. In our first town, Shkoder, the streets were full of cyclists and, especially as evening drew in, promenading pedestrians, walking and chatting in streets lined with well-maintained baroque buildings, small shops and workshops:

"A shoemaker whistles in his dark little workshop as he folds patent leather around the shoe-mould ... three men in another tiny shop laugh and chat together as they mend watches. The cafes are full of people drinking beer, coffee or spirits. A father with one little girl on the back of his bicycle, tows his baby in its pram as he pedals through town. Everyone is out enjoying the balmy summer evening."

The only slightly disturbing sight amid all this tranquil normality, was the presence at frequent intervals along the roadsides and around the town, of small round concrete gun emplacements, like pale mushrooms sprouting from the earth – no longer used, we were assured, but evidence of a paranoiac fear of outsiders or invasion which had dominated national and international politics until very recently.

The next pleasant surprise began on our first full day of sightseeing, when we were taken to visit the ancient Skodra Fortress, founded originally in the 4th century BC and enlarged again by 15th century Venetians and 18th century Ottoman Turks. Though there were only ruinous walls to see, I had not expected to find such historic sites in Albania – even if our guide could not (would not?) tell us much about it. Here, however, I encountered for the first time a quirk of Albania's recorded history: we were told that the original fortress was built by Illyrians, though it was clear that they were talking about the ancient Greeks. Albania was officially at war with Greece from 1940 until they finally re-established diplomatic relations in the 1990's (the state of war was not officially lifted until 2016), and throughout the 40-year rule of the dictator Enver Hoxha, he had tried to reinforce the nationhood of Albania by rewriting history to show them as a distinct nationality and culture since ancient times. It was not appropriate, in his view, that Albanians should be descended from ancient Greeks! We encountered this historical viewpoint in the museums we visited throughout the country, too, whilst several times we watched 'traditional Albanian' cultural events which featured men's white skirts more commonly associated with Greece, and dances virtually identical to their familiar Syrtaki dances.

Another totally unexpected sight for me, was the agricultural landscape of the country. I had been regularly travelling in neighbouring Yugoslavia and Greece with my tours and was used to the desolate, waterless 'karst' landscape of the region, where centuries of tree-felling has resulted in the loss of topsoil and exposure of porous limestone rock into which all surface water disappears, leaving land useless for growing crops. Yet here in Albania, we were seeing hillsides neatly terraced and irrigated, producing abundant crops of tobacco, maize, fruit, sugar beet and cotton. We were told that this was the result of the hard work of older schoolchildren and students, who spent one month each year in unpaid labour on national projects like terracing, or even railway building – recently there had been a special project for this unpaid labour force: tree-planting to help preserve the subsoil. A huge communal effort, but one which had certainly paid off in terms of the land. Yet clearly the government's priorities were different from ours:

"We pass fields of sunflowers, flanked by irrigation channels running with water ... but though there is plenty of water for the fields, running water for the villages seems to have a low priority. We often see women washing clothes in the irrigation channels or beneath leaks in aqueducts, and fetching water home in buckets and pots from the canals. What kind of strange philosophy puts irrigation before the health and comfort of the people?"

Later in our trip, we were woken on a Sunday morning by loudspeakers (located on every street corner in every community) calling the people to 'donate a day to Albania' and join special buses waiting to take volunteers out for a day harvesting cotton or doing other necessary farm work. At 6am, crowds were already flocking to the buses ... perhaps out of patriotism? ... or perhaps just for a day out in the country? Certainly, agriculture could only be successful by harnessing extra manpower when needed, since all the farming we saw was very labour-intensive: men and women working with hoes and mattocks, assisted only by donkeys and mules with a few ancient tractors and other machines.

Everywhere we went, the people were fascinated by us and openly friendly – crowds gathered each time we stopped (despite the efforts of our guides to keep us from all but the official contacts) and several times I was invited into people's homes, when I was spotted walking by myself without the presence of our guide/ guardian. Especially I remember an invitation to visit a home in Korca, where I had broken away from the group (sated with 'official sights') and stopped to photograph a typical house with overhanging upper floors:

"As I do so, two old ladies dressed in black skirts and cardigans spot me and excitedly tell each other 'Turista!'. One approaches to speak to me, and we try to understand each other using my limited Italian (Albania was an Italian protectorate during WWII and older Albanians remember a few words of their language). I ask to take a photograph of her, and she agrees, though she thinks I am mad since she is not dressed in her best finery. Then she invites me into her home – of course, I agree with alacrity!"

She took me through a garden hung with shady vines, up the stairs into her huge airy living room on the upper floor, adorned with bright carpets and good quality modern furniture, to meet her daughter-in-law. We sipped very sweet cherry wine together from tiny liqueur glasses, then chatted for a few minutes with another younger girl who spoke some classroom English. How privileged I felt, to be invited to meet a family in their own home!

As we progressed around the country, we were shown magnificent historic sites which were the equal of any major tourist attraction in other lands, yet seemed barely appreciated by the Albanian people and even by our guides. In the city of Durres, we explored the half-excavated 2nd century Roman arena and what appeared to be Christian chapels below it, decorated with mosaic representations of saints and angels. In Butrint, at the end of a rough track, we discovered an entire ancient city which flourished both under the Greeks in the 3rd century BC and also under the Romans in the first centuries of the Christian era. We were the only tourists here, led by a local guide who clearly knew little about the site – fortunately, we had an expert within our group who was able to explain the ruins to us:

"We all move on to one of the glories of Butrint – a huge, circular Baptistery with lines of columns and a magnificent mosaic floor. The guide tells us it was built as a Roman temple, but our expert informs us that it was built as a Christian baptistery – hence the cross inset into the mosaic floor. I am amazed by the colours and patterns of the floor, depicting 70 different animals. Apparently, it is normally kept covered with sand to protect it from the fierce sun – it was only uncovered a few days ago, so we are lucky to see it."

Another less well-preserved site was the ancient city of Apollonia, again founded by the ancient Greeks with a grand temple to the god Apollo, developed by the Romans as a major port and later (in the 14th century) the site of an imposing Greek Orthodox church, now lying in ruins but (according to our guide) due for restoration at some time in the future. Throughout the country we saw a few mosques and many Orthodox chapels and churches, almost all in ruins. Enver Hoxha had tried to ban religion completely and all religious buildings were abandoned in 1968: I questioned our second, more informative, guide about the implementation of this ban:

"I put to him the question burning in my mind – how did the government close the churches and mosques? Our guide tells us that 'it was a

spontaneous youth movement to abolish religion and keep the religious buildings only as cultural monuments. The priests/imams all gladly stood up and told their congregations that it had been a hoax all these years ... the people approved ... there were no public demonstrations or protests'. Can he <u>*really*</u> *believe that? What agony and heart-searching there must have been among the priests and imams. How many still rot in jail?"*

One lunchtime I broke away from the group to climb up the hillside to a deserted Orthodox chapel, passing two defensive dogs on the way. As I climbed, I heard the dogs barking again behind me – was someone following me? I reached the chapel, windowless and stripped of all furniture and decoration, but the door was open, and I stepped inside. As I was reaching for my pen and diary, I heard a noise outside:

"A young man comes in, blocking the door with his body. He reaches for me ... I grab his arms. He leans towards my face ... I grab for his sunglasses – maybe if I break them, he'll leave me alone. He moves forward to pin me against a wall, so I look him sternly in the face and declare 'Not in God's house!' A doubtful look crosses his face, but he tries again with a half-smile. I repeat 'Not in God's house!' and he steps back, letting me slip past him out of the doorway to head off down the path."

It is good to know that I have divine protection wherever I travel!

Highlights of our sightseeing were the two 'museum cities' which we visited. First, we spent a day in Berat, nicknamed 'the town of 1000 windows' because of the typical architecture where wide-windowed houses climbed up the steep hillsides, one on top of the other:

"I head straight off to the old part of town, already excited by the delightful appearance of Berat. Who would have expected such character and beauty? I head up the first steps I see and plunge into a rabbit warren of cobbled alleyways, lined with huge mysterious wooden doors behind which I can occasionally glimpse shady courtyards. The main passage runs horizontally across the hillside, but most of the alleys run almost vertically up and down, sometimes only just wide enough for one person to pass. And always spotlessly clean."

The second museum city was Gjirokaster, nicknamed 'the stone city' for its stone-slabbed roofs:

"The lower town is a jumble of grey stone as bleak as any Welsh slate

quarry when seen from above, but softened by large windows and trailing vines when viewed from the street. The upper residential districts, reached by steep, slippery, polished stone streets and steps, are filled with elegant villas, their eaves supported by huge wooden struts. The walls which face the valley are adorned with pleasant, terraced balconies, and shaded by vines and fig trees."

I was enchanted by the houses of Gjirokaster, though for our local guide its principal attraction was the (reconstructed) house where Enver Hoxha was born. It interested me only for the chance to see the interior of a traditional grand mansion, with small rooms on lower floors to allow for easier heating in winter, and high airy summer rooms upstairs with beautifully carved ceilings and screens. Outside Tirana (the capital city) we were also taken to admire Hoxha's tomb, beneath a massive red marble slab and guarded by 3 soldiers at all times. Our guide Lida told us that the bouquets adorning the tomb were 'gifts from ordinary Albanians':

"Can we believe this since no other tomb in the war cemetery behind is adorned with flowers? There is no point in trying to get Lida to tell us the true feelings of the people for their dead leader. Certainly he created a great sense of national identity and pride, certainly he implemented huge reforms in the land, economy and even the lifestyle of the people. But surely they must see what his style of leadership has cost them in terms of personal freedom?"

We were also introduced to another Albanian hero – a 15th century prince called Skanderbeg, who fought against Turkish invaders. Our coach stopped by a nondescript modern structure, which we entered to find that it enclosed a ruined mosque, burial place of this national hero … and a huge red Albanian flag featuring a double-headed eagle. Lida was horrified and disbelieving when we said we had never heard of Skanderbeg, but was finally persuaded to give us a brief version of his story – especially the fact that he unified north and south Albania in 1444, hence the double-headed eagle on the national flag.

Alongside the historic sites, we were taken to see model schools, farms and factories. Early in our tour we visited an exceptionally neat primary school classroom full of well-scrubbed and well-disciplined children who recited patriotic poems to us. We were told that schooling was compulsory until age 14, that priority at university was given to the children of workers or peasants, and that the subjects they then studied at university were allocated by the State according to the country's needs – resulting in a guaranteed job at the end of their studies.

At the farming co-operative we visited, I was again surprised by the level of centralised control. The farm was run as a huge co-operative, comprising 10 villages with a dedicated medical centre and every level of school. The State allocated which crops should be grown by each farm, though the co-operative leaders decided where on the farm each crop should be planted. Most of the crops were used to feed the co-operative, sold at subsidised rates in local shops, whilst any excess (plus cash crops like tobacco and sugar) was sold to the State in exchange for machinery, fertiliser etc. Each family had a small garden plot and was allowed to sell their produce locally at State-controlled prices. After the official visit, we had some time to explore alone:

"I wander along the dirt roads, past houses and walls built of stone or mud brick with wooden beams. Chickens wander freely, children gather to gaze at us – creatures from another world! By now the whole village knows of our arrival – we are invited into homes, and many women (and even a few men) come up to shake my hand in the street. Our bus is besieged by children asking for pens, though not insistently – they seem just as happy to pose for a photograph instead. As we prise ourselves loose and depart, we see many villagers running through the fields just to catch a glimpse of us."

On the other hand, the factory visits were an eye-opener – especially in the precision engineering factory, where any British health & safety officer would have been horrified:

"A man peers (with no safety goggles) into the furnace to extract a block of red-hot metal and drop it into a chute leading to another man, who puts it in the stamp. From there it is thrown (yes, thrown!) to another man across the room for another process, then thrown on to the next machine. The floor is rough and broken, with huge tripping potential. Our group picks its way warily around the room, dodging the deadly juggling act going on in the centre and praying for a Safety Officer to eject us into a more secure space."

Our tour of Albania was poorly planned, with many roads closed to us as foreigners because they were considered of inferior quality or else ran too close to the sealed Greek border. Consequently, we frequently re-traced our steps through the heart of the country, but I did not regret the chance to repeatedly enjoy the landscapes of terraced hillsides and forested mountains (which cover 75% of the entire country):

"We drive through undulating hills, leading up into high mountains. A few cows and donkeys, plus herds of brown goats graze nearby; shepherds drive flocks of sheep beside the road or along the course of dried-up rivers. Our track is barely wide enough for two vehicles to pass, but it's blissfully empty and in remarkably good condition – presumably because it is rarely used? We continue climbing, winding higher and higher with views back over valleys which cut deep into the mountains."

Twice we passed the amazingly blue, clear waters of Lake Ohrid, looking across to the mountains of Yugoslavia beyond, but perhaps the most glorious scenery was the Mediterranean landscape in the far south of the country:

"The road inexorably draws us up a steep ascent into the hills again, winding through narrow ravines and clefts, often above awe-inspiring drops. Finally, we descend to the marshy land around Saranda where they grow rice and farm fish. We cross a low range of stony hills dotted with cypress trees and suddenly ... there is the sea, bathed in the light of the setting sun. Now it is a gentle run down to the coast, through groves of olive, lemon and orange trees. Saranda stretches luxuriantly along the seafront, gazing across at the hazy outline of mountainous Corfu."

Against all my expectations, Albania was a stunningly beautiful country, full of magnificent historic sites and friendly people – I cannot wait to visit again and see how it has developed.

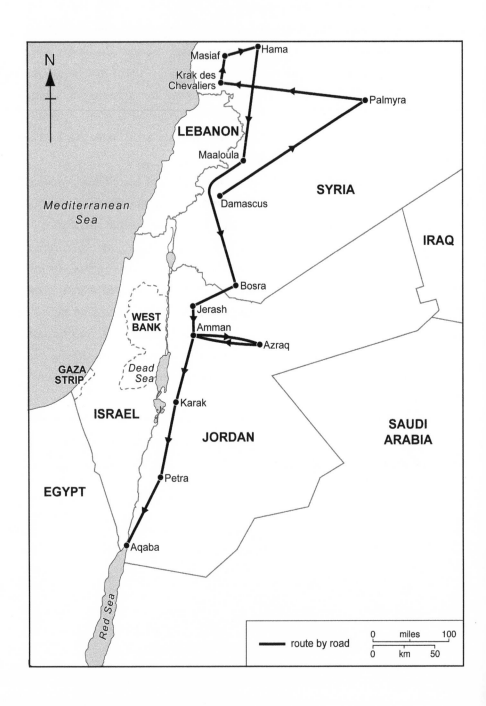

Syria and Jordan (March/April 1986)

SPRING 1986 SAW ME HEADING to the Middle East. I had already visited Egypt to see a friend who was married to an Egyptian, so I had experienced a taste of the Arab lifestyle, but now I wanted to see more. My tour took in the highlights of both Syria and Jordan – how much of what I saw still remains now, after years of civil war in Syria?

We started in Damascus, proudly claiming the title of Oldest City in the World – supposedly founded by the son of Noah, with Roman remains, early Christian sites and traces of both Arab and Turkish Muslim rule. At first sight I found it just an uninspiring jumble of concrete blocks, grey with dust and surrounded by arid brown hills, though once we had time to explore, I was fascinated by the narrow alleyways of the old city:

"I plunge into streets crowded with workshops of every type. Woodworkers sit making furniture and kitchen utensils, sometimes still on lathes turned by both hand and foot. Further on, sweet aromas drift from the almond sugarers – great copper drums turning like concrete mixers to coat nuts with sugar solution. I stop beside a black doorway leading down to an underground bakery, watching as they work with smooth co-ordination, slapping thin circles of bread dough on to a long wooden paddle, then pushing it into a great glowing oven where within seconds it puffs up. The baker's helper, excited by my interest and filled with hospitality, brings me one of his pitta loaves as a gift, insisting I accept it."

We were admitted into the sacred Omayyad Mosque, built on the site of a Christian church, in turn built on the site of a Roman temple – Damascus was full of these multiple layers of history. The Christian church housed the severed head of John the Baptist, re-interred by the Muslims into an ornate tomb because they revere him as their prophet Yahia. As infidels we were permitted to enter only by a side door ... as women we were supplied with a voluminous black over garment in which to swathe ourselves ... but once we were inside we were free to explore as we wished, despite the prayers taking place in the worship area. Later I searched out the House of Ananias (where the apostle Paul had his sight restored), hidden in back streets which required the assistance of a Syrian Orthodox priest and several local Christian ladies (wearing black jackets and cardigans, rather than an Islamic cover-all outer garment) to navigate. Ananias' House was now a shrine run by Catholic Franciscan monks – two stone-vaulted cellars set up as a simple church. Pre-Isis Damascus allowed all these different religions to exist side by side – who knows what is the situation today?

A few hours' drive from Damascus lay the ancient city of Palmyra, a wealthy staging post on the caravan routes between the Arabian Gulf and the Mediterranean since several thousand years BC, flourishing also under Roman rule and even creating its own empire in the early centuries of the Christian era. In the 3rd century it faded into obscurity until it was rediscovered in the 1920's. It was one of the most impressive ancient sites I have seen, built of warm yellow sandstone which glowed in the sunshine, rising from otherwise barren desert like a mirage. We visited the magnificent family tomb of Elahbel, its interior surrounded by a stone colonnade, its ceiling still painted in vibrant colours – sadly, the tomb was totally destroyed by Isis in 2015. We also saw the vast Temple of Baal, built in 32AD during the heyday of the city. Much of it was already ruined by an earthquake centuries before, but the 'Holy Room' still stood almost complete when we visited. Originally the heart of the Roman temple, it was converted into a Christian chapel, then a Muslim mosque. Once containing niches filled with Roman idols, it was then decorated with Christian mosaics, and later turned into a Muslim mihrab (prayer-focus). Sadly in 2015 Isis also blew up all this history and heritage – photos I have seen recently show only the gateway still standing. Palmyra is often called the City of 1000 Columns, with grand colonnades lining the access roads along which the camel caravans would have passed – at least Isis seems to have spared these, but how lucky I was to see the marvels of Palmyra before modern warfare destroyed them.

We stayed in the original guesthouse within the confines of the ancient city, a run-down fusty building with mouldy bathrooms boasting only intermittent hot water, but at least it meant that we could use our time at the site to its best advantage. After touring the ruined city, several of our group set out to visit the 13th century fortress towering over the ruins. There was no official access, so we had to scrabble our way up a scree slope, dislodging avalanches of stones, to cross a rickety wooden bridge over the moat and enter the fortress ...

"... a crumbling, multi-storey labyrinth of passages, doorways, vaulted chambers and mysterious holes. There has been no work done here to secure tourist access and it is with both excitement and unease that I pick my way through the labyrinth, never quite sure when the floor may give way beneath my feet and drop me into the black void below."

In one last orgy of destruction before leaving Palmyra in 2016, Isis seriously damaged this already fragile structure. With the efforts of world archaeologists fully occupied with restoring the ancient ruins, will the fortress be simply abandoned?

For us, Palmyra's fortress was a foretaste of the massive 12th century Crusader castles which line the Syrian coastline, each once housing over 1000 knights and all their equipment in a fortified chain designed to protect access to the Christian shrines of Palestine from the attacks of Muslim armies. Most imposing was Krak des Chevaliers – also damaged by bombardment in the Syrian War, though hopefully not irreparably. Even the approach to the castle was impressive, passing through fortified gates and passageways, up a ramp negotiable by horses, around a hairpin bend which acted as a trap for invaders. The sheer stone walls of the main castle soared up from the moat, enclosing a maze of vaulted halls including the splendid, arcaded Knights Hall, lit by delicately traced Gothic windows. We visited the more ruinous Marqab Castle too, perched on a rock in the forested hills bordering the coastal plain, then turned into the heart of the mountains en route to Masiaf, the former fortress of the drug-crazed Old Man of the Mountains and his 'assassin' followers.

More history awaited us in the town of Hama, filled with the agonised creaking and groaning of 12 huge wooden waterwheels (up to 600 years old), still functioning as an irrigation system:

"The force of the water flowing beneath them turns the wheels, flat paddles scooping up the water and carrying it backwards and upwards, hurling it into the irrigation channel at the top by centrifugal force. Most of the water sprays back down into the river – these are certainly not as efficient as a modern pump, yet they have worked adequately for thousands of years and similar wheels are still in use in many lands today."

Though there were reports that the waterwheels (called 'noria') had been burned in the war, more recently it has been claimed that they have survived – hopefully, one small fragment of Syria's history still remaining for future generations.

An abiding memory for me was our visit to the tiny village of Maaloula, hidden away in a narrow cleft in the mountains, its mud-coloured houses blending into the rocky background to render it almost invisible. This was one of only three remaining villages which still spoke the Aramaic language which was used by Jesus and his followers, so we were taken to a tiny room in the Syrian Orthodox monastery there, to listen to a battered old cassette recording of the Lord's Prayer in Aramaic:

"I am captivated! I am listening to the language of Jesus! The guidebooks say it is smoother and less guttural than modern Arabic, but spoken by the monks it sounds harsh, jerkily moving from one word to the next."

As we left Syria, we made one last stop in the town of Bosra, again rich in layers of history illustrated by a 13th century Arab fortress and the minarets of mosques built when this was an important stop on the pilgrimage routes to Mecca. Here we plunged into dark vaulted passageways which led us out into a huge sunlit arena – an ancient Roman theatre built in the 2nd century BC and later turned into a Muslim fortress. It was Friday (the Muslim holy day) and the arena was packed with holiday trippers, some launching into an impromptu Syrtaki-like dance while others crowded around us to practise their English.

The historical theme continued as we crossed into Jordan, though now the landscape was gentler with roads lined with yellow mimosa and fields planted with grain or fruit trees – and none of the military installations or army convoys which were so frequent in Syria, even in 1986. Our first stop was at the ancient city of Jerash, considered the most complete example of a Roman provincial city in the world (though I thought it lacked the stark grandeur of Palmyra, since it was set amid greenery and trees instead of burning desert). We spent hours here, walking through the colonnades of the main Cardo Maximus street to the Oval Forum and visiting the temples and amazingly preserved Theatre.

In Amman, I wore out my feet walking from end to end of this bustling modern city in search of ancient remains. I found the (heavily restored) Roman theatre and squeezed through a barbed wire fence into the jumble of stone which is all that remains of the Roman temple of Hercules, but I was impressed by neither. So I was glad to escape the chaos of big city life for an excursion into the nearby desert, where 8th century rulers built themselves mini-castles – 'holiday homes' where they could escape back to the simplicity of their nomadic ancestors for a short time. The 'castles' were abandoned by the 9th century and forgotten (until rediscovered in 1898) since there were no roads or regularly used tracks in the area – our trip was only possible because of a modern road built just 2 years before our visit. The excursion included a visit to El Azraq Fortress (one of the bases used by Lawrence of Arabia) and its nearby oasis:

"I am excited by the romantic idea of an oasis – palm trees and clear water against the sands of the desert. But when it appears, it is nothing like my image! At first there is no surface water, only scattered palm and fir trees and a concrete village bristling with aerials and washing lines, the streets cluttered with tin cans and pieces of plastic. The pool itself finally appears – the only permanent water for hundreds of miles, surrounded by tamarind, palm and pine trees and flowering reeds. But the tranquillity is spoiled by the constant clank and roar of the pumping station and the view is criss-crossed by huge irrigation pipes."

We headed south, stopping on Mount Nebo to gaze (like Moses) across to the Promised Land of Israel, and visiting the magnificent 6th century mosaic floors in Madaba. We wound around the mountains and deep gorges of the narrow Kings Highway, to visit the ruinous fortress at Karak. However, my chief memory of our visit to Karak was the free time I spent exploring the little town below the castle, meeting local people who not only smiled and greeted me, but in one case invited me to join them on their terrace for tea and biscuits: two sons spoke some English and explained that they were Catholic Orthodox, whilst their mother was Protestant, all living in harmony within a Muslim culture – emphasising the tolerant attitude prevalent in Jordan, at that time at least.

However, the overarching highlight of Jordan for me, in fact the definite highlight of the whole tour, was our 3 days in Petra. Most tourists are lucky to get a full day at this fascinating site, with many only managing a day trip out of Amman, so I consider myself so fortunate to have had time both for official sightseeing and also free time to explore on my own. I was also delighted to be staying, not in the newly built Forum Hotel but in the original Resthouse, composed of rambling terraces of rooms perched among the rocks and with a bar actually located in a 3000-year-old tomb! Petra's golden age began in the 3rd century BC when the formerly nomadic Nabatean people settled into a hidden valley in the heart of rocky hills, at first preying on passing trade caravans, then taking tolls from them. They developed an advanced form of agriculture based on amazing water engineering, and became fabulously wealthy from trade in spices, perfumes and silks as well as gold, silver, copper and bitumen (used by ancient Egyptians for embalming mummies). Finally trade routes changed and, by the time the Arabs reached Jordan in the 7th century, Petra had been forgotten, remaining no more than a legend until rediscovered in the 19th century. Our visit started in the former 'suburbs' of Petra, rarely visited by tourists:

"The landscape here is fabulous – weird formations of eroded sandstone in domes and knobs, and behind them the higher more jagged rocks of Petra itself, glowing with a reddish light. We squeeze through the rocks on a narrow path, beneath a colonnaded temple and past simple tombs dug out of the rock on various levels. The path is transformed into a flight of rock-cut steps leading through the ever-narrowing chasm towards a great stone – perhaps a representation of the chief Nabatean god?"

Next day we set off on our official sightseeing tour, starting with a compulsory (to contribute to the local economy) horseback transfer through the access gorge – the Siq. The valley beside the Resthouse was milling with skinny horses: my steed was a sad, broken-down old nag led by an elderly Palestinian, but at least he plodded slowly enough for me to relax in the saddle and enjoy the view. The Siq was awe-inspiring, a narrow chasm carved through the rock by a dry watercourse with walls up to 300ft high, suddenly opening into bright sunlight to be faced by the magnificent facade of the Treasury. Here we were allowed to leave our horses and walk off down a broad valley, hidden within the mountains, marvelling at the workmanship of facades carved into the rock walls. Most were open for us to walk inside, though it was a shock to realise that all the rock-carvers' skill was used on the outside, whilst inside there was no more than a single simple room – perhaps a tomb, though no-one really knows. The sandstone rock itself contributed to the artistic merit of the facades:

"We explore the Urn Tomb, climbing up through a labyrinth of low and narrow arches (called the Prison) to a sunlit colonnaded square. Opening on to this square is a large rock-cut room with arched niches set into its walls. The ceiling is covered with beautiful red and white ripples of stone, enhanced by traces of black from more recent fires, like the swirls of a fine silk shawl. Petra is famous for the colours of its rock, laid down as layers of sand a million years ago beneath a vast sea."

While many tourists had to finish their visit with this official sightseeing, we were able to continue on, climbing first up to the Monastery, one of Petra's two sacred high places, carved as a temple in the 3rd century BC and later used for Christian worship. We plodded uphill from the main valley, ascending via natural ledges and worn steps cut into the cliff to the immense facade (50m wide and 45m high), then followed the path used by the original masons to the top of the facade where sat a massive urn, three times the size of a man though seeming insignificant from below! After all this exertion, we were delighted to find that an enterprising local Bedouin lady had carried up a thermos flask of tea, plus soft drinks and water, to establish a pop-up tearoom for the few visitors who reached this height. The next day we climbed up to the second sacred high place, a hard climb on almost continual rock-cut steps to the High Place of Sacrifice (sadly no pop-up tearoom here) for a spectacular view over the mountain-ringed valley which formerly contained the (long disappeared) free-standing structures of Petra. The descent from this spot was via narrow steps carved into the brightly coloured rock to emerge into a tiny green valley, an oasis of peace ending with the colonnaded Garden Tomb, where lizards darted from one shade patch to another and birds whistled from the rocks above.

Our tour finished beside the Red Sea at Aqaba, where I was able once more to snorkel above a coral reef:

"... pale blue coral, mauve and pink blotches, huge green mounds, fleshy-coloured tentacles and the deep blue lips of clams embedded in the reef. Shoals of silvery whitebait or brilliant goldfish sweep past me, while deep purple fish with yellow tails drift around aimlessly. None seem interested in me, though a striped sea-snake lifts a lazy head and waves its tentacles at me."

But the reef could not compare with my experiences in Australia, and I felt that the tour could only go downhill after the glories of Petra.

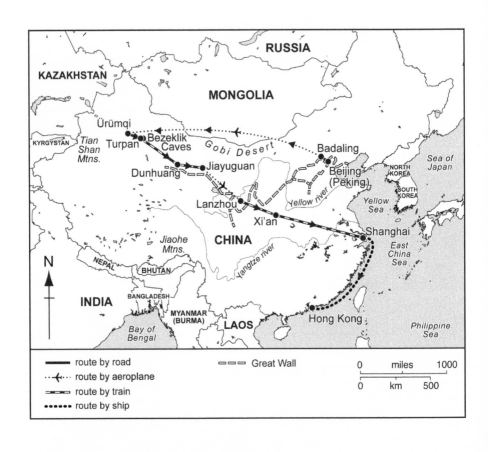

route by road
route by aeroplane
route by train
route by ship

Great Wall

0   miles   1000
0   km   500

China (October 1986)

AUTUMN 1986 SAW ME EMBARKING on a trip to China, braving the hospitality of China's national airline (where we were unexpectedly well cared-for) for over 7 hours en route to 'Peking' (as we called it then: now we use 'Beijing' to interpret the Chinese name). I was full of anticipation, yet my first impression of the city was disappointing – the air was thick and hazy with dust and exhaust fumes, the scene drab and colourless with grey rows of apartments beneath grey roofs and a grey sky. Everywhere there was noise, bustle and crowds:

"The main road outside our hotel is filled with traffic – buses hooting their way along the centre of the road, bicycle bells ringing along the side. How do I cross this unceasing tide? Nothing for it but to choose my moment and walk out decisively. It works! The bicycles avoid me (but I don't try it with the buses). Crowds of people are walking their children or buying vegetables from carts or cloths spread by the road ... but in a small park couples are spaced every yard or so around the walls, backs to the world, enclosing their small space with their bicycles, eyes only for each other – an island of privacy in a sea of humanity."

We were accompanied already by a British escort and a Chinese national guide who would be with us throughout the country, but before sightseeing could begin we picked up a city guide too, who took us first to pay our respects to Chairman Mao – since 1977 embalmed and on display in a mausoleum in Tiananmen Square. A huge queue was standing 4-deep right across the square, but we were permitted to push in and ascend the steps in compulsory silence, listening to a loudspeaker reciting the Thoughts of Mao:

"In a large crystal coffin lies the great man, his face illuminated. He looks yellow and shiny, more like a waxwork than a mummy, but there's no time to study him because we are hustled on with cries of 'keep moving, keep moving'."

This hustle set the tone for all our official Chinese sightseeing – there was rarely time to stop and absorb what we were seeing, except when we could escape our guides to explore on our own. All day we were harried from one 'sight' to another – the tunnels of the Underground City, dug by hand in a period of intense fear of Russian attack between 1969-1979 ... the 15th century Temple of Heaven, its decoration giving me a first sight of the gaudy colours I had expected everywhere in China (the photos we see always pick out these rare spots of colour in an otherwise drab land) ... and finally the interminable courtyards and halls of the Forbidden City, once the hidden and private residence of the emperor and his family:

"Our guide tries hard to enthuse us with the marvels of his Chinese heritage, but I find everything rather disappointing – huge featureless courtyards with dingy Great Halls, all overrun by hordes of chattering Chinese tourists posing for photos at every point. Only in the living quarters of the women do I find delightful patios surrounded by pretty pavilions and shaded by ancient, gnarled cypress trees."

By next morning I was far more positive, rising at dawn to investigate the crowds of citizens taking their daily exercise in the parks near our hotel:

"Across the road, a group of older people have gathered for tai-chi and are tracing poetry with their bodies (almost) in unison. As I approach, they break for a chat, smiling greetings to each other before recommencing at a command from one of their number, composing their faces once more into peaceful immobility. Further on, another group are whirling and lunging with tasselled swords, while yet others perform more familiar step-ups and hip-swinging. What an experience to watch this vast tableau, and to hear the park echoing to the thunder of a hundred hands slapping a hundred thighs."

We were taken out of the city to visit the Summer Palace – though (being Sunday and the weekly day-off for government employees) we were far from alone! Terrified that we might get lost in the crowds, our guide produced a musical megaphone which played 'Jingle Bells' to attract our attention (we hated it, but he was delighted with his toy!) and we allowed ourselves to be carried by the crowds on the official sightseeing route around the site. More throngs of excited Chinese awaited us as we visited Peking Zoo to see the pandas, then it was on to the Lamasery for another taste of Tibetan-style Buddhism (which I had already seen in Mongolia and Nepal) – starting a fascination in me which led me to visit Tibet itself, 30 years later.

Another day dawned wet and grey, but this could not dampen our excitement at the day's plan – we were off to the Great Wall, following a battered old road cutting through mountains shrouded in cloud and mist. We parked in a muddy field packed with other coaches – we were going to visit the only well-restored part of the 6000km-long wall which lies within easy reach of Peking, and thousands of Chinese tourists had the same idea.

"Up we climb, passing the photographing, chattering hordes, following a broad stone path which gets steeper and steeper until we are almost walking with our feet vertical. The Chinese are quickly fading from the scene and the last few give up when the path turns into very high and narrow stone steps. Now it is just us ... up into the clouds by now. I can only see 20 feet in either direction and all is utterly silent. The mist rolls and swirls, the wind catches my hair – I can imagine all kinds of half-seen devils. How fearful the emperor's troops must have been here, on the edge of their world!"

China is a huge country inhabited by 56 different ethnic groups, of which the Han are the majority. The first days of our tour had given us an insight into the lives of the Han people, but now a 4-hour flight took us to Urumqi in the far west, into the lands of the largest minority group – the Uighur people, who are Turkic in appearance and Muslim in faith. Their land seemed to be mainly a stony desert, dotted with mudbrick villages, but the people were so much more lively and cheerful than we had experienced in Han China, with much more colour in their lives. On our very first night, we took a stroll into the heart of the city where crowds of smiling people were gathering around innumerable outdoor barbecues and teashops:

"Plucking up our courage, we plunge in among the crowds. Stalls sell cold roast meat cut to order from the bone, shish kebab grilled over hot coals, or slices of juicy melon. One enterprising stallholder gives us a dish of tea made with cherries to sample, then sells us each a bowlful – the whole district gathers round to laugh with us as he flirts with the girls, producing a

few words of English to add to our few words of Chinese. Urumqi has the atmosphere of an Arab town – a lively bazaar, people who are not afraid to shout to us and peer at us. Yet there is an element of China too, in its cleanliness – by next morning there is not a single melon pip left on the pavements."

Whilst we were in Urumqi, a few of us decided to take a night off from our standard hotel dinners and try out a small interesting-looking cafe in the bazaar. We ordered the only food on offer, a huge bowl of vegetable broth in which floated pasta wontons. There were no spoons to eat with, but instead the owner pointed to the communal chopsticks standing in a jam-jar of water on the table.

"Ugh! But there's no alternative! So we immerse the ends of the elderly wooden chopsticks for a few minutes in the boiling hot soup, chatting nonchalantly all the while – that should sterilise them? Next problem – how to fish out the wontons, especially with locals now crowding around the door to watch how we manage the chopsticks. The wontons are too slippery to grab, so must be lifted between two sticks and then hurled into the mouth – avoiding putting the chopsticks between our lips. Altogether an unforgettable meal, and tasty too!"

Though there were few notable 'sights' in Urumqi, we persuaded our guides to take us out to the exotically named Lake of Heavenly Peace, hidden away in the snow-capped Tien Shan Mountains. Most of the journey took us through a landscape of hot, stony desert, cut by dry streambeds and dotted with patches of shrivelled yellow grass where flocks of scrawny sheep and a few horses and two-humped Bactrian camels were grazing. Finally, we climbed into mountains dotted with the yurts of nomadic Kazakh people – the tarmac disappeared and we continued in clouds of dust along a gravel track, snaking upwards in a long series of hairpin bends, tyres skidding on the loose stone around the corners:

"We crest a rise and there is the Heavenly Lake! An expanse of brilliant turquoise sparkling in the sun as its surface is rippled by a light breeze. Ridges of hillside, stubbled with pine trees, run down to the water's edge, framing the snowfields and snow-dusted peaks at the far end of a valley which winds off beyond the lake. It looks like a scene from alpine Switzerland – can we really be in the middle of a barren desert?"

Sadly, that first idyllic impression was dashed when we reached the lake, where a shabby concrete 'tourist centre' dominated the lakeshore, festooned with wires and pipes. At the water's edge a noisy diesel pump was sucking water from the lake for a restaurant and scruffy sightseeing launches were tied up to rusty floating piers.

Now we undertook hours of driving across featureless gravel desert where summer temperatures are high enough to fry an egg or to burn children who fall over on the ground – hours which were memorable only for the 'comfort stop' in a tiny village, where we trooped into the communal village toilet: a wooden hut split into 2 rooms, each with 5 holes in the plank flooring above a steep drop! But those interminable hours brought us to the amazing oasis of Turpan, located 150m below sea level, where a network of underground channels (dug thousands of years ago) bring snow-melt water from the distant mountains into the streets and irrigation ditches, allowing the production of super-sweet melons and grapes:

"The town is a delight after our hours in the desert. I join the local people as they stroll along dirt lanes flanked by sparkling streams of clear water beneath overarching shady trees. They are chatting quietly to each other, washing clothes or filling kettles from the water channels. Animals meander freely and geese paddle peacefully in the streams."

We could not stop to relax for long, however, since a hectic programme of sightseeing was planned for Turpan. We had now picked up another Han Chinese guide (the formidable Miss Li, English-speaking but with little interest in the sights she was supposed to show us) to add to our British and Chinese escorts and Uighur state guide – who frequently fell into dispute with Miss Li, evidence of the tense relationship between Uighur and Han peoples in the province of Xinjiang. We visited the ancient cities of Jiohe and Gaochang, flourishing for over a thousand years until the armies of Genghis Khan passed this way in the 14th century. Now all that was left were eerie passageways between mud-brick edifices which had been so compressed and eroded, that it was difficult to distinguish between man-made walls and natural mudstone cliffs. The Astana cemetery was more interesting: tombs from the Tang Dynasty still occupied by bodies which had been mummified by the dry desert air, lying undisturbed for centuries – though I was doubtful how long they would survive now that tourism was being developed in the area, bringing electric light inside the tombs and the damp breath of increasing numbers of visitors. I had especially looked forward to visiting the Bezeklik Caves of 1000 Buddhas, carved and decorated by the finest artists of the Tang Dynasty (6th century) and Yuan Dynasty (13th century), but sadly they were in an appalling state – partly the result of natural decay after they were abandoned, but also the result of defacement by 19th century Western 'experts' who cut the finest painted frescoes from the cave walls and took them to museums in Europe.

Our onward journey was by train, travelling overnight in a 'soft class' carriage. I was touched by the solicitude of our local guides and drivers, who all waited with us at the station for our late night embarkation (even when the train was delayed until 3am) in order to help us load our luggage on board and wish us goodbye:

"We are summoned to the restaurant car for lunch – a chance to pass through the locked door which keeps our 'soft class' couchettes separated at the back of the train. We walk through the mail-sorting coach, two coaches of 3-tier bunks behind curtains (hard class), then two coaches of upright seats packed with soldiers. In one carriage a wood-burning stove roars beneath a huge urn of boiling water to fill the kettles which provide constant hot tea for all who want it."

At 5.30pm (precisely on time despite innumerable delays), we disembarked at a remote station on the edge of the Gobi Desert, boarding a coach to continue with extreme caution over rough, broken tarmac and then loose gravel towards Dunhuang, swerving frequently to avoid convoys of donkey carts plodding off into the darkness as night fell.

Our reason for visiting Dunhuang was to see the Mogao Caves, carved out of sandstone cliffs over the course of a thousand years by Buddhist monks and filled with sculptures and paintings. They were abandoned in the 14th century, like the Bezeklik Caves, and were accidentally rediscovered in the 19th century. Again, many of their treasures were 'sold' to Western archaeologists, but since the 1960's China had been trying to preserve what remained, even diverting a nearby river and blocking off the cave entrances to protect them from wind and sand erosion. I was on tenterhooks – would we find the same destruction as at the Bezeklik Caves? This time there was no disappointment:

"We enter a dark cave. At first we can see nothing, then we turn on our torches to illuminate a large painted Buddha sculpture flanked by disciples, and walls covered with paintings where the figures flow with energy and movement, beneath an exquisite ceiling whirling with activity as demons fly across it. In another cave a huge Buddha sculpture reclines at the rear, wall paintings represent the legends of his birth, and ceilings are covered with tiny painted Buddhas originally faced with gold. On again, plunging into a pitch-dark entrance to climb steep high steps which lead us out to a clifftop terrace, looking down over a precipice to the 26m high Seated Buddha, its eyes gazing across the void to the very spot where I am standing – an eerie feeling to be examined by the unblinking stare of a creature over 1000 years old."

After such a day, there was no more to be said – we returned to our hotel in total silence.

Before we left the Gobi Desert, of course there had to be a camel ride! Not the bad-tempered single-humped dromedaries I had already ridden in Egypt, however, but a much more pleasant two-humped Bactrian camel. There was no grumbling complaint as I climbed aboard, no lashing about with its head or flashing of its teeth – and lovely fluffy humps fore and aft to lean on, perfect hand warmers on a cold desert morning. We rode out into one of the few areas of sand-dunes in the otherwise stony Gobi Desert, stopping to allow us to scramble up one of the highest dunes to look down on the clear waters of the amazing Crescent Moon Lake, nestled incongruously in a depression amongst the dunes.

Still out in the 'wild west' of China, we were faced with a bumpy 7-hour coach trip across vast expanses of gravel and dust, following the route once used by ancient camel trains to reach the westernmost end of the Great Wall at Jiayuguan, a (restored) complex of gates and courtyards surrounded by battlemented towers, rising from the desert. From here we continued by air, departing from a tiny remote airstrip and flying to another remote airport situated 75km from the city of Lanzhou (why so distant? who knows?). Lanzhou was a huge disappointment – a big soul-less city in the dusty Yellow River Valley, boasting only a few shabby 'attractions', though Gansu Provincial Museum displayed interesting relics unearthed from some of the sites we had been visiting, including the famous 'Flying Horse of Gansu': a small statue seeming to skip lightly into the air, tossing its head coquettishly. Otherwise our visit seemed just a waste of time, especially when our itinerary was once more altered at the last moment to give us an extra (unwanted) night in Lanzhou. Part of the time was spent with a visit to a local school:

"The bell rings for mid-morning exercise – children spill into the courtyard, assume their positions and begin performing a type of tai-chi accompanied by blaring music and commands from loudspeakers. What a difference from a British free-for-all playtime! Then the children return to their bare-walled, shabby classrooms to begin chanting their lessons in chorus."

We also visited a 'model' village home designed for 3 families – just one bed-sitting room each, arranged around a courtyard with a shared kitchen and toilet/ washroom (even this semi-private toilet was more luxurious than in most Chinese villages at the time, which had only a communal block in the streets outside).

Finally, we could escape the monotony of Lanzhou to board another overnight 'soft class' train carriage, arriving next morning in drizzling rain at Xi'an, one of the most popular tourist centres in China. The city was full of impressive architecture, though I found it hard to be enthusiastic – partly because everywhere was wet and grey, but also because I was sad to leave behind the colour and tranquillity of the Far West. There was no disappointment, however, when it came to a visit to the renowned Terracotta Army! When I visited in 1986, there was only one partially excavated pit housing just over 1000 statues to see (now there are 3 excavated pits containing 8000 warriors) but still it was an awe-inspiring sight:

"We hurry inside a vast vaulted building like a great railway station – but instead of trains and railway lines, there are chariots and ranks of soldiers standing facing us at attention. There is no movement, but it seems they only await the command of their emperor to surge forward. Some are serious, others smile, but all are ready for the order, hands reaching for weapons which have vanished into decay or into museum showcases, leaving them grasping at air. A few ponderous static horses stand in front of heaps of earth, their wooden chariots and harnesses rotted away, leaving no more than the imprint of a wheel in the tight packed earth."

One more long train journey (over 24 hours this time) brought us finally to Shanghai, a terrible culture shock as we returned to the hustle and bustle of modern China. The streets were full of traffic – 4 lines of vehicles squeezed into a 2-lane road, weaving back and forth to dodge stationary buses and broken-down trucks. The pavements were packed with people walking or waiting at bus-stops, mostly dressed in yellows, pinks and reds, rather than the drab blue 'Mao suits' still worn in many rural areas. The river alongside the elegant Bund street was crowded with sampan houseboats and convoys of barges. In the residential part of the city, families were allocated just one room each – not surprisingly, most of life was lived out in the streets:

"People wash clothes on washboards in bowls, or wash dishes under a tap at a communal stone sink ... food cooks in woks on the outdoor iron stove, heated by coal-dust briquettes ... grandparents nurse children, sit and doze on stools or lie on padded cotton bedding spread over a lounger ... mothers sit and knit, or reach up to add more washing to dry on bamboo poles above the street."

The people of Shanghai seemed different from those we had met in other cities, perhaps because of their long history of trade and communication with the outside world, when the rest of China was cut off in self-imposed isolation. As I walked along the Bund, several well-educated and immensely polite citizens asked to walk with me, seizing the opportunity to practise their precisely accented English.

Our last days in China brought plenty to see, but the highlights for me had been left behind in the Far West. Finally, we boarded an ancient ferry for the 2-night journey to Hong Kong – still independent of China back in 1986:

"The harbour waters are thick with great container ships sitting sedately as tiny junks, launches and ferries skitter about between them, and powerful hydrofoils and jetfoils plough their routes, heedless of the smaller craft. On land, isolated clumps of sparkling new skyscrapers have spread out to fill the entire shoreline and start to reach up towards the cloud-shrouded hilltops. What a change from drab, single-storey China!"

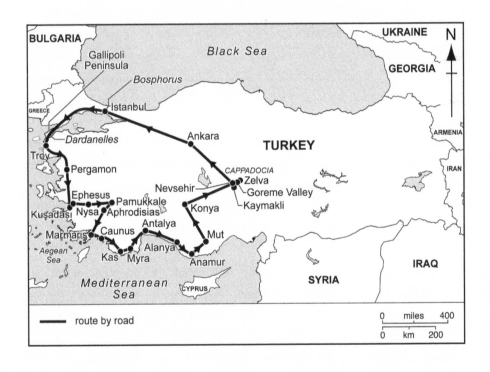

Turkey (August/ September 1988)

UNUSUALLY, I HAD A GAP in my professional touring to allow a holiday during the summer period and chose to go to Turkey. A word of advice – NEVER go to Turkey in August! It is way too hot! We often had temperatures ranging from 40°-50° C, and in those days, air-conditioning was not usual in coaches or the smaller guesthouses and hotels where we stayed. I have another regret about my visit to Turkey too – my chosen tour operator offered a range of tours to all parts of the country, and I was particularly tempted to see the mysterious Giant Heads of Nemrut Dagi in the far east of the country. However, I decided to take a tour of the more popular west and centre of the country first – I thought there was plenty of time to travel to the east on another occasion. Unfortunately, the war in nearby Syria developed and tour operators stopped offering tours to this area – I have still not reached Nemrut Dagi, though it remains in my sights.

The tour started by following the Turkish coastline, first alongside the Dardanelles to visit the infamous Gallipoli Peninsula where so many Allied troops died during the 1st World War: 36,000 died, 22,000 bodies were found and buried ... just 9000 of those were ever identified. Lone Pine cemetery was a sobering sight, cut from the cliffs where the troops were trapped, now silent and windswept with lines of headstones – the most moving inscription reading just 'believed to be buried in this cemetery'.

Then we started on a crash course in ancient history, visiting the sites of innumerable lost cities which once flourished along the Aegean coast, some famous and well-developed for tourism, others still hidden away as they had been for centuries. I had heard of Troy, of course, though the site was difficult to understand, even with the assistance of a special guide. The city was destroyed and re-founded up to 10 times between 3000 and 500 BC, so all I could see were scattered walls and ramps, earth mounds and trenches. I came away more confused than enlightened!

Pergamon was a completely different story – its glory stretched from 3rd century BC to 3rd century AD and many ruins remained from this period, so that Turkish archaeologists had been able to reconstruct some of the most impressive structures for tourists to admire:

"To one side lies the Roman Temple to Zeus (now being reconstructed), then we continue across an open space littered with fallen columns (the remains of a library, world-famous in its time) which are not being restored – yet? We descend a superbly formed, covered stairway of dressed stone blocks to emerge among the almost vertical seats of a vast theatre, stretching down the Acropolis cliff to the place where the magnificent Pergamon Altar once stood, before it was removed (stolen, in Turkish eyes) to a museum in Berlin."

In 2006, after failed negotiations to have it returned, it was decided to recreate the Altar on its original site.

There was considerable controversy about the reconstruction of ancient ruins, with international archaeologists believing that conservation should do no more than preserve the ruins from further decay, whilst the Turks firmly believed that it was better to re-create the buildings, using both original stones as well as new-made sections. From a tourist's point of view, I appreciated the reconstructions, which helped me see better how the city once looked. This applied too in ancient Ephesus. I had been in Ephesus before, one of the stops on a short cruise making up part of one of the European tours I had conducted, and remembered the site as an incomprehensible jumble of ruins. Now it seemed that the ancient city was coming back to life:

"Rounding a bend, the Marble Way stretches off below us towards the distant Library. I am fascinated by the beauty of the decorations on arches and pediments, by the intricate designs of mosaic floors in the houses of merchants. Finally, we come to the Library, now reconstructed so we can actually go inside (though it is still roofless). Mysterious mounds suggest more buildings as yet not revealed – this is a site which will provide new thrills for generations to come."

Excavations at both Pergamon and Ephesus began in the 19th or early 20th century, whilst the excavations at Aphrodisias did not start until 1961, so were still in an early stage when I visited in 1988, with less than one third revealed. Yet already my diary records that ...

"... this will be better even than Ephesus one day! The Temple of Aphrodite – rows of columns still erect, standing side by side around the holy area ... the enchanting Odeon – a gem of marble, with dolphin arm-rests on the posh seats and lions' feet decorating the end of each row ... but my breath is taken away by the Agora being revealed and restored at the foot of the hill. I cannot stop gazing at this vast paved, colonnaded area with fragments of marble fountains and podiums peeping from beneath unexcavated soil where workmen are wielding their pickaxes."

These were the famous sites, but our guide was passionate about the history of the Turkish coast and often took us off up dusty side-tracks to ancient ruins like Nyssa, built in the 3rd century BC:

"We climb through the olive groves where a few stone vaults emerge from the trees. No tourists come here normally, so welcoming villagers wave to us enthusiastically as we pass. We follow a dusty path to where the Bouletarium (council chamber) suddenly looms from a massive hole in the ground, past rows of ancient shops which are now just gaping mouths of stonework by the trail. A donkey brays, a bird sings ... otherwise all is silent. Where has the bustle of an ancient city gone? What caused the population to disappear entirely, leaving not even a peasant village?"

Further south, we took a boat ride on the Dalyan River through reedbeds alive with birdlife to ancient Caunus:

"This is a sad site – no-one cares for it and no-one excavates it. Just a few blocks of stone bear mute testimony to a lost people, while nature reclaims everything: geckos dart in and out of cracks in the stonework, earthquakes shake loose the keystones of massive arches which must once have seemed solid enough to stand forever."

Continuing to the Mediterranean coast, we visited the ancient site of Anamuryum:

"I push through vicious thorns and thistles towards a complex of rooms with mosaic floors which must have been the Baths. Next door, an uninteresting-looking building only tempts me to look inside because of its

semi-circular flight of steps – but what a surprise! Falling away at my feet are rows of theatre seats; far below is the mostly subterranean stage – a Roman-style free-standing theatre, invisible from outside."

Fortunately, there was more to our tour than ancient ruins – I am interested in ancient history, but within limits! I was pleased to explore some of the Orthodox churches still remaining, though there was no sign of any of them being used since the entire Greek population was removed to Greece in 1923 (one of the causes of the ongoing tension between Greece and Turkey). At Myra, we picked our way past sheep and chickens in the village street to find the partially buried Basilica of St Nicholas (Santa Claus), probably the oldest church in Turkey (4th century) with recycled Roman columns and well-worn marble mosaic floors – I had hoped to find the former tomb of St Nicholas (his body is now in Italy) but no-one we could ask seemed to know where it was, or even to care. More impressive was the Church of the Evangelists in the mountains near Mut:

"We walk up a dirt road – the air is cool and fresh, scented with pine; the ground beneath our feet softened with pine needles. The view grows more spectacular as the ascent grows more difficult ... pairs of eagles soar acrobatically above us ... huge caves in the hillside are being used as overnight shelters for goats, safe from wolves behind thorn fences. We reach the two churches, one in ruins but the other complete except for its roof. Stepping through a doorway beneath a beautifully carved lintel, we find columns and arches soaring skywards."

The Turkish coast offered different types of sightseeing opportunities too. We visited the gleaming white cliffs of Pamukkale, which feature on every advertisement for the country. At the top of the cliffs was yet another ancient site (Hieropolis) which once enclosed a sacred thermal spring of water – still accessible (when I visited) within the confines of a motel:

"The water is blood-heat, making the air feel cool on the skin in comparison, and full of tiny bubbles of gas, rising with the water from the spring. Near the source, the bubbles are so thick that I can barely see through them – the water fizzes like champagne."

The cliffs themselves were amazing! Calcium in the water was deposited on the cliff-face as the water from the spring flowed over it, creating a series of terraces where the water collected in shallow pools. When I visited in 1988, it was still possible to walk across the calcium-coated rock and through the white mud or gravel at the bottom of streams and knee-deep pools – now special artificial pools have been created to allow the tourist experience whilst protecting this natural phenomenon.

The tour included lots of chances to cool off in the sea, and even a couple of full days to spend on the beach. By the time we reached the Turquoise Coast, I was weary of archaeological sites and carpet shops, and decided to spend a day on the beach at Kas, finding an idyllic inlet with a tiny pebble beach, even boasting a small cafe with sunloungers and umbrellas:

"I walk down the steeply shelving beach into the water, and it is COLD! What agonising bliss! Further out to sea there are some warmer patches, but the surface stays icy all day. I am surrounded by a turquoise transparency through which I can see black fish circling to investigate my white toes. All day I move between sea and beach umbrella shade ... but the sun burns me right through the umbrella to a lurid shade of red."

In Kusadasi a group of us tried out a traditional Turkish Bath – 20 minutes sweating in a steam bath, followed by a vicious scrub with a loofah then with soap, and finally a massage, before retiring to a lounger to rest and sip tea whilst being tenderly dried off:

"We were all a bit shy while sitting naked together (mixed!) in the steam bath, but by the time we have been laid out two at a time on a marble slab for massage, we have lost all modesty and the merest wisp of clothing is enough for us."

Whenever possible I explored alone the communities where we were staying, usually choosing a time when the heat of the day was fading into evening and the population were emerging to enjoy the coolness. I watched as people hosed down the streets (the Turks were incredibly clean, the streets outside the cities immaculate and litter-free) ... as men in baggy black pants with red waistbands chatted in men-only cafes, whilst their women, also in baggy pants and headscarves, squatted to chat on their balconies ... as little boys (supposedly over 12 years old, though they looked only 9 or 10 to me) carried trays of tea for customers in shops, balancing trays of sesame buns on their heads. Children chatted to me in the streets, showing off their few words of English, while shopkeepers lured me to their shops with German, French or Italian phrases, offering me tea or fruit whether I bought or not. As a woman walking on my own, ladies invited me into their homes to share tea or a bunch of grapes – often in the hope of selling me a piece of embroidery or a silk scarf, though I never felt hassled. In one town, a teacher of French asked to accompany me as I walked then invited me for tea, talking all the while about his worries about the political situation in Turkey. I did not feel threatened in any way by his attentions (though my roommate allowed herself to be invited to stay for several days with a man she met in Kusadasi – I would not have gone that far!).

After two weeks on the Turkish coast, we turned inland, visiting first the city of Konya where the famous Whirling Dervishes have their base. We were able to visit the tomb of Mevlana, the poet saint who started the movement, but the Dervishes were officially banned by Ataturk in 1925 because he feared their influence and so now they were only allowed to perform their ceremony once a year, whirling themselves into a trance and so nearer to God.

We were heading into the heart of the country now, to the region of Cappadocia – for me, the most memorable part of the entire tour. The region was once volcanic and was covered with a fine ash which solidified into a rock called 'tufa', soft enough to be eroded over time by wind and rain into the incredible rock formations for which this region is famed. Soft enough, too, to be carved into cave homes and churches, safely hidden in the difficult years after the coming of Christianity from the 4th century onwards:

"Suddenly, out of a monotonous landscape rises a rock honeycombed with caves and holes – this is Uchisar, set in the heart of the Goreme Valley, filled with spires and pinnacles of tufa rock, with troglodyte dwellings cut into the hillsides wherever we look. The rock is shaded in layers of white, pink and even green, dotted with the vivid red tile roofs of more recent village houses."

Our hotel was in one of the old villages where precipitous (and rather smelly) alleyways clambered up and down the hillsides, houses squatting behind closed courtyards, broken vaults and arches everywhere, stone stairways now leading nowhere as cave homes had been abandoned and left to decay. Yet our hotel was enchanting – a network of courtyards and stairs, with most rooms (including mine) actually cool vaulted caverns dug into the hillside. I loved it! Hopefully in the ensuing years since my visit, someone has realised the potential of these abandoned cave homes and has rescued them from dereliction. As the sun began to sink, the village streets filled with men returning home with laden donkeys, children playing together and women sitting outside their doorways, knitting and chatting. All responded cheerily to my greeting of 'Merhaba', and some invited me over to talk and laugh together for a while.

We had two days to explore this fascinating region, starting with a walk high above Goreme Valley – a place from which we could best appreciate the unique geology of the landscape:

"Below us are forests of rock pinnacles, each peppered with cave entrances (though many are now blocked off or transformed into pigeon lofts), topped with dark stone 'Noddy hats' of harder rock which does not erode so easily. The scene stretches on and on, new cliffs being eroded into gullies which may yet become pinnacles – a whole plateau on the move, its sides melting away into an eroded jumble."

Down in the valley itself, we entered the Goreme Open Air Museum, a convoluted system of valleys full of painted and carved entries to chapels, some no longer accessible because their steps had eroded away, others made accessible by modern concrete or iron steps – some hermitages reached only by shallow footholds carved into the rock:

"The Apple Church: its original entry has fallen away so we squeeze through a narrow modern passageway into a tiny but perfect Byzantine church nestled beneath multiple rock-cut domes. Everywhere is richly painted, with portraits of Christ and many saints looking down on us from every wall and vault, coloured mainly with russet and sandy shades, highlighted with black, white and the palest aquamarine blue."

In Zelva, our guide offered us an exploration 'for the courageous only' – how could I resist? We entered a cave-house with a solid front wall and windows, then climbed out through a hole in the wall on to a precarious ledge across the cliff-face to reach several otherwise inaccessible houses. Then on to the monastery … up a metal ladder … then stone steps … into a chimney which we could climb only using footholds cut into each side … dropping 3m through a hole in the floor to a chamber below … down another chimney … then some vertical stone steps which finally led us back to the valley floor. We had certainly experienced the Goreme Valley in a way which Health & Safety rules would probably reject today. In fact, one group member landed awkwardly after the drop and we had to help her out of the labyrinth – later a doctor confirmed that she had broken her foot.

Some miles away, we explored the Underground City at Kaymakli, a maze of underground passages and chambers with mysterious origins – perhaps it was built as individual cellars which finally linked up? Or perhaps it was always intended as a refuge in difficult times? It was a huge complex: 8 storeys deep, reaching a depth of 40m below ground, with narrow tunnels specially designed to force fresh air into every corner – there was no mustiness inside:

"We bend into a crouch position and set off through narrow tunnels and even narrower doorways, sometimes flanked by massive 'millstones' which could be rolled across to block entry, and smaller holes at knee-level to cut at the legs of a passing enemy. We follow a well-lit trail, but occasionally I shine my torch up enticingly mysterious steps and passages leading off to other rooms and levels. In places, over-enthusiastic builders have dug too close and broken through into earlier diggings, revealing a labyrinth all around us – thank goodness for the arrows marking our trail!"

We were also taken off the beaten track to the Soganli Valley, wandering through a village past donkey enclosures and houses partly cut from the rocks and partly built above ground. Here were more beautifully carved and painted churches, especially the spectacular Church of the Dome, its domed roof carved inside the pinnacle of a rock tower – though that tower was crumbling fast. It was obviously once part of a massive complex with several other churches and tombs – sections of the church had been roughly restored and patched with lumps of rock, but many stairways now led nowhere, and many rooms had lost their outer walls. In such a huge area, what chance might there be to preserve everything? Or will the Turks manage only to conserve the principal sights of Goreme Valley, leaving the rest to erode away?

Back to the modern world now, following highways full of speeding impatient traffic, which was often a hair's breadth from collision, into the thick polluted air of Ankara. The only highlight to record in Turkey's capital was the Anatolian Civilisation Museum which led us step by step through the country's long history, from gold jewellery 4500 years old, through Hittite and Phrygian treasures to the arrival of the Romans. The museum's collections stopped there – as if Turkey had nothing from the last 2000 years to boast about. That is certainly not true, as our last few days were to prove – our tour culminated in the fascinating city of Istanbul.

I am normally not a fan of cities, but Istanbul was enchanting! The Grand Bazaar: covered by a beautifully painted vaulted roof … glistening with stalls selling gold, jewels, finely painted camel bone trinkets and brightly coloured cloth … vendors listening out for the language of potential customers, then asserting they had visited at least one city in their client's country to engage them in conversation (one even began an exchange of Shakespearean quotations with us!). The Blue Mosque: looking through the wires supporting the lamps, to the ethereal beauty of the roof … its tiles delicately coloured in blue and red, warming into deeper red and gold in the main dome. Hagia Sophia: great Arabic roundels tacked on to the walls, yet still an image of Christ Redeemer sitting above the main door … thick swathes of angel wings supported the dome, yet their faces had been painted out and replaced with Arabic holy words – Islam had not managed to erase all traces of Christian heritage from this 6th century church, turned mosque, turned museum. The harem of the Topkapi Palace: dark stone passageways leading into the Sultan's luxurious rooms … stained glass windows gleaming like jewels … richly carpeted floors and benches … glowing tiles on the walls, ornate baroque paintings on the ceilings. The Underground Cistern: descending steps into a mysterious vaulted chamber … dim lights reflecting off oily black water … softly illuminated arches stretching into the distant gloom.

Most of the city was a solid mass of traffic crawling through a haze of pollution, yet below the Galata Bridge we found clearer air and innumerable barrows and snack bars selling fresh fish, newly caught from the Bosphorus. The bridge itself was lined with fishermen using everything from marlin-rods to bits of string, baited with bread or mussels. Walking out one evening, I spotted a large sign proclaiming 'Water-pipe Garden':

"I find an arcaded courtyard, perhaps once a caravanserai, full of Turks chatting and puffing on their 'nargilehs' like a band of demented clarinetists struggling to produce a tune. Cheerful waiters serve apple tea (one even carrying the tray on his head) and assist tourists to get their pipes to light

and draw properly. The owner emerges to charm me with jokes and a warm welcome, then leaves me to sit as long as I wish."

A delightful way to spend my final evening, with another taste of the warmth and hospitality of the Turkish people.

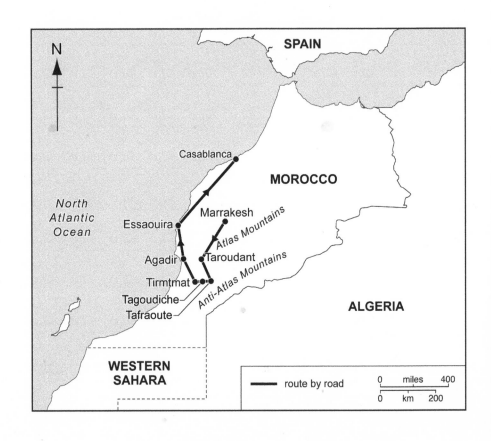

Morocco (March 1989)

I WAS OFF TO MOROCCO, this time in the company of a friend though usually I prefer the selfish independence of travelling alone. Our first and last nights were spent in Marrakesh, which remains a magical city in my memories (though heavy rain rather washed away my enthusiasm when we returned at the end of our tour). Especially the souk (market) enchanted me, walking into the cool, dark shade of a canvas roof, absorbed in a world of unfamiliar sights and scents:

"... spice stalls rich in enticing aromas which hint at exotic flavours ... carpenters' shops giving off the fragrant scent of fresh sawdust ... stands of dried fruit, the owner squatting in the centre like a genie appearing from the ether – however did he get in there? Butchers selling heaps of pungent sheep heads, ox feet and offal, one dismembering a cow's head with the careful precision of a surgeon peeling back the scalp. Pharmaceutical stalls offering heaps of hedgehog skins, dried lizards, tiny horns or herbs – while a chameleon clings to a stick at the entrance, tasked with catching flies which try to pollute the wares."

In the quieter back streets of the souk were the wool-dyers' workshops where young men were plunging long poles into steaming vats of colour, emerging with forearms dyed indigo or lurid red. In the leather souk, hordes of boys were working in tiny booths, stitching and cutting leather surrounded by their wares.

Alongside the souk lay the large open space at the heart of the old town, the famous Jemaa el Fna. In the daytime the square had no particular charm, but at night it seemed to come alive with entertainers, each individual act surrounded by a dense ring of fascinated spectators. In one corner I spotted the heads of acrobats rising above the crowds as they clambered up into a human pyramid; elsewhere there were musicians or comedians evoking gales of laughter with jokes which (of course) I could not understand. At the heart of groups of people seated on the ground were storytellers or political orators, holding their audiences entranced. Unfortunately, our white faces were everywhere recognised as potentially generous donors and, though it meant we were encouraged (or even pushed) to the front of the crowds, we were repeatedly milked of our money before we even had time to work out what the act was about. As darkness fell, swarms of begging women and children snatched at us for alms and a snake charmer demanded money from us when we just glanced in his direction … it all became too much for us and we had to retire to our hotel.

The highlight of our trip was to be a week walking in the Anti-Atlas Mountains, though first we had to cross the higher Atlas Mountains, bouncing in Landrovers across a landscape dotted with miserable terraces of wheat enclosed within hedges of prickly-pear cactus and adorned with orchards of blossoming olive and almond trees. We passed tiny villages of simple mud-brick houses where flocks of black goats wandered freely. I was amused to see some of the goats climbing into the branches of small, twisted trees – Argon trees, we were told, producing a fruit which can be used for oil. Our road twisted its way back and forth *'like a demented hosepipe flicking out-of-control across the hillside'* (as my diary describes it), climbing up to the Tizi n' Test Pass (2100m) amid snow-flecked mountains, entering the lands of the Berber people who occupied this area long before the Arabs arrived. Now we started to see women who were not heavily veiled, but instead wore brightly coloured lacy cloths over their heads and lower face only.

Finally, we slithered down an often washed-out, muddy road into the Souss Valley, to reach the walled town of Taroudant. Here I again made my way into the narrow alleys of the souk, roofed with matting for shade – but what a difference from Marrakesh! No hassle here from shopkeepers trying to force us into their shops, no insistently begging children – just a few smiling faces calling 'Bonjour' to us as we passed. On our way through the

High Atlas, we had stopped to see the ruined fortified mosque at Tinmel; in Taroudant we were taken to the abandoned fortress Tiout Kasbah – for centuries the Berbers had fought for independence from rulers in distant Fez, and the mountains in this area were studded with the remains of fortresses. Fortunately, we found a local guide to escort us through this Kasbah:

"Inside is like a maze – I have no idea where I am going but follow blindly up heaps of stony earth and through doorways so blocked by rubble that we must bend almost double, under ceilings where even the beams are cracked or splitting. Occasional finely-cast plaster archways or painted domes give a hint of former glory, but today the Kasbah is no more than a heap of crumbling mud and splintering timber."

There was no money to restore monuments in these remote areas, especially since the Berbers were still considered to be an inferior race (though they had inhabited Morocco longer than the Arabs), so I imagine many of these fortresses will simply crumble back into the mountainsides.

Whilst in Taroudant, some of our ladies decided to try out the local 'hammam' (bathhouse) – open in the afternoons for women, and evenings for men. We were lucky to arrive at the same time as a couple of local ladies who took us under their wing and showed us how everything worked, organising our payment and leading us through winding, pitch-dark passages to the first room (still at normal temperature) where 20 women were relaxing on platforms in various stages of undress, eating oranges:

"Here we remove our clothes, and our new friend Fatima finds each of us a big black bucket, then leads us through increasingly hot rooms full of naked ladies and children – all sitting on the tiled floor, splashing desultorily in buckets. The women are massively obese with pendulous breasts, protruding stomachs, vastly rounded hips, immense legs – we are like starvelings beside these ideals of Arab beauty. They are completely unembarrassed, proud of their shape (and sympathetic that we are so thin!), showing off their stomachs and hips with the tiniest of bikini briefs which vanish beneath rolls of fat. In the hottest room we find the hot water tap, where Fatima fills our buckets and fetches mitt-loofahs and ceramic scrubbing discs for us, before smearing us all with her treacle-like black soap (which turns red on our skin) and beginning to scrub the nearest of us energetically, We all follow suit until the heat becomes too much and we

retreat back to the relaxation room to rest. Finally, we depart, our skin smooth as silk and squeaky clean!"

A memorable experience, and possibly the only time in my life when I have felt slim!

We drove on deeper into the Anti-Atlas Mountains, the land much dryer and stonier than in the Atlas, with no verdant valley bottoms or lush irrigated fields – just clouds of red dust infiltrating everywhere and rocks scattered across the land and the road. Only the Argon trees and cactus-like succulents seemed to survive here. Our road passed high above deep valleys, beneath peaks and cliffs eroded from the mountainsides – spectacular scenery. The only traces of humanity were tiny villages of flat-roofed mud-brick homes, clinging to hilltops and straddling knife-edged ridges, or fortified kasbahs (now often used as grain stores) guarding the valleys. Finally, we descended to the sleepy little town of Tafraout where our group fanned out in search of food supplies for our week-long trek, overwhelming the few shops available. We had hoped for a quiet night, but our hopes were dashed when the sound of drums and pipes playing lively tunes, informed us that a wedding party was taking place nearby:

"As the evening progresses, the dogs join in – howling and yipping in a diabolic chorus backed by the steady rhythm of the drum and the shrill voices of chanting women."

Having finally fallen off to sleep, we were woken at 5am next morning by the call of the muezzin – being Friday, the call was extended into a long harangue over loudspeakers. No chance for a lie-in before we started our trek!

However, nothing could spoil our excitement as we began to walk, first across fields of bright green barley then following a dusty track between rocky spires and mounds, a jumble of red stone broken into a thousand pieces. The only sound was the scrunching of our feet on gravel and sand eroded on to the path from the rocks around, with occasional exclamations as we spotted lizards flitting from crack to crack, or large black beetles fleeing frantically from our approach. The track began to climb a serpentine route uphill, beneath ridges of rock like petrified waves surging up the mountains, with the sun growing ever hotter and the patches of shade ever rarer:

"What a delight as we round a bend to see before us a huge bowl of green fields nestled beneath the peaks, in which clusters of multi-coloured houses

cling to the hillside like swallow nests. This is Tagoudiche, our first destination. As we walk in, we are greeted from all sides – one unveiled graceful girl in an embroidered black sari, hurries over to shake me by the hand. By the time we reach the cool concrete hut which will be our base, I am in love with this village!"

This warm welcome was repeated wherever we went in the remote villages of our trek, especially from the women. The men were out in the fields, the children usually in school, but we met women everywhere as we explored the villages, often clustered around the drinking-water pipes or irrigation channels. Most spoke little French, some none at all, but they were keen to communicate by sign language and even to teach us a little of their Berber language (though all I remember now is 'Bislama', meaning Goodbye).

The walk on to our next village was cooler, with cloud to temper the heat of the sun, and colourful wild flowers scattered like a rock garden across the sides of the path. There was no urgency, so we ambled gently along – until a crowd of begging children appeared, throwing stones at us when we gave them nothing. However, by the afternoon we had reached Tirmtmat:

"A green oasis with palms and argon trees ... a broad river bed and a few enticing pools of water to bathe our aching feet ... an enchanting, pink-washed village ... a silence broken only by the croaking of frogs and chattering of birds. Flat stepping stones take us dry-footed across the river, where two little girls solemnly shake our hands, then lead us to their homes where their mothers also wait to greet us with a handshake. As the sun sets, herds of goats and sheep are brought in from the hills, and mating frogs begin their creaking chorus. What a fabulous place to relax!"

We spent two days in this idyllic valley, scrambling into the nearby hills seeking out summits which offered the best views, then returning to bathe in a deep green pool of icy water in the stream, stretching out to dry in hot sunshine on nearby rocks. Our accommodation was very simple, sleeping side-by-side in sleeping bags on the concrete floor of our hut, cooking our meals on a pair of camping stoves in the doorway, washing in the stream – yet the tranquillity of the setting and the friendliness of the local people ensured that this place became the highlight of my tour.

You can perhaps imagine my sadness when our time in Tirmtmat came to an end and we had to shoulder our bags for a final hour's walk back to the road (accompanied by an affectionate village dog which had adopted us ... and kept us awake at night defending us from imaginary enemies) to catch the local bus back to Tafraout. After days of tranquillity, Tafraout was a hurly-burly of people attending the weekly market – donkey carts and trucks picked their way between clusters of men selling olives and dates, almonds and vegetables, baskets and any other saleable goods (from donkey saddles to hubcaps). Only when the market disbanded and the tourist coaches (on a day-trip from Agadir) departed, did some calm return to the town, allowing a shopkeeper we met last time we were here, to invite us to join him for some 'Moroccan whisky' (actually just mint tea) and a chat.

In a cloud of depression, not helped by grey rain-laden skies, I rejoined our Landrovers to leave the mountains and head towards Morocco's Atlantic coast. Our drivers seemed to be delighted to be returning to 'civilisation', hurtling at top speed along die-straight roads, yodelling with glee as they swooped up and down gullies, every part of their ancient vehicles vibrating as if about to explode. We reached the coast at the internationally-known resort of Agadir – lines of glamorous Western-style hotels set amid gardens beside sandy beaches and a dull grey sea which reflected the sky. It might have been a dream resort for many holidaymakers, but for me there was no trace of Morocco in it, and none of the beauty of the mountains – I just wanted to stay longer in Tirmtmat, not come here! Fortunately, our destination was not Agadir, so we continued on along the shore to Essaouira. What were we going to find there? I was not hopeful – oh to be back in the Anti-Atlas!

"Cath and I reach our room and fling open the shutters. In front of us the sun sets into golden clouds behind the clock-tower. On benches beside the walls sit clusters of ladies, entirely hidden within heavy white serge overgarments and heavily veiled – only their eyes flit energetically back and forth. The streets are full of strolling people: women in veils; women in Western garb; men in djellabas; men in trousers; black men; white men; even the occasional tourist. I can't wait to explore, rushing into the old walled town by the first gateway I find. Before me, a labyrinth of darkening passages and alleyways opens up, hung with brilliantly coloured carpets. Workshops stretch back from tiny entrances ... artisans are working at leather or

woodcarving in the gloom. Beside the harbour, men set up handcarts ready to fry fish dinners for their clients on the spot, while huge herring gulls wheel overhead."

As you will gather from my diary extract, my mood was transformed by my first sight of Essaouira – I had no idea of what to expect, but was totally transfixed by the exotic atmosphere of the town from the first time I looked out of my hotel window.

The next morning, we woke to grey skies and heavy rain showers, but decided to swathe ourselves in waterproofs and go out to explore. The town was slow to wake on this soggy day, but already men were out in the streets wearing sacking-like djellabas with pointed hoods (like pixie-hats) and women were scuttling about their business beneath umbrellas. We joined them wandering in the bazaar, ducking under archways to avoid sudden showers and delving into shops selling unique thuya-wood items when the rain became too heavy. Finally, we reached the residential parts of the city:

"... a maze of narrow alleyways twisting and winding between tall white buildings, each adorned with blue painted shutters and elaborately decorated doorways which open to tiled lobbies. Frequently the alleys dive beneath arches or into tunnels roofed with massive beams which support a house above. Workshops are interspersed with homes, many resounding to the hammering and planing of woodworkers. A craftsman takes us aside to explain the different types of wood he works with. A little boy invites us in to watch him trimming tiny pieces of mother-of-pearl with wire-cutters, before hammering them into the holes he has drilled to make the pattern on the table he is decorating. A woman spins wool with a bicycle-wheel, while 2 men work a wide loom, turning out striped blankets. Men sit cross-legged on the floor stitching garments."

In the end Essaouira was enchanting, and I would not have missed it for the world – despite all the complaints I had stored up in my diary when we left the mountains!

One last Moroccan experience awaited us as we assembled at the local bus station for our public bus back to Casablanca. A huge storm had passed in the night, so the bus station was awash with muddy puddles amongst which lines of buses, together with donkey carts and camels, waited patiently for their loads. Men and handcarts scuttled back and forth carrying heavy bundles to the buses to be man-handled up rickety metal ladders to the roof. Our guide ensured we arrived early so that there was space under the tarpaulins on the roof for our baggage, and so that there were seats for us, squeezed in among local people who stared at us, open-mouthed with amazement and curiosity. Though I had loved the scenery and architecture of Morocco, what really made the trip special were these Moroccan people.

▬▬▬	route by road
··✈···	route by aeroplane
NP	National Park

0	miles	800
0	km	400

North America – the West (September/ October 1990)

BY 1990, I HAD DECIDED it was time for another big trip – this time taking on an entire continent (North America) with an organised coach tour in the west and self-drive in the East. The coach tour was chosen because it visited as many of the National Parks as possible: I was keen to see the natural wonders of the continent, without having to suffer too much city life (nor to spend too much time experiencing the overindulgent – it seems to me – American way of life). Even a first glimpse of the traffic and pollution, advertising billboards and beggars in Los Angeles was enough for me to rejoice that our coach was carrying us as fast as possible away into the nearby mountains of Yosemite NP. Yet that proximity was a threat to the Park itself; the National Parks in USA were leased to commercial companies who were supposed to protect them from over-commercialisation, yet instead I saw big hotels (one even with its own golf course) right at the entry to the Park and innumerable campsites inside. Our guide told us that there were discussions going on, whether to close the area entirely or to limit access only to buses and shuttle buses, banning access by cars. As far as I know, neither option was ever actioned, and commercialisation continues unabated.

Before we entered the Park, we were introduced to California's massive and ancient trees in the National Forest which surrounds Yosemite:

"A shower of rain just before we reach Mariposa Grove brings out the scent of pine and cedar as we stroll on soft beds of needles and rotted bark, between massive trunks of Ponderosa Pine and Incense Cedar, occasionally stopping to marvel at the vast red Giant Sequoias glowing in the darkening

forest, or to mourn beside fallen giants – their roots winding inwards to form the inadequate base which brought the tree's downfall."

We drove up to Glacier Point for our first view over the forested Yosemite Valley, looking down on a panorama of canyons, cliffs and rock domes, then continued into the Park itself. Sadly, I had only 3 hours to explore – just time to follow a rough path of sand and pine needles to the base of Yosemite Falls (with only a trickle of water left after a dry summer). Birds chattered in the trees, jays flashed across the path in a burst of blue plumage, squirrels ferreted noisily through the undergrowth – the natural world stilling visitors into quiet reflection. Overall, Yosemite seemed a lot smaller than I had expected – basically just one protected valley ringed by some impressive cliffs, yet so over-exploited that it was hard to get away from people and the facilities they demand.

No chance yet to escape into the wilderness, since our next stop was one of only 4 cities which I visited in depth during my whole 2-month trip: San Francisco – though it was an interesting city both for its situation and its population. I walked in the narrow strip of public gardens called Golden Gate Park, full of people roller skating, cycling or strolling in the sun, surrounded by vans selling coffee, sausages and cupcakes (to undo any healthy effects of the exercise!). I jostled the crowds for a clear view of the Golden Gate Bridge (considered an 'impossible' bridge to build, so plaques talked of the 'eternity of the bridge representing the eternity of mankind' – let's hope it never collapses!), then walked the precipitous streets, including Lombard Street (the world's crookedest street) where cars wound slowly downhill amid the scent of overheated brakes. And of course, I rode on one of the famous San Fran cable-cars:

" ... clanking precariously up and downhill, one man in the front driving, another at the rear hauling on the brake; passengers packed inside or hanging on the outside, screaming and shouting in excitement, especially when 2 cars pass and the 'hangers-on' brush against each other."

Now at last we could head northwards, leaving behind some of the crowds as we made our way along the Redwood Highway, stopping to admire examples of the tallest of the Sequoia family – the Coastal Sequoia, which grows up to 100m high, living for thousands of years thanks to a tannin in its bark which can resist the fires which regularly ravage these forests. I could not help but reflect on the history of these trees, witnesses to the earlier lifestyle of native tribes and to the arrival of white men with their destructive ways – living monuments! Modern suburban sprawl was left behind as we followed the thickly forested coastline past quiet fishing or lumber settlements, admiring traditional homes with wooden facades reminiscent of Wild West movies, shocked by the number of people apparently living permanently in trailer parks:

"We stop high on the cliffs, whipped by the wind, peering over the top of ranks of Christmas trees to the turquoise sea and creaming breakers far below. Bays and headlands alternate their way into the distance, punctuated by massive basalt rocks which lie offshore, while the beaches are littered with bleached tree trunks washed down by floods long ago. Others lie around the edges of lagoons and marshy hollows, cut off by drifting grey sand."

As we moved through Oregon and into Washington State, the weather worsened to bring veils of rain blown ashore on strong winds, which set the traffic lights in Seattle bobbing and jigging in a wild dance above the road junctions. I was not impressed by Seattle, mostly a plain and purely functional city, though I rode their unique monorail out to the illuminated Space Needle, pride of the city. Only the harbour interested me – a bustle of ferries plying in and out, dodging a freighter casting free from its tugs and heading off to sea, sounding its horn against the thick layers of mist and rain obscuring its path.

The rain escorted us all the way across the Canadian border and into Vancouver, causing the cancellation of all our planned sightseeing trips, yet when I woke next morning I was greeted by a sky clear of cloud and washed a pale pink by the rising sun – what a transformation! With all official sightseeing cancelled, I resolved to spend the whole day seeing as much as possible on my own, starting with a dash across town by Seabus and local bus to the cable car up Grouse Mountain:

"The cloud is pursuing the cable car up the mountain, but the summit is clear. There's no view since all the hills and valleys below are draped in swirling cloud but at the top, wooden cabins hum with activity as they prepare for the ski season. A mule deer and her fawn graze without fear amid the buzz of chain saws. The cloud finally rises to cover the summit, clearing

the lower slopes for a fine panorama of watery inlets and city skyscrapers as I descend again."

I sped around the city on foot and by bus, ascending the Harbour Centre Tower for crystal-clear views, then traversing elegant (and touristy) Gastown into Chinatown to visit Dr Sun-Yat-Sen's Garden – vaunted in my guidebook, but a disappointment with ponds full of thick grey water, like a sewer! The huge Stanley Park was more interesting, though I have not forgotten the sight in the 'free zoo' of a sad polar bear licking his cage bars disconsolately (I hope that, in these more ecologically-friendly times, he has been sent home). On the other hand, the (expensive) Aquarium was amazing, especially for its underwater viewing chambers where I could watch pure white Beluga whales, drifting like silent ghosts around their sunlit pool, eyes closed in an apparent trance until suddenly one opened its eyes to fix me with a curious stare. Though I am not a 'city person', Vancouver is an exception – full of colour and variety, its wild environs reaching deep into the heart of the city as a constant reminder of nature unconquered by man.

From Vancouver we were heading off into the wilderness of western Canada, already deep into autumn or even the start of winter. We followed the twin lines of the Grand Trunk Railway and the Canadian Pacific Railway (described as a 'triumph of construction over geography' when it opened in 1885), along the narrow gorge of the Fraser River beneath tree-covered cliffs which rose steeply above us, looking down over fast-flowing rapids in the grey, silt-filled river below:

"The river roars over white-water rapids, the railway cuts through tunnels or passes below protective roofs, while in the distance a snow-capped mountain reveals itself from the cloud. The river is full of rocks, the hillsides crumbling into gravel scree – this part of the highway (built 1962) cost a million dollars per mile, needing concrete foundations and frequent retaining walls. Extra-long trains wind like serpents along their respective tracks – we count 123 coal wagons on one, with 2 extra engines in the centre to boost the power. Because of these 2 railways, they could not build the highway where they wanted, nor even blast the rocks at will, for fear of blocking the rails."

As we approached Kamloops, the land became greener and the river clearer – so clear now that we could see the salmon migrating. Later we learned that this was the largest Sockeye salmon run for 77 years, with 21 million salmon making their way back from the sea to the place where they were born up to 5 years previously, in order to spawn ... and die (they adapt so well to conditions at sea that they can no longer live long in fresh water). At first, we only noticed the surface of the river stirring as they passed, but our guide spotted a sign pointing to a 'fish festival' and diverted from our route to investigate:

"Down at the river bank, at first I see nothing – no leaping fish, just a few fins here and there, but as my eye becomes attuned to the scene, I realise that just below the surface are thousands of dark red fish swimming upstream in energetic bursts followed by a minute or so rest. A few leap out of the water but they're not interested in feeding, just forging on with dark green heads and white jaws straining forwards. Further on, the water is shallower and less peaty so that the fish are revealed as a vibrant red carpet across the entire river bed. A few have grounded in the shallows and have died, their lurid brilliance now fading through pinkish grey to the colour of mud."

We were in the heart of the Rockies now, with scenic wonders all around us: Spahat Creek, where a stream flowed from a dark hole to plunge headfirst into a massive rocky gorge, rushing on in creamy turmoil to join the main river valley ahead ... Rearguard Falls (at 800 miles from the sea, the furthest point which the massive Chinook salmon can reach) where we scrambled down a slope slippery with a dusting of snow, to a broad rock step over which tons of green water were gushing in a smooth unbroken chute ... and Maligne Canyon:

"The snow on the roads has been cleared, but that's not true of the footpath – some of our group make it no further than the first steps before sliding out of control. After that, we are all slip-sliding away down to the bridge over the chasm. The river is out of sight far below us, hidden by a jumble of rocks, holes and eroded cliffs – only its roar confirms it is there. A couple of us slide on further for a view back up the gorge towards the bridge, where our group (brightly coloured in woollen caps and gloves) hangs excitedly over the ravine."

Now for the first time we were seeing wildlife too – black Douglas squirrels with orange bellies, chattering at us furiously as we walked through the forests; a single grey coyote trotting unconcerned across a snow-covered meadow; a family of stately Wapiti elks calmly watching us from the roadside; at Maligne Canyon, a group of Bighorn sheep sitting on a rock above us, confident enough of their superior foothold on the snow to be unafraid of our slithering approach. When I emerged from our motel in Jasper early one morning, I found Mule deer nibbling delicately at a willow tree outside the door, and a female elk and her calf breakfasting on a rowan nearby – though we were warned not to approach too closely, since elk can be dangerous.

Jasper National Park was full of scenic highlights: we saw the Athabasca Falls, a narrow cleft in the rock which compresses the river into a torrent before releasing it again to spread across a wide stony bed … the Endless Chain, a ridge of continuous peaks and cols, spattered with greenish glaciers and coated with gleaming white snow ... then continued to Columbia Icefield. This was one of the best-known sights in the Jasper NP, its visitor centre crowded with Japanese tourists, yet it was a disappointment to me: the 'concession' on the access road to the glacier belonged exclusively to the Glacier Tour Co. so we could not use it, and the cloud had sunk low enough to obscure the view from the main road. Forget the Columbia Icefield! Instead, we made frequent photo stops as we moved through a white world (snow by the road, snow-frosted forest, snow-capped mountains vanishing into thick cloud in the sky) to a viewpoint overlooking Peyto Lake:

"We descend a slippery, snow-packed path... will the view be worth the effort? Oh yes! Suddenly a great vista opens out before us – the vast valley of the Mistaya River that we have been following for some time, and below us a vivid green lake seemingly inlaid into the dark green of the forest."

Peyto Lake was named for the leader of a packhorse train who always declared he would rather move his bedroll down to the lakeshore instead of remaining in the crowded company of the (just 6 or 7) traders in his train. How would these early residents have coped with the onslaught of mass tourism? Our tour was one of the last of the season, yet still we were finding crowds in some of the most popular spots, especially as we descended from the remote mountains into the resorts of Lake Louise and Banff.

Morning in Banff dawned with sunlit mountains and clear sky, perfect for a busy scenic day which started as we took the first cable-car of the day up Sulphur Mountain (2300m), looking out over the town and valley from an icy-cold viewing platform. Our coach next climbed through forests of tall skinny Lodgepole Pines, seeing lakes and dramatic rock pillars like the Tower of Babel and jelly-mould shaped Castle Mountain, stopping at midday to eat a sandwich in a chilly picnic spot beside the Emerald Lake:

"The day is darkening now, cloud descending to hide the mountains, perhaps bringing more snow? I hurry to explore the lakeside, gazing into the clear depths where every fallen twig, now hazy with algae, is visible beneath the water. Then on into the oppressive silence of the forest. Occasionally a bird twitters ... more often the trees resound with the furious chastisement of squirrels – one by the path attempts to chatter its defiance through a mouthful of mushroom, then gives up, rushing up the tree where its drey is located. Having deposited the mushroom, it deafens me with a loud cry like a pneumatic drill, then runs off, leaping from tree to tree, leaving me in moss-deadened silence."

Plans to drive up the hair-raising Kicking Horse Pass were stymied by the news that it was snowing hard up there; an attempted visit to Johnson Canyon had to be aborted when the rangers officially closed the path: our day was cut short by the onslaught of winter, so we returned to Banff. Wandering in the town, I strolled into the 'Indian Trading Post' shop to admire displays of cured pelts of squirrel, deer and bear, and an odd curiosity in a glass case at the back of the shop – supposedly a mummified merman with an ape-like torso and a huge fishy tail, though no-one could tell me anything about it.

Crossing the Rockies back from Alberta to British Columbia, we entered Kootenay NP, negotiating fresh snow on Vermilion Pass then descending to view Marble Canyon:

"... a deep cleft cut partly through white and grey dolomite (not real marble) by a rushing stream far below. Snow has settled on paths and bridges, freezing so that it crunches nicely beneath our feet; a spider's web strung across the path has caught a few flakes of snow, gleaming like diamonds. The river roars below us, at times invisible because of projections of rock eroded away in centuries past, though in one place an exceptionally hard piece of rock remains to form a natural bridge. As we climb, I notice a white cloud creeping silently through the trees towards us. A few flakes of snow begin to fall, becoming ever thicker till we return to the coach amid a real snowstorm."

The snow ceased as suddenly as it started and by the time we left the NP, we were back into a land of colour – blue sky dotted with swirling white clouds, dark green pines and autumnal golden aspens. The mountains were briefly left behind us as we returned to the USA, then we continued back into the Rockies at Glacier National Park. Unfortunately, much of it was inaccessible because of the winter weather (the fascinatingly named 'Go to the Sun Road' through the middle of the Park was closed) but we were able to walk in the forests beside Lake McDonald:

"Strolling in crisp sunshine beneath light blue sky, beside dark blue waters filled with reddish pebbles, surrounded by golden and green trees, with meadows dotted with white frost – this is an artist's dream! Everywhere the sunlight filters through the trees to pick out a twig or fern-leaf, as autumn leaves twist gently down to carpet the ground."

The Park is famous for wildlife including wolf, wolverine, cougar and bear – in fact before we went walking we were given instructions on what to do if we met a bear (back up slowly talking softly, climb a tree if it follows, and as a last resort curl up on the ground and protect head and neck), but we met nothing!

Crossing Montana, we were in the heart of 'cowboy country': wooden barns and farmhouses dotting meadows where beef cattle grazed peacefully – the little town of Drummond proudly declared itself 'World Capital of Bull Shippers'. Once this was a vast open range where cattle roamed free under the care of mounted cowboys, now the meadows were fenced, and cattle management was done by helicopters. Yet still we were surrounded by mile upon mile of open rolling lands covered in thin grass with no trees and few bushes, the Rockies just a distant range of snow-sprinkled hills – I could easily understand Montana's nickname of 'Big Sky Country'. The film-set scenery was completed when we spotted our first herd of bison (American buffalo) grazing peacefully in a valley just beyond the mining town of Butte – too far away for a photo, but we were assured we would see more once we reached Yellowstone NP. Our thoughts were increasingly beginning to drift towards Yellowstone now, with our guide explaining the geological formation of the Park in detail (and in two languages – this was a bilingual tour in English and Dutch). My diary talks of ancient sediments ... geological uplift ... volcanic activity with geysers and hot springs ... earthquakes. Yet it was hard to absorb all this information since we were still driving through a landscape of hillocks and gullies, bush-lined creeks and rocky outcrops, all covered in the golden pastures familiar from a hundred Wild West movies. Finally, the grazing cattle were replaced by campsites and motels – we had reached Yellowstone, first National Park in the world, founded in 1872.

I had expected to be among ranges of mountains, but the approach to Yellowstone was so gradual that there was no sensation of height (though we were already at 2100m), just mile upon mile of sparse forest (much of it still blackened and dead after a big fire two years before, just beginning to regenerate with grasses or Lodgepole pines) and featureless grassy plains where a few bison were grazing. I was puzzled: why was Yellowstone so famous? ... What was so special about it? Then, in the distance, I saw the first plumes of steam announcing the Geyser districts. We stopped to stroll on the boardwalk past a cauldron of boiling mud, an energetic geyser which was hurling itself enthusiastically into the air, and a smaller geyser gurgling to itself from time to time. Vents of steam (fumaroles) were creeping from every crack in the ground to fill the rapidly chilling air with sulphuric clouds. Signs ordered 'Do Not Leave the Walkway' – as if we would dare!

We drove on as the sun set into the swirling mists – whiffs of steam appearing in the most unexpected places, mostly near the river but sometimes even in the middle of a meadow or amongst the forest trees, until we reached the Upper Geyser region, home of Old Faithful herself. Alongside this most famous of geysers stood a historic wooden lodge, the oldest (built 1903) and most characterful of the Park's hotels – and our base for the next two nights (we were the last guests for the season – the lodge closed as soon as we departed). This first evening we waited around hoping to see Old Faithful erupt; at one time this geyser was completely reliable, erupting every 64 minutes exactly, but since an earthquake in 1959 it had been less regular. We saw nothing on our first night except a constant plume of steam but did get to see a full eruption of super-heated water the next day. I believe that these days, the NP wardens time each eruption and use the statistics to calculate fairly accurately when the next eruption will be.

Our visit to the sights of Yellowstone were again curtailed by winter weather and snowfall – it snowed repeatedly during our stay and roads in the eastern part of the Park were closed, but at least it meant that we were virtually alone as we toured (normally this very popular Park would have been overrun with tourists). I started my own sightseeing with an early morning saunter on the boardwalks outside the hotel:

"Deep pools of clear water, some still and others bubbling gently, changing from pale blue or green into deep blue as my eye reaches down to the point from which the water issues. Most geysers are quiet, though Sawmill constantly coughs out spurts of sparkling droplets. Many geysers are surrounded by self-made walls of lime and calcium deposits, sometimes just a simple lip but sometimes (as in Tower or Grotto Geysers) a great wall of deposits like an artwork, surrounding a plume of steam which wafts according to the wind in every direction. A few geese warm themselves beside the pools after a freezing night. A strange contrast to see snow lying alongside the hot pools and streams, crunching beneath my feet on the boardwalk, beautiful as it clings to the trees."

Our coach sightseeing took us along roads covered with ice and snow (with the Park closing on the very next day, there had been little gritting), cautiously making our way towards the 'Grand Canyon of Yellowstone' where the Yellowstone River crashed over a spectacular waterfall into a deep gorge worn into soft yellow sandstone. Pinnacles of rock protruded from the valley sides like weird modern statues, while streaks of reddish scree flowed down towards the river – the viewpoint was accurately described as 'Artist Point'. As the road conditions worsened, our driver let air out of his tyres for better traction – but he continued (reluctantly) down a steep road which clung precariously to the hillside:

"I really had no idea what Yellowstone is about – I had expected mountains and views, like Yosemite. I had never heard of the Grand Canyon of Yellowstone, and now we were heading for another unknown marvel: Mammoth Hot Springs – hot calcium-laden springs flowing or trickling down the rocks to create terraces and pools like those at Pamukkale in Turkey. Where the water flows, it deposits a smooth and gleaming white travertine; where it no longer flows the cliff is grey and crumbly. Algae grow beneath the water, creating a confectioner's delight in pink and green, or swathes of orange."

We crawled on towards the Norris Geysers, the world's largest and most active geothermal region, to walk down to a viewpoint across Porcelain Basin – a vast white expanse dotted with blue pools and drifting steam, though all was quickly obscured when snow set in again with renewed fury. Finally, we abandoned our sightseeing, returning to the hotel in time to watch Beehive Geyser erupt – a water volcano shooting from a narrow funnel high into the air.

We were unsure which route we would be able to take to escape from snow-bound Yellowstone, but fortunately a night without snow opened the roads for us to head due south, crossing Craig Pass (2500m) with a sight of Yellowstone Lake, a vast expanse of water backed by the great snowy ranges of the Rockies. We could only glimpse the peaks and ridges of Grand Teton NP, looming black and forbidding in parallel to our route, like a line of prehistoric flint tools honed to a sharp edge, before we descended again into the wide meadows of cattle country, heading for the resort of Jackson – slightly depressing with its summer season finished and its winter season yet to commence. Now our goal was the Mormon state of Utah, dotted with small farms scraping a living from difficult land, and little towns of wooden shacks clustered around their imposing Mormon churches. Our guide gave a long discourse on the origins, beliefs and scandals of the Mormon faith before we reached Salt Lake City, where we were given another version of the story by an official 'missionary' as we toured the Visitor Centre and Tabernacle (the Temple was considered too sacred for non-Mormons to enter, so we could view only from outside).

We were not visiting Utah because of its Mormon connections, however, but instead for its stunning National Parks. Our first visits were in Zion NP, a confusing tangle of valleys, chasms and walls of multi-coloured rock, with great stratified cliffs rearing up above us, eroded into weird red formations topped with white sandstone. We were on a tight schedule so there was little time to explore:

"Lunch stop here, but no time to eat! I have just one hour to explore as far as possible. A path leads over the river then winds uphill, following a line of feathery yellowing tamarisk trees towards a rocky pass. Time is running out, so I turn back – butterflies flit past, crickets leap and chirrup, cedar trees by the path give a little welcome fragrant shade from the sun searing down from pure blue skies. I am surrounded by sheer red cliffs, crowned at the narrowest point of the valley by a natural rock arch."

We left Zion's inner valleys via the Carmel Tunnel, built in 1930 and only high enough for coaches in the centre – so Park rangers had to stop the traffic whilst we picked our way gingerly through over a mile of rock, straddling the central line to avoid scraping the roof. It brought us into the outer Park, a wonderland of erosion which had left the surface of every rock-face covered in decorative whirls and swirls, surmounted by pinnacles wearing caps of harder, impermeable stone. Innumerable gullies twisted and wound through the rocks, filled with brilliant red maple trees – our first real autumn colours.

Ultimate goal on this busy day was Bryce Canyon (at 2700m), aiming to arrive in time to see sunset illuminate its pinnacles. Bryce is not really a canyon or a valley, but what is known as 'badlands' – a vast cliff-face crumbling away with erosion. Our first sight of the cliff was outside the National Park, at the 'Red Canyon' where I was dazzled by cliffs of such a brilliant orange hue that it was hard to look at them. Then it was on into the Park itself, to 'Sunset Point' for a steep walk – our guide stressed that we should walk only if our hearts, lungs and circulation were in order. What were we letting ourselves in for?

"We set off steeply downhill, plunging into the myriad pinnacles at the base of the cliff, descending on a tight hairpin path of beaten earth. It grows colder and a cool breeze blows through the sudden shade. After the first steep descent, the path levels off to meander through a fairyland of pinnacles, glowing orange where the sun catches them. The bends of the tortuous path absorb the sound of voices and leave me walking alone in deep silence amid a maze where innumerable tempting trails lead off to one side or the other. Let's hope the trail markers are all in place, or I may be here all night!"

Fortunately, we all climbed safely back up to the clifftop, for one more fine panorama over the whole Bryce Amphitheatre, looking out over hundreds of pinnacles like crowds of tightly packed spectators in an arena, waiting as if frozen in time for the arrival of a mega-celebrity.

One more scenic highlight still awaited us, the most famous of all – the Grand Canyon. Most of our group had elected to join an optional flight in a convoy of small planes, over the convoluted waterways of Lake Powell (brilliant blue channels, dotted with houseboats chugging over the water like beetles, beneath vertical red cliffs) into the Navajo Indian reservation to visit

Monument Valley (a vast red plain familiar from the movies, dotted with rocky mesas and buttes eroded into incredible shapes), then on over the Painted Desert admiring patches of coloured rock cut by erosion into swirling patterns. The air was heating up by now, and we were bumping and swerving through severe turbulence – the pilot turned to survey us all with a worried look, but plenty of deep breaths and tranquil thoughts were just about holding the contents of our stomachs in place. Yet this was a wonderful way to approach the Grand Canyon for my first view, crossing the eroded streambeds of future canyons to the greatest of them all:

"At first, the Grand Canyon is what I expected – a huge cliff running down to the green waters of the Colorado up to a mile below. But as we fly on, I am instantly lost ... what is this vast maze of gullies, valleys and peaks? Where is the far side of the Canyon? I had thought it was simply an extra-deep gorge, but it certainly isn't that! Even from the air, it is totally incomprehensible. The plane twists back and forth (staying high, since flights into the Canyon are no longer permitted) to show us groves of trees growing on top of mesas or nestled in remote valleys deep inside the Canyon – I have lost all sense of direction, and my stomach grows more uneasy."

That evening we joined the crowds enjoying the classic sunset view over the Canyon, with a glass (or rather a plastic beaker) of wine in our hands:

"Ahead lies ridge after ridge, valley after hanging valley, mesa after butte – who could ever map this complexity? Shadows creep inexorably across the landscape, making every valley seem even deeper. Far below us, the Bright Angel Trail hurls itself in tight hairpins over the edge of a flat promontory, reaching through a deep cleft towards the lurid green Colorado River, barely visible from where we stand."

Inexplicably, my tour of the National Parks did not allow for any extended exploration of the Grand Canyon – we were supposed to content ourselves with a sunset view and move on the next day to the bright lights of Las Vegas. Determined to see a little more, I rose at 4.30am next morning to pick my way by torchlight to the top of the Bright Angel Trail, scrambling down a steep dusty path dotted with mule dung (its semi-sweet smell reminded me strongly of Nepal) into the Canyon itself. At this time of day, all was still cool (temperatures can reach 40°C), with just a light breeze arriving with the dawn to rustle the dry leaves of the trees. Otherwise the only sound was the distant roar of the river … until I passed a tent squeezed in beside the path and heard a tourist's alarm clock going off, followed by the clatter of rocks and distant cries from the first of the day's hikers. I had no time to go far (it takes two days to complete the whole hike), but I am so glad that I took the chance for my own tiny adventure into the Grand Canyon.

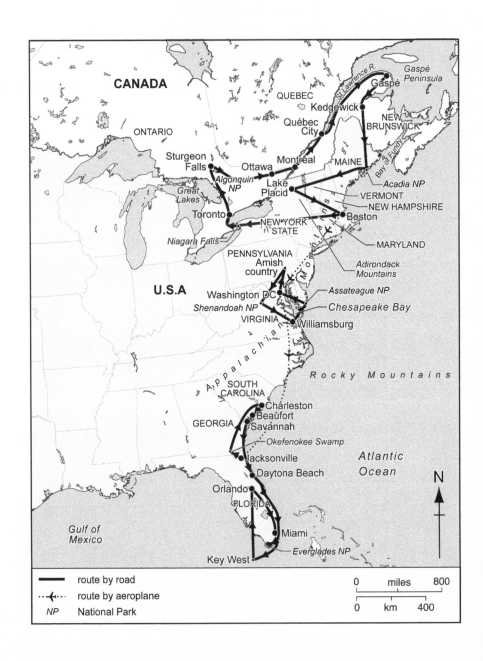

CANADA

ONTARIO

QUEBEC

St. Lawrence R.

Gaspé
Gaspé Peninsula

Kedgewick

Québec City

NEW BRUNSWICK

Sturgeon Falls

Ottawa

Montréal

MAINE

Bay of Fundy

Algonquin NP

Lake Placid

Acadia NP

Great Lakes

VERMONT

NEW HAMPSHIRE

Toronto

NEW YORK STATE

Boston

Niagara Falls

MARYLAND

PENNSYLVANIA
Amish country

Adirondack Mountains

U.S.A

Washington DC

Assateague NP

Shenandoah NP

Chesapeake Bay

VIRGINIA

Williamsburg

Rocky Mountains

Appalachian Mountains

SOUTH CAROLINA

Charleston

Beaufort

GEORGIA

Savannah

Okefenokee Swamp

Atlantic Ocean

Jacksonville

Daytona Beach

Orlando

FLORIDA

Gulf of Mexico

Miami

N

Key West

Everglades NP

	route by road
...-+-...	route by aeroplane
NP	National Park

| 0 | miles | 800 |
| 0 | km | 400 |

North America – the East (October/ November 1990)

MY TWO MONTH EXPLORATION OF North America continued, this time driving myself (alone) through three separate areas – a circuit out of Boston, crossing into eastern Canada ... a circuit out of Washington DC, including Virginia ... a circuit out of Jacksonville, including the 'Deep South' and Florida itself.

The first segment started with a glimpse of New England, where I had been hoping to catch the famous autumn colours (though as it happened, I was too late for autumn this far north and did not find the full spectacle until I reached Virginia). I headed quickly northwards, though I could not resist a stop in a little town called Lee (with a typical, white-painted church and spire, and elegant clapboard homes) before hurrying on to the Canadian border to visit Niagara Falls. I wanted to see the Falls first from the American side, so I drove into Buffalo ... only to be frustrated by an inability to find the river! I cruised past strings of motels and restaurants, each with hoardings screaming their offers, yet could not find any signs pointing me to the Falls themselves. Finally, I simply parked the car, got out and listened for the sound of rushing water:

"I hear a roar as I get out of the car, which leads me to the river – racing along, churning and tossing in a headlong dash to oblivion. I follow the channel till suddenly it vanishes across a cliff into a deep rock bowl. The base of the Falls is lost in a swirl of mist as the water crashes against a jumble of rocks, then flows out into a gorge where the famous rainbow rises serenely upwards to frame the scene."

The Canadian side was easier to access, looking out over a vast expanse of water dotted with islands and rocks thick with seagulls. I watched the Maid of the Mist sightseeing boat plodding steadfastly out into clouds of spray, struggling to hold position as its passengers snapped photos while huddled in plastic capes on deck, but my schedule did not permit me to join them ... actually I preferred to watch from the comfort of dry land, anyway!

I was due to stay with an aunt in North Ontario for my first nights in Canada, so hurried onwards past the glass skyscrapers of Toronto into the forests which line Lake Huron. Here at last I escaped from the trappings of busy cities and could turn off the main road towards the lake, hidden amongst thin forests of spindly trees dressed in sparse red and orange foliage:

"I follow a winding narrow road through the forest to the waterfront where tiny cabins nestle beside peaceful inlets, each accessed only by dirt tracks marked 'Strictly Private'. All is tranquil, the water totally calm ... marshes shelter noisy ducks, but otherwise this is a delightfully quiet place to recover from city life."

The simple town of Sturgeon Falls, where my aunt lived, was equally tranquil – especially since many of the residents had departed to spend the winter as 'Snowbirds' in Florida. The silence was broken only by the calling of ducks ... and the sound of spring-rakes as everyone cleared the leaves from their lawns in preparation for winter. My aunt explained that the leaves turn to slime beneath the snow and was proud that she had collected 44 bags of leaves from her own lawn alone.

Refreshed by my family visit (and with all my washing done), I set off to explore North Ontario (which my aunt loved to call 'the start of the wilderness'), heading into Algonquin National Park. What a joy to be fully independent, after a month of organised sightseeing in the west – able to turn off when I spotted an interesting side road or an enticing sign. One side trip took me up a dirt road and along a muddy path to Ragged Falls, a huge torrent of water leaping through a narrow cleft in the rock ... another led me along a rough track between tree roots and boulders – the Beaver Trail:

"Tiny red squirrels chirp worriedly to themselves as I pass but cannot bring themselves to cease their frantic ferreting for winter supplies among the dead leaves. Their pine squirrel cousins churr stridently yet invisibly from the trees nearby. The path leads to beaver-made lakes and dams – perfectly

still lakes mirroring clouds and trees, with humps and mounds of beaver
lodges in the centre. Suddenly I spot an animal swimming! Might it be a
beaver? It pulls itself out on to a branch for a minute ... but it is only the size
of a kitten, with a pointed nose, clearly too small for a beaver – probably just
a muskrat?"

I was so absorbed in the sights and sounds of the forest that I sat watching
until the sun began to set, reluctantly then returning to my car to hunt out a
motel for the night. In fact, I could only find a single motel still open so late
in the season, and I was the sole guest.

Into the valley of the St Lawrence River now, passing through Canada's
capital city Ottawa – the grandiose hilltop Parliament buildings were
supposed to be modelled on our British Palace of Westminster, though they
reminded me more of St Pancras station. I stopped just long enough to view
the Canadian collection in the National Art Gallery, though the images of
wide-open spaces and Arctic light reminded me that I really just wanted to
get back to Canada's natural scene, away from their cities. A stop in a Bird
Reserve on the windswept marshes beside the St Lawrence was much more
to my taste!

"Suddenly a jackrabbit (longer back legs than our rabbit, shorter ears
and no 'powder puff' tail) leaps out almost at my feet. I freeze and so does
he ... finally he decides I am not dangerous and lollops off in a series of
leisurely but far-reaching leaps. The undergrowth crackles with activity as
birds forage for seeds; the air is full of the constant cacophony of Canada
Geese; the waters in the marsh are rippled by fish and disturbed by the plops
of frogs."

Sadly, as I drove on, I frequently saw dead porcupines lying by the
roadside – victims of speeding drivers like our hedgehogs back home, though
surely far more visible since they were as big as cats!

Next day I continued into Quebec, though there was no indication of a
border, just a sudden transformation of the road-signs from English into
French. Passing Montreal (and its Olympic Stadium from 1976) without
stopping, I found myself travelling through a string of enchanting villages,
mainly built of brilliant white clapboard, surrounded by raised verandahs
with ornately carved fascia boards and often a cosy wooden 'love-seat' – all
neat and crisp with carefully trimmed lawns. Many were proudly flying the

blue & white flag of Quebec (since I left Montreal, I had not seen a single maple-leaf Canadian flag):

"This really is an awe-inspiring land! The sky grows clearer with the flat stark light of the North. The countryside, except for a few patches of forest, is covered with rolling hills where dairy cattle graze – and always there are views out to the wide slate-grey St Lawrence River. To mark their presence in this vast monochrome land, people paint their roofs in bright colours – red, orange, green or blue, whilst luridly painted roadside Virgins or Crucifixes scream devotion on a large scale."

I had decided to devote a full day to Quebec City, but ended up struggling to fill the day. I found it a pleasant but unexpectedly small city, where the solid, stone-built Lower Town reminded me strongly of Breton architecture (the first settlers here were from Normandy and Brittany in the 17th century): inside the cathedral of Notre Dame, alongside a very un-Breton wedding-cake altar of white and gold, hung a typical Breton-style votive ship. I rode the ancient funicular as it groaned its way up to the Upper Town, but by mid-morning I was finished with sightseeing and sitting in a French-style patisserie eating cherry tartlets! I filled the rest of the day with an organised tour out to Montmorency Falls, a powerful torrent falling over black shale cliffs, and to the pilgrimage church of St Anne, festooned with crutches donated by the disabled who were healed after their visit. The best part of the tour was when we took the old road back to the city, past traditional houses with outdoor bread ovens and wooden shacks set in groves of maple trees, where maple sap was boiled to make syrup or maple butter. A snack of fresh bread and maple butter made a welcome treat to round off a dark and chilly day.

The weather now was becoming colder and more wintry – fresh snow sprinkled the hills as I made my way out to the Gaspe Peninsula, and ice coated the roadside rocks where seeping water had frozen overnight. I stopped to walk down to the tidal flats in the Parc du Bic NP beside the St Lawrence, visiting a tiny hamlet of summer chalets nestled among a few bare rowan trees still laden with scarlet berries:

"I stop at the beach to crunch over snow-covered sand to the water's edge, lapping peacefully against bleached driftwood and huge clumps of seaweed. The air is full of the smell of seaweed and a little woodsmoke from

a cabin which is still occupied. A flock of black and white Eider Ducks take fright as I approach the water, flapping wildly away from me out towards the sea, but the seals which the information boards promise, are not present today."

As I drove further, the landscape became wilder, the communities rarer. The properties I did see were 'winterised' with cabins and motels boarded up against winter storms, garden trees and shrubs wrapped in sacking against the frosts. I was surrounded by the scenery I had been hoping for: the road clung tightly to the shore, with signs warning of slippery conditions when waves rose to sweep the tarmac ... inland were towering cliffs of multi-coloured sediments, twisted and convoluted by geology ... any water trickling down the cliffs had frozen, sheathing the rock in a veil of icicles ... snow dusted the branches of fir trees, deformed by years of fighting the wind. It was a black and white scene, relieved only by the soft pinks and blues of sunset creeping over the sea – but that was a worry, since I did not want to be driving by night as the temperatures dropped well below zero. There were only a few villages tucked into sheltered coves, and none offered any accommodation. Finally, just as darkness fell, I spotted the welcoming red sign of a motel, with a friendly lady owner who informed me that this was the only motel still open in the area – and it would have been over an hour before I found any other accommodation on this road.

Clear skies and bright sunshine greeted me as I set off at 6.30am next day – I have always loved the morning hours and did not want to waste a minute of precious good weather. I intended to finish the circuit of the Gaspe Peninsula today, through delightful fishing villages like Cloridorme which I stopped to explore even before I had found anywhere for breakfast:

"A wide-spread cluster of small homes reaching down to the harbour, where nets dry on special wooden racks on the clifftop, lobster pots are piled at house doors and fishing boats (ranging in size from dinghies to small trawlers) huddle up against the quay under the benediction of an old wooden cross on the hill above."

In some ways these villages reminded me of Cornwall, though here there was little sign of a developed tourist industry. I presumed the inhabitants must have lived totally from fishing, which seemed to provide a decent income since the homes (while small) were well-kept. Later, chatting to other guests in the next motel, I learned that in fact the fishing season lasted only 4-5 months and residents lived on social security for the rest of the year!

Leaving Quebec, I entered New Brunswick, officially Anglophone though many of the rural people I met spoke French. My road took me through mile upon mile of forest, with only occasional clearings for very poor-looking cabins (some still with wells for water and no indoor plumbing – I spotted the toilet huts at the bottom of their gardens). The poorest communities seemed always to have French names, while the commercial centres on the coast bore the names of Scottish towns – my fellow motel-guests had commented that the Anglophones were usually rich, while the French-speakers struggled: my observations seemed to bear that out. In Canadian history, it was the French who wandered the forests as trappers, whilst the British set up trading posts. Was this part of the cause of the resentment felt by Francophones against the dominant Anglo-Canadians?

For hours I drove through unending forests, asking myself why I was seeing no timber yards or piles of maturing logs. The answer to that question was revealed as I passed the community of Kedgwick where a huge pulp mill was belching out smoke and steam over the forest – clearly most of the timber was grown for paper-production. Curious to learn more, I offered a lift to a young man just leaving his work in a small timberyard where a huge fire burned in a tower – he told me in halting English that the fire was to burn the bark and twigs once the best timber had been taken for planking. As he struggled to speak to me in English, we switched to French (better for him, though I now struggled to understand his thickly accented French) and he told me that everyone in this area worked in the timber industry – even his mother and sister were involved in de-barking the logs. I drove him all the way to his front door, expecting perhaps to be invited indoors for coffee, but he left me with barely a thank-you – apparently lift-giving was part of normal life here and deserved no particular thanks. Driving onwards, I had to change my plans again – I had hoped to reach the town of St Johns to experience the world-famous tides in the Bay of Fundy with up to 15m tidal difference, but again I had planned more than I could achieve in one day (I was pushing myself even harder than our coach tour in the west had pushed us). So, with minimal daylight left, I decided to turn instead towards the border, re-entering the USA beneath a spectacular sunset – a fiery sun lighting swirling red clouds above the darkening trees, like a forest fire raging on the horizon.

The first US state was Maine, back to real wilderness – mile upon mile of forest, interspersed by open patches of bilberries and marshy river valleys ... few signs of human habitation, not even holiday cabins. Breakfasting in a truck stop, I was fascinated to listen to some roughneck local hunters chatting casually about moose sightings – though I saw none. Very soon I was entering Acadia NP, travelling through glorious forests where the red and gold colours of the trees were set off by the deep blue of sky and sea. I couldn't resist the opportunity to take a walk in this awe-inspiring landscape:

"My path stumbles and trips over the convoluted roots of spruce trees which run right down to the rocky coast. The shoreline is a jumble of pink granite broken into rectangular chunks piled up like a child's building blocks. The sea eddies and gurgles in and out of the rocks ... a buoy clangs its mournful bell to warn shipping of a semi-submerged reef ... a fishing boat chugs between the bright floats which mark its lobster pots."

I sampled some of that lobster (though I could only afford the cheaper claw meat) in the charming village of Bar Harbour, and also found time to ascend Cadillac Mountain (at 450m, the highest point on the Atlantic coast) for superb views over a blue sea studded with islands, and multi-coloured forest broken with lakes.

I headed back into the heart of New England to see more of the picturesque villages of white-painted clapboard mansions, so for one night I decided to lash out on a B&B in an elegant mansion, proud to be listed on the National Historic Register (instead of the usual cheap motels I was using most nights):

"It's lovely! A fine example of a New England sea captain's mansion (now the home of a Massachusetts dentist), furnished with antiques and Victorian knick-knacks – warm and cosy, complete with a Yorkie Terrier and a cat to sit on my lap as I relax with a book in the elegant parlour."

By now it was Hallowe'en, a big festival in the USA with all the homes decked out with bright orange pumpkins at their doors. In the early morning, I watched in amazement as kindergarten children were paraded in a neat crocodile through the town to collect candies from every shop. By the evening, neighbourhood children were rushing excitedly from door to door demanding 'treats', never expecting to be refused nor to be asked to perform a song or poem to earn them.

I meandered through New Hampshire and Vermont into New York State, seeking out the White Mountains, the Green Mountains and the Adirondacks in my search for mountain scenery; passing ski resorts still shuttered in this pre-season period, including the Olympic (1980) resort of Lake Placid:

"The town is a mess! A glamorous modern Olympic Centre is squashed into the grounds of a 1930s school building; the houses are a mixture of modern cubes, alongside mock Alpine chalets, alongside New England clapboard stores and motels. Everywhere is hung with strings of tattered and faded flags from around the world. Perhaps the winter snows will bring some glamour – it certainly needs it!"

The mountains and ski resorts were a disappointment, but the back country of tranquil villages, babbling streams and autumnal forests was a delight, especially the 'mirror lakes' where dark peaty water (when unruffled by a breeze) was so still that it was hard to tell where the edge of the pond lay – birch trees appeared to grow both up and down from the same root, houses were reflected in every detail.

This part of my tour concluded as I made my way back towards Boston, stopping occasionally to investigate 'historic sites' from the 18th century revolution against Britain. After returning the car, I spent a full day exploring Boston, following the Freedom Trail (a red line set into the pavements, taking tourists past the major historic sights of the city) to view the shady quadrangles of Harvard University; the naval yards and museum ship USS Constitution (guided by a modern marine in historic costume); the house of American hero Paul Revere. However, the Red Line also took me past beggars and rough sleepers at Boston Common; strings of take-away food stalls frequented by seriously overweight citizens at Quincy Market; dingy buildings surrounded by litter and drunks asleep in the gutter at North Station:

"Boston: not as glamorous or genteel as I had expected. I've heard Jewish accents, Italians, Polish – the whole melting pot, together with each cuisine and culture. I've seen the American Dream and American Disillusionment. Success, hope, enthusiasm, national pride ... and those who are faced only with despair."

A short flight took me to Washington DC to collect another car, first driving northwards into Amish Country ... like another world:

"An excited flurry of oddly dressed children rushing down the road to school, many of the boys pushing themselves along on wooden scooters. Tightly closed-up buggies, like boxes on wheels, pulled by high-trotting horses. A young man skilfully handling a team of 6 powerful horses as he ploughs in the maize stubble. He gives me a strange look as I take a photograph – I didn't realise they don't like photographs ... sorry!"

I visited the Amish Farm museum and the information centre at the People's Palace, gradually collecting the information to help me understand this unusual and strict religious sect. They refuse to use electricity or own cars (though they will ride in them) because they think both will drag them into our modern consumer society. They refuse advanced education because it will pull children off the land – farming is the lifeblood of their way of life. They preserve traditional costume to enhance the sense of community. But no-one is forced to be Amish – young people are allowed to sample modern American life (pop music, beer, dancing...) until their early 20's but must then choose to fully adopt Amish ways or leave the community. I liked the sound of their philosophy with its simplicity, emphasis on human kindness and mutual help – though perhaps you have to be born into it, to be able to live the way they do?

Heading southwards again, I followed the Skyline Drive along Virginia's Blue Ridge Mountains, looking for examples of autumnal colours in the trees – surely winter had not yet come this far south? At first, I was disappointed: strong winds had stripped the trees of their leaves, carpeting the ground with red and gold – though at least the bare branches allowed more splendid vistas over forests and meadows from the top of the ridges. However, as the Skyline Drive brought me back down from the end of the ridge, I spotted huge patches of vivid red in the valleys on the northern side of the mountains:

"I make my way to the village of Waynesborough and its trailer-park suburbs. Here the trees are still in full foliage – vibrant red oak, interspersed with yellow larch and green spruce. I go mad with the camera! Every way I turn there are banks of colour so rich, I almost begin to wish for the soothing green of summer!"

Virginia is one of the most historic states in the USA, so here I was able to visit some of the 18th century plantations with their elegant mansions and imposing grounds (US equivalent of British stately homes) before continuing to Williamsburg Living Museum. It was my first taste of this style of museum and I was very impressed. Instead of the guides explaining or pouring out facts, they were actors who talked to their guests as though we were actually living in the period:

"As we wait to go into the Capitol, a guide chats about the fears of the people that the Capitol may be moved; in the George Wythe House the guide talks about the ferment in the air as the people get fed up of paying taxes when they have no representation in government; in the Wythe kitchen, a cook expresses the worries of a real-life slave cook who worked here for 20 years. Out in the streets, I am invited to join a discussion between a group of costumed characters about the philosophy of the Revolution, as if we are thinking of fomenting a future rebellion."

To head back to Washington DC again I decided to follow the coast, first having to cross the impressively engineered road across the mouth of Chesapeake Bay – 18 miles of bridge, tunnel, causeway, tunnel and causeway again:

"The road runs straight out to sea, surrounded by surging, windswept grey water. Seagulls are everywhere, soaring along the up currents by the bridge, barely skimming the guardrails in their mastery of the air. I stop at Seagull Pier viewing terrace, where hundreds of gulls and a few huge cormorants rest on the rocky foundations or bob on the sea, as massive freighters and nippy fishing boats ply back and forth across the top of the tunnel. It's rather odd to be racing an ocean freighter!"

On this eastern side of Chesapeake Bay, we seemed to be far from the rich farmland and exclusive mansions further west. Here many of the historic mansions had been abandoned to decay and instead people were living in trailer parks. I turned down a track towards the seashore expecting to find sandy beaches and dunes: instead I found only reed inlets and a huddle of shabby buildings redolent with the repulsive smell of an oyster port.

Finally I found a sign pointing me towards the National Wildlife Refuge at Assateague, where I spent some hours walking on trails beaten through the forest by the hoofs of wild horses (seeing a few as I walked) and down to the shore where tidal marshes were alive with herons, egrets, geese, muskrats and deer. A delightful end to the second part of my tour.

A final flight took me to Jacksonville, though after collecting a car I left Florida, turning north towards Georgia and South Carolina, into 'Gone with the Wind' country. My very first morning I stopped in a roadhouse for breakfast and was persuaded by the waitress to sample the local speciality – 'grits' (white and grainy cornmeal porridge, eaten mixed with butter and salt). I was the centre of attention from the other (local) customers as they all explained what I was eating and then began to give advice on what I should see in the neighbourhood: a great introduction to southern hospitality. One of their recommendations was the Okefenokee Swamp, taking a half-hour ride in a flat-bottomed boat:

"... past bulbous-based Pond Cypress trees with their weird 'knees' of root rising from the swamp like mangroves. There are fly-trap plants too, and a jungle of vines. Hawks and songbirds swoop and flutter through the trees, but there's no sign of alligators or even frogs – perhaps too cold for them? But it's not too cold for the mosquitoes!"

Much of coastal Georgia seemed to be comprised of swamp, together with forest where often the trees were hung with Spanish Moss, growing like long shaggy locks of grey hair. I noticed a stately avenue leading to one mansion, lined with broad spreading oaks whose branches were so heavy with Spanish Moss that its fronds brushed the top of passing trucks.

In search of the 'Deep South' I aimed for Charleston, though it turned out not to be the perfectly preserved architectural jewel I had expected – much of it was still suffering from the destruction brought by Hurricane Hugo one year earlier. Many of the old houses were run-down and in places modern monstrosities and parking lots had popped up, but there were still plenty of examples of the typical 'single house' – rows of tightly packed, thin oblong homes of brick or clapboard, just one room wide, facing a tiny garden. These were formerly the homes of servants and even slaves, working in the grander free-standing porticoed mansions on the edge of town, which once belonged to families made wealthy from cotton.

As I explored the town, I met four people strolling in fine 19th century costumes – they told me that one of the colonial mansions (Boone Hall) nearby was holding a reconstruction of a Civil War battle later in the day (hence the costumes) so I decided to make my way there:

"There are crowds everywhere, most in costume – women in hooped crinolines or long skirts, men in frock coats or the uniforms of soldiers from both sides. Horses with army saddles are hitched to rails beside an encampment of white canvas tents, some housing the troops but others selling anything from souvenirs to a full uniform. The house itself sits serenely, ignored by tourists who today have eyes only for the 'living history' all around. I get the impression that, for the local people, this is not just 'dressing up' but that these are real Confederates and Unionists slipping back into the role where they feel most comfortable: this is their real life."

The battle began with small groups of cavalry charging up and down the field, while infantry marched forward to the accompaniment of clattering volleys of musket fire and the occasional boom of cannon. Clearly it was set to continue for hours so I returned to Charleston, stopping for a photo of a particularly rickety-looking bridge. Underneath the bridge, my eye was caught by row after row of basic tenements, reminiscent of the slave quarters at Boone Hall, festooned with lines of washing – and every resident was black. What a contrast to the gorgeous mansions in the southern part of the city, all inhabited by wealthy white people. Clearly there was still a racial distinction here in the 'Deep South', though I could find no-one willing to discuss the situation – in fact, by now, I was getting desperate to find someone willing to hold a deeper conversation with me. The Americans I was meeting were all very friendly and hospitable but seemed so shallow. Perhaps it was getting time for me to go home?

Still in search of the 'Deep South' I moved on to Savannah, a working port with heavy Victorian-style warehouses by the river – not yet the atmosphere of 'Gone with the Wind'! But finally I discovered the enchanting town of Beaufort, where I found the gorgeous historic mansions set in tranquil gardens which I had failed to find in Charleston or Savannah, mixed with smaller houses with neat little gardens, and even tiny cabins with no gardens ... yet all shared the peaceful shade along roads lined with palms, beeches and oaks hung with moss. At the end of every street ran the river, thick with golden reeds and glinting in the warm sun. At the waterfront was a promenade lined with swinging benches where residents, old and young, black and white, were all enjoying the cool river breeze together. This was what I had been seeking.

Now I could return to Florida, which seemed to be struggling to preserve its natural environment in the face of persistent development. I found areas of coastline where the beaches and their wildlife were undisturbed because they were protected as Nature Reserves or State Recreation areas, but wherever there was no official protection, there were restaurants, motels, holiday homes or at least signs offering development sites. In a few places, like Daytona Beach, the ubiquitous condominiums were replaced by huge resort hotels, though more often the facilities were smaller and simpler. I travelled to the very tip of Florida, stopping first in the Everglades – not a swamp like the Okefenokee, but rather a vast river often just a few inches deep but 50 miles wide, dribbling from Lake Okeechobee towards the sea through a vast plain of sharp-edged sawgrass. In this winter period, the water levels were low, so I was able to see alligators and many types of bird in the few pools which remained. Then on along the string of coral islands which make up the Florida Keys, linked by bridges which stretched out like lace across a brilliant turquoise sea, becoming longer and longer as the distances between the islands increased. The longest was 7 Mile Bridge, where I felt as if I had been whisked out to sea, surrounded by innumerable seabirds, with no land in sight.

Of course, many people go to Florida just to visit the theme parks – not really my scene, but I thought I should sample at least one. So I made my way to Epcot, entering with the very first visitors of the day and moving speedily to keep ahead of the crowds. In fact, it was more enjoyable than I had expected. I was not sure if it would be all serious science, or all tacky entertainment – in fact, it was a clever mix of the two: enough science to satisfy my desire to learn something new, enough entertainment to keep it interesting. Different pavilions offered a dash through the history of mankind, or a glimpse into the deep oceans, or a survey of the influence of man on the surface of the Earth – all accessed by exciting 'rides' in the true tradition of Disney's parks. Alongside was the World Showcase, with copies of buildings and cultural events from 11 different countries. I had expected it to be superficial and stereo-typed, but in fact the buildings were carefully recreated (I had already seen many of the originals, so was surprised by the accuracy of the structures) and even staffed by nationals from the represented countries. The only inaccuracy I perceived was in the American display:

"*I am surrounded by the real article – fat, gaudily dressed, unintellectual and loud. Yet they portray themselves as refined gentlefolk from the colonial period, living in a superb Georgian mansion. The 'show' in the American pavilion presents them as the most courageous pioneers, the wisest philosophers, the most advanced in development of technology, the most responsible in the defence of the world. Do they really see themselves this way? I've been trying to understand the mentality of the USA while I've been here – is this it? Is the famous 'American Dream' really a self-image of perfection, which never looks at reality? Do they really believe that their land is perfect? Are they blind to poverty, prejudice and hamburger joints?*"

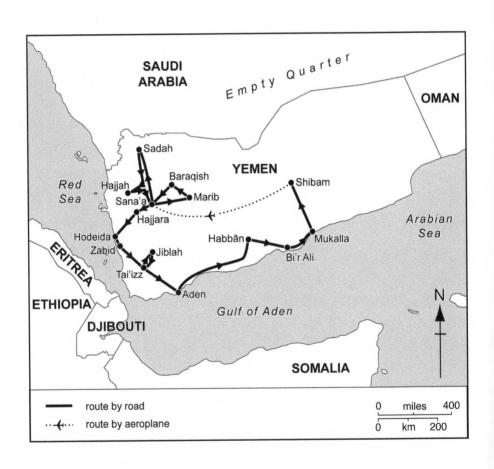

Yemen (November 1992)

IN 1991, I WAS LEAFING THROUGH the brochure of one of my favourite 'Adventure' tour operators, when I spotted a new tour to a destination described as 'a sight seen only once in a lifetime' – Yemen. That was enough for me … I resolved to organise myself on to this tour, finally departing at the end of 1992.

Once again, what a privilege to have seen this amazing country before it was torn apart by a civil war which (with the interference of Iran and Saudi Arabia) has been raging since 2015 and now (in 2020) shows no sign of abating – a war which has virtually closed the only port which the outside world can use to send humanitarian aid, leaving almost the entire population starving and at risk from unstoppable health epidemics. Yet when I visited, the country was full of hope for the future. It had been divided into two different nations since the 1960's, yet in 1990 had rushed through a unification so that newly-discovered oil reserves in the former border area, could be shared and not fought over. Soon after my visit, there were to be elections – the first multi-party, universal suffrage elections in the Arab world (though the boundaries of the constituencies had not yet been worked out – so chaos was expected). Though there had been a long tradition of in-fighting between different tribal groups and between Shi'a and Sunni Muslims, as well as the diametrically opposed politics of Western-oriented North Yemen and communist South Yemen (first and only Marxist state in the Arab world), those differences seemed to have been resolved and the introduction of tourism was a sign of willingness to leave behind centuries of isolation and open the country to modern development.

Our tour started in the capital city Sana'a, a city unlike any other I have ever seen:

"An amazing first view of the jumble of mud-plastered 5 or 6-storey towers, with windows topped by a half-circle of coloured glass (some even still using the original alabaster instead of glass), each window highlighted in white gypsum. Some houses are run-down, but many boast fine new wooden window-frames and massive painted wooden doors. The alleyways between the towers are partly cobbled with blocks of stone, but partly just litter-strewn dust. Peering into a dark hole between a couple of small shops, I see a huge grinding stone being driven by a patient camel, plodding round and round with basket-blinkers over his eyes, his lips moving as if muttering a constant mantra ... or a stream of abuse!"

We picked up an ancient guide at the entrance to the old city, who inexplicably stopped outside one of the tower-houses to rap long and hard on the door. Eventually a cry from the roof acknowledged him and a rope leading down from the living quarters on the 3rd floor was pulled to lift the latch and allow us to enter. We picked our way nervously up multiple flights of immaculately washed stairs, edged with white for clearer visibility in the dark stairwell, past firmly closed doors leading to storage or living rooms – all the way up to the roof. Why were we there? Ah! ... from the roof we could peer down into the Great Mosque, closed to infidels like us (an ingenious way to get around the ban), though in fact, the mosque courtyard was not really worth seeing; totally bare, like a school playground. However, we could enjoy the rest of the view, gazing out across acres of decorated tower-homes, peering into domestic courtyards – in one, a small flock of sheep was penned, in another a man was tending huge pots of mint. Back down in the alleyways, we negotiated hordes of small children just released from school, who called out 'Hello' or 'Salaam' (one tiny girl mixed the two into 'Hellaam'). Everywhere, we passed men chomping on leaves of the local drug Qat, one cheek already swollen with chewed leaves, ruminating like camels until the leaves finally disintegrated to be spat out as a fine green dust. As our tour progressed, we came to realise that just about every man in the country (including our driver Salah) spent the afternoon and evening hours

Qat-chewing. Salah offered us a few leaves to sample – I decided against it, but others in the group tried ... and said it tasted like a privet hedge (when did they eat privet?).

The first part of our tour took us northwards, skirting the edge of the coastal mountains, almost to the border with Saudi Arabia. The landscape was striking – mainly ancient, heavily eroded sandstone, frequently crumbling into boulders blackened and oxidised by the sun, sometimes laid out as wide expanses of flat pavement, split by cracks which often deepened into ditches or chasms. The tops of the ridges were desolate and dry, dotted only with cactus and thorn bushes, yet frequently our eyes were drawn to green or yellow patches of 'dillah' corn nestled on hillside terraces or in the bottom of shallow valleys. This part of Yemen was referred to by the ancient Romans as 'Arabia Felix' (Happy Arabia) because of its fertility, and the newly formed unified government of Yemen was talking about making the country into the 'breadbasket of Arabia'. Yet I suppose, when you come from a green country with plenty of rain, 'fertile' is a relative description – to me, these grain fields looked to be more suitable for feeding a single family than feeding a nation or a sub-continent! Water was clearly a precious commodity and the fields were enclosed by low ridges of mud, to ensure that no drop of irrigation was lost. The markets in villages we passed, were selling only small quantities of vegetables and fruit ... though often large quantities of Qat (clearly the most desirable commercial crop).

The villages were often difficult to spot, composed of tower-houses built from the same rock as the hilltops where they perched dramatically, as if they were sprouting organically from the terrain. Yet they gave us a glimpse of the life of the local people: a young veiled girl throwing stones at her flock of goats to guide them; a man casually strolling along a path with his rifle over his shoulder; a threshing ground amid the rocks, where a woman chased 3 yoked donkeys around in circles across sheaves of corn while a man swept the grain back into the centre:

"We stop for lunch at a little cafe in the village of Huth. I decide only to drink a cup of tea, strongly flavoured with cinnamon, and to spend my time exploring instead. The village is charming – tall houses built of sandstone blocks; two houses linked by a rickety bridge between their top storeys; walled courtyards adorned with flowers creeping along their walls. The main

thoroughfares are paved with rock, worn smooth and shiny, though the side alleys are paved only with litter! A black-scarfed (but not veiled) girl of 8 or 9 years old shyly begs for a pen but when I refuse, she still leads me to the wall of her house to show me some ancient lettering carved into the stone ... then pulls back her scarf to display proudly her safety-pin earrings. She is delighted when I reveal that I am also using safety-pins – to stop my light shawl from slipping off my shoulders. But maybe I should also be covering my head? A group of little boys throw a single stone at me, perhaps in rebuke ... or perhaps just as a game, imitating their rebellious older brothers?"

As we progressed northwards, we encountered more military – the Saudi border had always been a flashpoint, not even clearly demarcated, and there were often skirmishes with semi-independent mountain tribes in this region. At one point we passed an army encampment overseen by armed guards on a ridge above the camp. In a narrow cutting through a ridge, we noticed a small tank pointing its cannon at us (though the mouth of the cannon was encased in a plastic bag). We also encountered fairly frequent army checkpoints, though we were usually waved through – they were only interested in armed rebels, not camera-toting tourists. A particularly large and modern army camp heralded our arrival in Sadah – most northerly point of our tour. The entire town was enclosed within a massive crumbling wall over a metre wide, giving us a perfect platform from which to look out over the town's well-maintained mud-brick homes. On some, workers were building an extension, so we were able to see the building technique – a stone foundation topped by layers of half-metre deep mud blocks laid on top of each other, waiting for each layer to dry before continuing, so that the lower level could suck moisture from the new layer, creating a solid bond.

The town suk (market) was almost closed up by the time we reached Sadah, though the silversmiths, for whom the town is famous, were still at work – many of them Jewish men distinguished by shaved foreheads with tight ringlets dangling beside their faces. I still have a pair of silver earrings bought here, forced bloodily into my ears on the spot (using brute strength) by a helpful veiled lady shopper. Next morning, we had a little free time to explore:

"... wandering through the maze of alleys which meander around the

jumble of houses. The women are out in force this morning and are pleased to stop and talk to me as a woman on her own. Several unveil for me and one even speaks a few words of English. Though most of the older children are at school, the streets are full of toddlers – the girls wearing 'pixie hats' as a head-covering which cannot fall off. As I photograph two little tots, a pair of young Yemeni men appear, demanding that I also take their picture. I am delighted to oblige!"

In the former North Yemen, many of the men were smartly dressed in sparkling white 'futa' (men's skirt) and jacket, with an ornate ceremonial dagger (jambiya) tucked into their belt. Once we entered the South the costumes became much less formal but more colourful, with a bright-hued futa and tasselled headscarf – but no jambiya: they had been banned by the former South Yemeni government for security reasons. The men were delighted when we admired or photographed them, as were the children, but the women were shy. Even when they unveiled for me or took me into their homes, they were not willing to be photographed – after all, a strange man might look at those photos and undo all the modesty their veils had offered.

We turned southwards again, at first retracing our route along the same road – there were few good roads in Yemen (until the 1960's there were no paved roads at all), although the Chinese were providing both engineers and workers to improve the network in this period of hope for a brighter future. Our driver Salah was clearly glad to be leaving the tense atmosphere of the north and treated us to a burst of music from his cassette player as we drove, a wailing female song accompanied by repetitive drumming which set my hips and shoulders twitching uncontrollably into dance. He was even more delighted that we found a restaurant for his lunch at a sensible hour – the main meal of the day in Yemen was lunch, and Yemeni men seemed mostly to eat out at midday instead of in their homes. We were happy with a picnic or just a drink and a snack, but our British escort had frequent disputes with Salah when he could not find his hot lunch!

While he ate, I took the opportunity to explore the town of Amran, which had seemed so attractive when we sped past on the way north:

"It looked so inviting before, but now I find it unattractive almost to the point of being unpleasant. The alleyways are paved with rubbish, and in places with sewage, instead of stone. The houses are unadorned mud-brick

with windows which seem just to have been punched through instead of carefully placed with artistic care. The 'shops' on the ground floors are actually just dark holes closed off with battered wooden doors or shaded by an awning of torn blue plastic. A few young men contrive to brush against me as they pass, or to fondle my backside as I walk as far as the main square – an open refuse-strewn space where goats and chickens pick through the litter. The children (mostly boys) plague me – obviously they have seen too many tourists and are interested only in the handouts we might give them (though some adults drag them away by the ear: many parents do not like to see their children begging)."

This problem of litter was to be seen everywhere we went in the country, seemingly a new phenomenon since the advent of the consumer society. Traditionally the people had thrown their refuse into the street to be eaten by goats roaming freely – a system which worked well when the refuse was fruit peelings and other edible items. Now Yemenis had discovered the joys of plastic but were still throwing this refuse into the streets. The goats, of course, did not eat it, so instead it built up into a thick impermeable 'pavement' which no longer absorbed the rainwater (or sewage) but instead directed it in torrents from top to bottom of steep village streets.

Now that we were more familiar with the generally arid landscape, we could better appreciate the patches of fertility in the broad valleys, especially as we descended a series of steep hairpin bends down to Amran Plain:

"... an oasis of verdant cultivation nestled at the foot of arid mountains, with fields as far as the eye can see – what a sight for ancient, parched, desert travellers as they reached Arabia Felix! But the corn and barley are short and grow sparsely – what would these people make of our tall dense crops? And as men and women squat side by side to harvest with hand sickles, what would they make of our monstrous combine harvesters? They would be no use here, where each tiny patch of arable land is enclosed behind mud dykes to aid irrigation."

Our escort Steve told us that Yemen was once the model of efficient farming for arid lands – rain which fell high up in the mountains was caught by the highest terraces, held by mud embankments to soak the soil for a period of time governed by a 'water-master', then channelled to the next level, and so on, all the way down the mountains to the coastal plains, which received not only water but also extra topsoil washed down with it. The move into a modern market economy had apparently shifted the emphasis to cash crops on the plains, leading some mountain farmers to abandon their land and allow their terraces to disintegrate and erode.

We were able to see for ourselves this ancient system in action as we left the plains to drive westwards into the mountains, since we were accompanied by storms with heavy rain and lightning (though November was supposed to be the dry season). The water was gushing off the mountain-top rocks to fill the upper terraces with water, as if they were paddy fields, ready to be released to flow on to the next level. I had seen terraced mountains already in the Himalayas, but nowhere had I seen terracing on quite such a scale – up to a thousand metres of mountainside cut (by hand) into steps reaching almost from the summits to the coastal plain far below:

"We drive among jumbled rocks and great pools of water (some spilling over the road), between a few waterlogged terraces, then climb again. We reach the crest of the hill for a spectacular view of terracing which stretches to the horizon – acres and acres of stepped fields running into the hazy distance of the valley far below. Jagged peaks loom from the mist (oh, for clear weather!) and water cascades over the rocks by the road, filling distant terraces with a silvery gleam. Tiny waterfalls are beginning to flow as we descend, though the fields at this level are not yet full. What a contrast from the arid land we saw only this morning – it is almost wet enough to be England."

The rain followed us all the way along a convoluted Chinese-built road (past incongruous pagoda-style roadside shelters they had left behind) to our mountain-top hotel above the town of Hajjah, accessed by an ever steeper road which strained the engine of our coach to its utmost. We unloaded the coach with trepidation – our baggage was all loaded on the roof ... and Salah had not been provided with a tarpaulin! To add to the difficulties, the hotel suffered power cuts repeatedly throughout our stay (a situation we found everywhere in the country, including in the capital Sana'a), but we had just enough daylight on arrival to open our luggage and spread the soggy contents all around our room:

"Of course, it's the smallest room we have had so far – by the time we've used every knob, ledge and hook, plus my washing line strung from window

to glamorous (but non-functioning) chandelier, it looks like a Chinese laundry!"

By next morning, everything had dried to the grade of 'dampish' and could be repacked and loaded (this time beneath a tarpaulin hastily acquired by Salah overnight). The morning was to be spent in the spectacularly located village of Kohlan, a short drive away – except that the rain had loosened a massive rockslide which had covered the road. Local 4x4's had smashed a path through the rocks, but the gap was too narrow for our coach, so we had to leave it behind and walk to the village:

"But it's definitely worth it! We follow a narrow stony track that contours the rock beneath a 17th century Turkish fortress, to find a huddle of stone houses linked by steps and alleys. The flat rooftops are crowded with children who deafen us with their chorus of 'Sura, sura' (photo) or 'Kalam, kalam' (pen), with an odd 'I love you' thrown in – obviously not many attend school in this village."

With so few good roads in Yemen, it was inevitable that we would have to pass Sana'a again as we returned from the north, though this time only for a lunch-break, extended when Salah and Steve went to search out camping gear for the second part of our trip – tourism was still very young and there were few hotels available, especially in former South Yemen. Yet the delay allowed for a little more people-watching – one of the delights of foreign travel:

"We sit on the step outside the (posh) restaurant, watching the parade of 4-wheel drive Jeeps and Landcruisers, Mercedes and Volvos, disgorging upper-class men to eat. There are Egyptians and Lebanese in Western garb, Saudis in pure-white djellabas, Yemenis in smart futas with prominent jambiya knives ... but all men. As mere women, it takes a bit of bravado to use the restaurant's toilet (there is no 'Ladies' since women do not eat in restaurants), marching in one by one to dash behind the only lockable door. But the men do not look too surprised by our antics ... after all, we ARE degenerate Western women."

With the coach roof now piled even higher with baggage and equipment, we headed off into the western mountains again, our road snaking like a living creature across hillsides seemingly composed of little more than scree and sand beneath eroded rock pillars, yet all neatly chopped up into terraces.

We struggled up one steep pass after another, trying to avoid heavily laden trucks hauling their weary way uphill, honking wildly before each village – they could not afford to lose any impetus by having to brake for a child or an oncoming car. The scenery was stunning:

"Wow! A sudden glimpse below us of our road, sparkling with new tarmac, twisting in 3 successive hairpins one above another, while the old road (a track barely wide enough for a laden donkey) plunges straight on over the abyss. Across the valley, hillsides are terraced from top to bottom, studded with tower-house villages and gashed by occasional cliffs. The valley grows narrower ... jagged peaks and pinnacles tower above us ... trucks fill our lungs with the stink of their exhaust. There are far more trucks on this road than yesterday's – many are empty as they descend to Hodeida port to load, so they roar past in a swirl of fumes. Does Yemen have no exports to fill these descending trucks, only imports to bring inland?"

Our hotel for the night was in a tiny village at the end of a turn-off from the main road – a newly-built 'funduq' (basic hotel) with a tiled lobby (my diary describes it as *'like the entrance to a swimming bath'*) boasting a few fold-up seats, each bearing an elderly local man with a cheek full of Qat when we arrived. The lobby was pervaded by a strange smell, like stale stew, though the rest of the hotel was adequate and even reasonably clean. Our group had two separate rooms (one for the men, one for the women) with carpet and mattresses where we could lay our sleeping bags, and the hotel boasted running (cold) water in the only bathroom plus two lockable toilets. What more could we want? We were even entertained in the evening by 3 local musicians and 3 dancers – joined enthusiastically by the drivers of another group staying in the funduq (Salah refused):

"The dancing involves rhythmic steps, the odd crouch and spring ... and lots of ferocious waving of jambiya knives! Repetitive perhaps, but they are so obviously enjoying it that I can't fail to enjoy it too."

Next day brought the chance to walk along a rocky mountain track to the village of Hajjara – a welcome change from constant coach travel and snatched photos through the windows. What a joy to have time to stop and admire the vistas of misty reddish-brown ridges reaching off to the horizon, dotted with tiny hamlets seemingly rooted into hillsides which were carved into sickle-shaped terraces, parading steadily downwards in neat steps. The village itself was fantastically perched on a precipice, accessed only by rock-cut steps, its streets almost vertical ... though, sadly, again paved with litter and running with water. Many of the windows in the tall stone white-patterned houses were open, so I could see the women inside – and they could see me:

"The women quickly emerge to invite me in – hoping for gifts or to sell embroidered headbands, though they are not pushy. A couple of charming teenage girls persuade me to enter their home, up dark and worn earthen steps to a landing and a tiny room where mattresses are laid around the walls. All the younger females of the family are there, unveiled now, and are delighted when I produce some little stick-pin brooches for them. They even agree to have their photo taken, until they see Mother approaching – she permits a photo only of the tiniest children."

Of course, we could not tarry long in Hajjara – our itinerary was driving us onwards, down out of the mountains into the steamy heat of the Tihama coastal plain. What a contrast! Not just in the climate but in the villages, which were now composed of simple dry-stone circular huts with conical thatched roofs (instead of the imposing stone towers of the mountains). All around us were expanses of thick, fertile earth (carried down by centuries of water from the terraces), divided into fields of tall, strong corn within high embankments to hold the irrigation water – though nearer the coast the rich earth was replaced by infertile sand-dunes.

We passed a few small towns too – filled with modern concrete structures festooned with TV aerials, and the first slums I had seen in Yemen: tents and shanties clustered in the suburbs. In the city of Hodeida itself I saw many rough sleepers, wrapped in a blanket or constructing a 'home' from a couple of pieces of cardboard. The men here were dressed in a motley array of clothing, sometimes wearing a distinctive flat-topped turban or else a cloth wrapped around a white skullcap, but rarely displaying a jambiya knife – a source of such pride with the highland Yemeni men (perhaps the Tihama had lost that respect for their heritage as foreign influence flooded in from the sea?). The women wore brightly coloured dresses and turbans, often topped with small conical straw hats. Many of the people even looked different – I saw frequent African-looking negroid features (descendants of slaves) among the hook-nosed Arab faces.

Hodeida offered little of interest to me, though I spent the evening wandering in the suk (yes, I admit it … I got lost!). Even at 8 or 9pm, there were still many stalls open – selling clothes and plastic buckets, mangoes and sticky dates, dried tobacco leaves and toothbrush twigs … and of course, Qat (though here sold only in tiny bunches, instead of the huge branches on offer in the highlands, where it is grown). Next morning, we were taken to the fish market:

"The laden boats seem to carry mostly hammer-head sharks, being hauled ashore with much heaving, shoving and sluicing with water, from the hold to the quay, then on to ancient wheelbarrows to be hurried to waiting trucks or donkey carts. Some are being cleaned and gutted on the beach alongside the market, beneath the watchful eyes of hundreds of gulls. Men and women are haggling enthusiastically and loudly with the porters who transport the fish. Motorbikes putter noisily up and down, donkeys stand half-asleep, resigned to their lot. Everywhere there are people, people, people – all in a hurry. Only the net-menders sit quietly in a companionable semi-circle under a shady awning, sucking at small plastic bags of fresh water."

We did not stay long in Hodeida, moving on along the coastal plain to Zabid – reputedly the hottest town in Yemen … and we arrived at midday! But it was a fascinating town, which I would not want to have missed. We were led by a small boy who appointed himself our guide through a rabbit warren of whitewashed stone alleys – some lanes barely wide enough for a single person to pass, twisting and turning on themselves to give access to the arcaded courtyards of the 80+ town mosques (Zabid was once considered the cultural capital of South Arabian Islam, possessing 286 mosques!) and to mysterious mansions hidden behind elaborate wooden doors:

"Flashes of gorgeously decorated facades catch my eye above the high whitewashed walls, and we are taken inside one courtyard, filled with corded beds hung with washing. Another invitation takes us up steep steps on the outside of a house, to visit the elaborately decorated 'mafraj' room at the top of the building, where men gather after afternoon prayers, to smoke mada'a water pipes and chew Qat."

As we continued south, we were buffeted by strong sand-laden winds blowing from the Red Sea – apparently, they were common in this area, and we were lucky to have avoided them until now. Reaching the end of the

Tihama coastal plain, we turned away from the port of Al Makha (better known to coffee drinkers as Mocca) to return to the mountains at Ta'izz, briefly the capital of Yemen in the mid-20th century and still third city of unified Yemen when we visited. In fact, Ta'izz seemed better adjusted to 20th century life than Sana'a had been – and our hotel here actually had unlimited hot water in the shower (oh, the simple pleasures of life!), but there was little to see beyond pleasant shops and restaurants. The land around the city seemed much wealthier than further north:

"The road cuts into the rocky hillside, looking down over scenes of rich cultivation spattered with large villages. Even the terraces are much larger than the tiny patches of land we saw near Sana'a. The red stone villages sprawl over the land – very different from the compact sites of the north which try to use up as little precious land as possible. Here there is more land available ... and perhaps, in the past, less danger from marauding desert tribes, so less need for fortress-like hilltop sites. Gaudily dressed women move about the fields, vivid as flowers compared to their black-swathed northern sisters."

We were en route to the historic town of Jiblah, notable for its connection with the redoubtable Queen Arwa who (in the 11th century) took over the government of south-western Yemen when her husband died, ruling with extreme compassion and wisdom for over 70 years – and still greatly revered, despite the fact that in this strict Islamic country, women are hidden from public life. Well done, Queen Arwa! The beautiful mosque which she built was still functioning and we managed to find a local resident who persuaded the imam (a small worried-looking man) to allow us to peep into the courtyard. After a moment's thought, our guide took us right into the courtyard to look inside the mosque itself, until the imam appeared again and shooed us out. Our itinerary allowed just a single hour to explore this fascinating town, so I launched at top speed into the Old Town, up the narrowest and busiest stairway which I could find. It turned out to be the suk, with a row of tiny shops perched in the walls above steep rock-cut steps:

"From there, ever upward via steps and rough stone paths thick with litter and (in places) running with the fast-flowing water of a stream. Tall stone houses rise above me, built as solidly as our Norman castles – do some of them date back to the time of Queen Arwa? Small doorways lead to dark

vaulted lobbies ... children hang out of windows and run down to meet me, but I am not invited inside. Men and women are trudging down to market or back uphill, laden with produce or live chickens. Many of the women stop to talk, though all are firmly veiled – this is stern Ismaeli country here, and we are all well-covered too, despite the heat."

Both here and in the nearby city of Ibb, we found many people dressed in their best clothing for the Friday holy day – crowds of men were sitting in porches outside many of the mosques, listening to the preaching of the imam, relayed at volume across the town. Once more, the men sported finely embroidered belts holding their traditional jambiya – even the little boys sometimes wore miniature versions, while the little girls were dressed up in frilly, sparkly dresses (totally unsuited to playing in dusty alleys). The women, of course, were invisible within their black overgarments. Back in Ta'izz, I launched again into the suk, stopping as usual in a quiet corner to record my thoughts and observations in my diary:

"As I stand to write this, a crowd of adults and children gather – a few English-speaking men ask to read a bit, a couple of boys want to show me that they can write their names – though it is a girl who writes with most confidence. One up for the girls!"

A few hours further on, we reached the former border with South Yemen – no controls since unification, but such a vivid contrast from the relative wealth of the north. The first villages were no more than clusters of tiny one-room homes, sometimes only made of woven straw, each with just a small plot of cultivated land growing potatoes or maize. When we stopped to photograph an impressive range of rock pinnacles, we were approached by an unveiled woman dressed in faded cotton cloth – in this desiccated landscape, there was none of the rich agriculture or trade we had seen near Ta'izz, and no money for new brightly-coloured clothes. She was carrying a bundle of grass on her head, no doubt to feed a goat (the area looked too poor to support a cow) and she dropped her load to mime her hunger to us, begging for food (we gave her what we could). When we passed the first larger community, the town of Lahij, we saw densely packed concrete homes, including some drab blocks of flats which would not have looked out of place in East Germany – the functional 'homes for the people' supplied by Communist governments throughout the world, with no attempt to refer back to the traditions or heritage of the country. We were taken to visit the palace which had belonged to the former Sultan of Lahij:

"The 'palace' is nothing! It was once a complex of mudbrick and concrete buildings, of which a few remain. But the enclosing walls have been broken through, and new homes are springing up higgledy-piggledy. My impression of Lahij is ... hot and dusty, a jumble of concrete buildings going up and mud-brick ones crumbling down. But the people are friendly – the children watch us silently with no begging ... a woman replies to my 'Salaam' and encourages her son to do the same (though he is too shy)."

Unfortunately, my impressions of Aden were not a lot more positive. First sight of the city was a huge garbage tip (though perhaps that was a sign that in South Yemen, they were trying to solve the problem of plastic waste?). Then the outskirts: piles of sand, military barracks and plain concrete apartment blocks ... a few more glamorous modern houses with balconies and oriental-style windows ... a shanty town made of corrugated iron and wooden slats (taken from packing cases in the port, I assumed). All linked together by a jumble of messy dirt alleys where sheep were foraging. What a contrast then to drive in to the former British settlement on Aden Peninsula, with neatly paved promenades, smooth dual-carriageway roads and the posh high-rise Aden Hotel – nothing at all to tell us that we were in Yemen, except perhaps a few Arab-style dhows in the inner port. We passed the Fortress, a valuable site obviously still in use by the military, and Steamer Point with its red-spired Christian church – an ex-pat on the plane from Britain had told me that the bishop was to be permitted to reclaim his churches (closed by the Communists) and re-open them: certainly we did see some workers clearing rubble from a derelict church. On into Crater district, where the tiny fishing port beside Sira Island was now filthy with litter and lined with slums – the beach beyond reclaimed as the building site for a Saudi-financed hospital. Here we found a few old colonial buildings (from the time of British occupation in the 19th and 20th centuries), though their balconies were crumbling and their plaster peeling. Even our hotel at Gold Mohur Bay was a disappointment, run-down and dirty – though an evening walk revealed a beach of pure golden sand with not a piece of rope nor a plastic bottle in sight ... just shells, crabs and pebbles, beside blood-warm, deep turquoise water. Such a relief to paddle here after weeks of litter and dirt!

I was not sorry to leave Aden, heading along the coast past beaches where a few families eked out a living in driftwood shacks with a few animals wandering the dunes nearby, and scattered isolated 'fields' scraped from the sand to grow a scrawny crop of corn. We turned inland, following a tongue of ancient lava flow towards the distinctly volcanic black cone of Jabal Al Urays, streaked with red minerals and patches of green vegetation. Poor Salah (our driver) was not enjoying this day. The road was becoming harder and harder to drive, following dry wadis (valleys) through the mountains, travelling roads littered with axle-breaking potholes – on and on for hours with no settlements to provide refreshments and especially nowhere to eat that (for a Yemeni) vital lunch! At last, after 7 hours driving, we reached a non-descript settlement of shops and garages beneath a range of awesome 'inselbergs' (free-standing rocks) – a whole line of pinnacles, blocks and pedestals eroded in myriad shapes, which had us all reaching for our cameras. Of course, for Salah the only goal was that single restaurant in the midst of the shops!

Unfortunately, we were running late, so sightseeing time was very limited when we reached one of the highlights of the day – the 'mud Manhattan' village of Habban. This was our first taste of the amazing mud skyscrapers of South Yemen – towering homes up to 10 storeys high made only of mudbricks, preserved for centuries by a regular renewing of their protective coat of mud plaster. I had been impressed by the stone towers in the western mountains, but Habban seemed even more impressive because it was so unexpected in this otherwise poverty-stricken land. The houses were originally built by merchants made wealthy from the trade routes which led from the southern coast through the heart of Arabia to Egypt and Europe, at first carrying precious frankincense (which grows only in southern Arabia) and then goods brought into ports on the Arabian Sea from India. Now these amazing structures seemed to survive simply for want of money to change them – I could only hope that their value would be appreciated before an increase in disposable income persuaded their owners to replace them. We bounced down a dirt track into Habban village square, totally silent in the midday heat, watched by wide-eyed children and a few men sitting quietly in the shade. I was desperate to explore, but Steve tetchily told us that we were running hours late and must make do with a quick photograph before leaping back on to the coach to continue the journey. The locals looked at us as though we were mad – I agreed with them!

There were no hotels available in this remote area, so tonight we were due to camp. As the light faded, I saw innumerable flat areas where we could have erected our tents, but Steve was determined to reach the seaside – and he was right! We bounced off the road several times seeking a beach hard enough to take the weight of the coach, before arriving in Bir Ali in total darkness, swerving around fishing boats and nets pulled up on the sand before choosing our spot. I sited my tent as close as possible to the seashore (as it turned out, just inches from the line of high tide!):

"Tonight, we are bedded on soft coral sand with the sea lapping ever closer to my tent door. In the beam of my torch, myriad ghost crabs scuttle at top speed in and out of the waves, unnerved by the light."

Next day we were woken before dawn by the fishermen living in shacks along the beach, watching as they launched their boats into a brilliant red sunrise, followed by flocks of gulls. The children arrived to watch us preparing breakfast – one little boy waded into the sea to fling out a net for his own breakfast; another brought a ghost crab on a string to show us, while his brother towed a toy truck made of an oil can and a bit of wood. Otherwise the brilliant white beach was empty, inhabited only by transparent ghost crabs, huge dragonflies ... and annoying sand flies. An idyllic scene – except for the back of the beach, beyond the regular washing by the waves. This area was thick with rubbish: old cans, rotten fish-heads, bits of rope and plastic – the detritus of a society moving into the modern world.

We continued along the coast, past tiny communities scratching a desperately poor living from the sea and a few goats – with a brief stop when we spotted the tracks of a turtle which came ashore the previous night to lay its eggs in the sand. Finally, we reached the town of Al-Mukalla, an impressive chain of white houses decorated with finely carved wooden doors and ornately plastered windows, which once rose directly from the sea. In 1989 the authorities had built a mole of huge stone blocks around the town, so that the fortress-like structures now rose sheer from mounds of litter instead of from the water – yet I loved the town's atmosphere:

"Hot ... so hot ... as I walk along the shadeless road towards the town, so I turn into the parallel street where shops still hum with activity as midday

approaches. There are no specially interesting shops, just cloth and grocery,
but there's a unique atmosphere – ornate whitewashed buildings with
arcades giving a faintly colonial air. In a back alley I find a couple of stalls
selling a few spices and some piles of aromatic lumps – toffee coloured
myrrh and golden frankincense ... and another dried substance which turns
out to be chewing gum. The stallholder is amused that I cannot tell the
difference!"

However, I was glad that we were not going to stay overnight in this
fascinating, but smelly and fly-ridden town. Instead we drove on ... and
on ... along a featureless coast and then inland following a pipeline (perhaps
carrying the oil we had heard about?), passing a group of warplanes sitting
amid the thorn bushes, thickly covered in dust – presumably an air force base?
Finally we reached a prosperous-looking modern town with tree-lined
avenues, but our hotel was not here; instead we continued along a dirt trail
into the original village, through an oasis of palms and greenery to enter a
lovely walled garden full of trees and flowers ... this was it! Before us rose
an enchanting 'sugar plum' structure painted green, pink and white – the
former summer palace of the Sultan, our idyllic (if rather run-down) rest
house for the night ... and the furthest point eastwards which we would reach.

North again, amid clouds of dust from extensive road-building
construction sites; through eroded mountains and up slopes so steep that our
coach struggled to keep moving; across desperately dry land where the only
vegetation was straggly thorn bushes. Yet a few miserable villages survived
here, subsisting only from small herds of goats or camels. In one place we
spotted a complex of portacabins and a dirt airstrip beneath a large Total flag
– presumably prospecting for oil? They did not appear to be bringing any
wealth to the local people yet, though their empty oil barrels were proving
useful as fenceposts in this land without trees!

Suddenly a stir of excitement rippled through the coach as we reached
Wadi Hajareyn, a deep cleft in the rocks, lined with lush palm groves and
villages of whitewashed mud-brick homes – such a relief to our eyes after so
many hours of monotonous stony desert. Soon this smaller wadi led on into
Wadi Hadhramawt, the largest wadi (valley) in the whole of Arabia, with
enough water hidden deep below it to allow agriculture and settlement over a
period of thousands of years (tradition said that Noah's grandson settled here).

We were visiting because this valley was on the ancient trade route carrying frankincense and other valuable goods northwards, and merchants were wealthy enough to build whole towns of mud-brick skyscrapers like the ones we had glimpsed earlier in Habban – and this time, our itinerary was planned to give us time to explore properly!

Our goal was Shibam, seen from a distance as a solid mass of earth-coloured skyscrapers squeezed together like a giant mud pattie, their top storeys frosted with white gypsum like icing. On the edge of town, we passed rows of workmen who were smashing gypsum rock into powder, selling it in sacks to be mixed with the final mud plaster as a whitewash for the houses. Finally, we hurtled through the massive South Gate (it was lunchtime and Salah was hungry!) to find the old town shut tight for siesta, its streets inhabited only by dozing goats and browsing sheep … joined swiftly by a few persistently begging children:

"The town is impressive from a distance yet once inside, it is drab and run-down. However there are some superb doors, barred with ornately-carved crossbars and secured by elaborate locks, and many of the windows are veiled with 'keyhole' carved screens. I walk around part of the walls, but it is like walking in a sewer, so I cut through a dark passage to wander the alleys together with the goats. After all I had hoped for in Shibam, I am disappointed."

Rather disconsolately I crossed the broad sandy bed of the wadi towards the so-called 'New Town'. In the wadi I encountered a group of boys, aged only 12-13, busy collecting wheelbarrows of mixed mud and straw, tipping it into moulds to dry into bricks. They cheekily tried to shake hands with me, laughing with me as I stepped back from their mud-smeared fingers saying 'Yuk!', but then one of them guided me up a rock for a better view of the old town – not a very good view, but he was trying so hard to be helpful that I was happy to give him the pen he shyly requested. Now another, older, pair of lads took me in tow to show me the New Town – walking along the main street, hung with tin baskets on wires over the streets, where chickens roosted, and through a backyard where a woman was making straw brooms. There was a nicer atmosphere in the New Town, and a fresh breeze from the hillside restored my spirits.

There was no accommodation in Shibam, so we moved on to an official camping site in the neighbouring town of Say'un – certainly not the most comfortable campsite I have experienced on my travels!

"Our site is a hard, stony terrace. Putting up the tents is already agony, pounding pegs into the ground with stones as hammers – my first attempt foiled by poles which do not fit the tent, so I have to pull it all down and start again. As we retire to bed, the wind rises – ferocious gusts tearing down the wadi to rattle the pegs loose and envelop us in billowing fabric, forcing dust and sand through two layers of tentcloth to coat our faces, arms and sleeping bags. All night the campsite resounds to the plod of feet collecting up kitchen equipment which has blown away, and the ringing of stone on iron pegs as rescue efforts continue on the tents."

Next day we were told that this had been a 'catabatic wind' – cool air rushing downhill from the highlands to roll along the wadi. Nice to know we were part of a scientific phenomenon, but a few hours more sleep would have been good!

The combination of a difficult night and searing daytime heat, mean that my memories of our day's sightseeing in Wadi Hadhramawt are tainted. I remember the turrets and ornate plasterwork of Sayun's palace (entirely built of mud), rising above the town like a sugar-candy confection in cream and pale green; Tarim, with its fine mud-brick mansions and Al Mudhar Mosque's elegant arcaded courtyard and soaring minaret; lunch in another of the Sultan's summer palaces, painted in the most gaudy colour-scheme imaginable. Yet the best part of the day was simply relaxation in the palace gardens, amid palms and bougainvillea – it was just too hot for sightseeing! All was well again next day, though, since the night had been cooler – I even spent some time lying outside the tent beneath a clear sky dappled with stars, gazing at mountains which gleamed ethereally white in the starlight. We were sad to leave our characterful driver Salah in Say'un, abandoning him in the desert as we flew back to Sana'a across the infamous Empty Quarter:

"The play of light and shade on the ridges and hummocks, combined with patches of black stone and thin ribbons of greenery which trace the line of dry river beds, make an abstract design on the khaki scene below us, scratched repeatedly by a complex of dirt trails. Just at the point where a few rocks peek through the rolling sands, a few tiny green fields surround a couple of houses – what a place to eke out a living! Then nearby I spot an oil

pipe snaking across the desert – perhaps these are the homes of maintenance men?"

Our tour was not yet finished. Now we were supplied with 4-wheel-drive Landcruisers (and drivers who loved to push them to their limits!), heading north again, passing the palace of Wadi Dhar, perched high on a spur of rock, star of innumerable posters extolling the glories of Yemen. Imposing, but we had seen so many other wonders that this merited only a quick photo. More impressive was the great clifftop fortress of Kawkaban, its walls almost invisible from a distance, built of the same reddish stone as the mountains where it stood. Inside the fortress walls, we found only a few historic remnants (the town within the walls was heavily bombed during the civil war of the 1960's), but we were given enough time to walk down from the fortress to the market town in the valley below:

"A vertical wall of rock drops to the grey town of Shibam, its drabness helping it blend into the plain below – only the mosque, picked out in white, is clearly distinguishable. The voice of their imam echoes clearly up to us in the still cool air, blending with the calls of Kawkaban's imam – the Koran in stereo!"

We continued through the mountains north of Sana'a to emerge into a vast sandy desert, pierced by ancient volcanic cones – the edge of the Empty Quarter. Our goal was the modern town of Marib; characterless, but boasting the best hotel we had used throughout the tour – a pleasant place to sit out the hottest part of the day. Here, in the heart of the desert, constantly throbbing water pumps were bringing up ground water to irrigate the land and produce abundant crops of oranges, mangoes, potatoes and barley – seemingly a modern miracle. Yet the first dam here was built as long ago as the 8th century BC and for over 1000 years it irrigated crops which permitted Marib to develop as a major city, capital of the ancient kingdom of Saba and, according to legend, ruled at one time by the Queen of Sheba. Once the heat of the day had abated, we visited the archaeological ruins of temples probably built in 400 BC (though excavations were only just beginning when I visited, and information was sketchy):

"We climb the sand-dunes which encircle the excavations to see several sets of columns, smooth polished monoliths cut from warm golden sandstone – agile children swarm up some of them, trying to impress us enough to earn

a tip. An oval line of dressed stone, laid perfectly without mortar, lies half-buried in the sand – but it is hard to visualise how this site once looked, as the desert sands work to reclaim it all. There are no explanatory signs … just a Kalashnikov-toting youth who indicates we may photograph the ruins, but not the irrigation machinery nearby."

We returned to our Landcruisers to bump across the desert to see the remains of the historic dam (which finally collapsed in the 6th century AD). There were still two sluice gateways to see (though the gates themselves were long gone) – stone-faced rubble walls with solid stone gateposts, standing high and dry amid the sand at the mouth of a deep wadi cut into ancient accumulations of silt. Astounding to see relics still bearing witness to a Yemen which was once a powerhouse of the ancient world – and how sad to compare that history even with the Yemen I was visiting, never mind the disaster zone which the country has later become.

Our last destination took us into the region of Al Jawf, right on the borders of Saudi Arabia, described in my guidebook as: "… formerly inhabited only by nomadic Bedouins. Tourists are usually neither allowed nor wanted in the province. The local sheikhs still consider themselves to be in charge and are hostile to strangers". Even in Marib, a few hours' drive away, we had encountered innumerable armed men, toting Kalashnikov rifles and wearing bandoliers of ammunition … now we passed the time as we crossed monotonous desert scenery, counting the numbers of tanks and sub-machine guns hiding behind stone embankments by the road. We stopped to pay our dues to the local sheikh and pick up guides (or rather guards), one to each Landcruiser, who perched on our bonnets with their guns as we travelled on to visit the fortress of Baraquish. It all sounds very scary and impressive, but in fact I never felt any threat at all – most of these armed guards were no more than young, bored lads.

"Climbing on to the walls, we are approached by more and more armed guards – some glowering and silent, but most smiling and inviting us to photograph them. We spread out across the site, now targets for the next stage of their plan – individual guards squat in hidden corners to reveal treasures for sale: a terracotta lamp, pieces of pot, even a gold wedding ring! It seems strange to find this ancient fortress, still guarded by men on every turret – yet they have only ruins to guard."

They encouraged us to scramble up banks of scree to view a frieze of Minaean inscriptions inserted into the fortifications on stones re-used from a more ancient site (a notice in Italian told me about recent excavations by Italian archaeologists, who had discovered a small Minaean temple (500-200 BC) underneath the fortress ruins). Then we crossed the walls at a point where they had crumbled, to look out across the site – just a jumble of ruined stone buildings and heaps of collapsed mud structures, though all between 300-800 years old. The visit to Baraquish was not memorable for the sights we saw, but for the people we met – an insight into the precarious world of the northern borders where guns were part of everyday life rather than an immediate threat.

As we returned through the mountains to Sana'a one last time, my diary reflected on our weeks touring in Yemen:

"A last reminder of the incredible landscapes of Yemen, eroded by wind and polished by sandstorms or floods into spectacular peaks and wadis – any one of which would be a major attraction in our own country. The contrast between seemingly barren arid wasteland and the sudden lush green of crops – a reminder of the value of water, which we so profligately waste. Passing a few more mud villages, I am reminded of the Yemeni talent for making a living in places where we would just curl up and die. Whatever I may think of their standards of hygiene, driving or the place of women – Yemenis have plenty to be proud of, and are (so far) still a proud people, not reduced to begging for arrogantly-given Western help."

How tragic those words now seem, knowing what has happened in Yemen in the years since my visit.

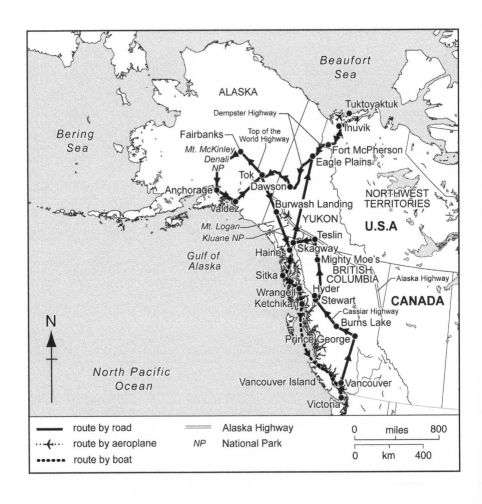

Beaufort
Sea

ALASKA
Tuktoyaktuk

Dempster Highway
Inuvik

Bering
Sea
Fairbanks
Top of the
World Highway
Fort McPherson
Mt. McKinley
Denali
NP
Eagle Plains
Tok
Anchorage
Dawson
Burwash Landing
NORTHWEST
TERRITORIES
Valdez
YUKON
U.S.A
Mt. Logan
Kluane NP
Teslin
Haines
Skagway
Gulf of
Alaska
Mighty Moe's
Sitka
BRITISH
COLUMBIA
Alaska Highway
Hyder
Wrangell
Stewart
Ketchikan
CANADA
Cassiar Highway
Burns Lake
Prince George

N

North Pacific
Ocean
Vancouver Island
Vancouver

Victoria

route by road	Alaska Highway	0	miles	800
route by aeroplane	NP National Park			
route by boat		0	km	400

North America - Yukon and Alaska (July/August 1993)

BACK IN 1990, I HAD BEEN entranced by a quick taste of North America's wilderness, so in 1993 decided to join a camping tour heading deep into that wilderness, both in Canada's Yukon territory and also the American state of Alaska. Of course, the only suitable time to visit is during their brief summer, so I took a high-summer break from my usual schedules of tour work. I had been frustrated in 1990 to have so little time to explore Vancouver, so flew out to Canada ahead of the start of the tour, for an extra few days on Vancouver Island. Even the ferry journey across to the island proved memorable:

"The Gulf Islands come nearer – ridge after ridge of thickly forested land; thinly grassed rocks reaching out of the trees to the water's edge; posh waterside homes or simple huts, mostly adorned with a proudly fluttering Canadian flag. An announcement from the captain causes a flurry of excitement: 'Killer whales off the bow!' and there they are – three Orcas cruising past, their fearsome dorsal fins rising and sinking in the water in a leisurely fashion ... no hurry, no fear of our ferry."

My main goal on the Island was to visit Butchart Gardens, which Canadian travellers had lauded so often – an old limestone quarry transformed into a riot of colour with formal beds of geraniums, begonias, wallflowers and marigolds, all surrounded by magnificent ancient trees. Otherwise, the town of Victoria (incongruously the capital of British Columbia, despite its isolation on the island) had a very British feel, with 'olde English' style buildings housing antique shops and estate agents, and

Craigdarroch Castle, a Victorian mock-medieval fortress on a hill overlooking the town.

Returning to the mainland, I joined my tour group for in-depth sightseeing in Vancouver itself – including the infamous Capilano suspension bridge:

"It's the wooden steps down to the bridge which worry me most – they look solid but are, in fact, attached to the cables and so they bounce as much as the bridge itself. It tilts too, especially when we all turn at the same time to peer down into the abyss below – eek! But I tell myself that I can trust Canadian technology, and the steel cables and netting must be solid. 70 metres below, the river runs peacefully between high tree-clad cliffs ... now I have to screw up my courage to tackle the 140 metre walk back across the gorge."

Vancouver was proud of its gardens too – we walked among the carefully designed flowerbeds and lawns of Queen Elizabeth Gardens, though most impressive were the people we saw there. Saturday was Wedding Day and innumerable wedding parties were vying for the best photo opportunities, with Asian brides dressed in traditional white and Indian brides in red and gold saris, each surrounded by a multi-coloured garland of guests and bridesmaids.

Our journey into the wilderness started along the same route I had used three years before, the road squeezing alongside twin railway lines to follow the narrow gorge of the Fraser River through the mountain ridges of the Coastal Ranges, which had proved an almost impassable barrier to the first white settlers in this region. This time we continued north along the valleys of the Fraser and Thompson Rivers, passing through constant forest broken only occasionally by a swamp or lake (usually created by the work of beavers to dam the streams) – perfect breeding grounds for mosquitoes! The only signs of human settlement were cabins for fishermen, hunters or trappers, plus remote campsites where we could pitch our tents – though the road remained busy with huge trucks and even larger American campervans (Americans seem to take everything, including the kitchen sink, when they travel). A massive timber yard and pulping mill at Quesnel provided the only major industry in the area, though there were some permanent residents making a living by providing for the truckers and other travellers on this major highway to the North:

"A moment of amusement when we stop for coffee and toilets at a roadside service centre – a notice on the Community Board, advertising a festival last weekend, featuring ladies' axe-throwing, ladies spike-driving and a baby crawling competition. Even the women and children are tough up here!"

In Prince George, there were enough shops for us to stock up on mosquito repellent, and for me to acquire a rather natty mosquito hat – like a cross between a fish-net and a parrot-cage (but who cares how it looked if it could repel the mosquitoes!). Then on through forest ... and more forest ... and more forest – only rarely were there gaps in the trees which gave a glimpse of mountain peaks in the Coastal Ranges which we were following. Campsites were located amid the trees – I was lucky to have a tent to myself, so that I could pitch it in a cosy hollow between the tree roots, just nicely wide enough to fit my hips. Dinner was cooked over an open fire, barbecue-style, sometimes with a session of marshmallow-toasting on pine twigs afterwards for dessert. At one of these campsites, I rose early in the morning to walk to a nearby lake to read my Bible and try a bit of wildlife-spotting:

"There is little activity at first, though there are crackles of noise and flickers of movement around the lake. A strange gnawing sound draws my eye to the far shore ... and there is a beaver, sitting in shallow water gnawing busily and methodically at a thin branch which is slowly turning white as he strips the bark from it. He must know that I am here, but he seems unconcerned. After his snack, he swims off underwater, stirring the waterlilies in a wild dance."

As we followed the River Bulkley, it suddenly narrowed to become a small rapid leading into a short gorge, forcing the massive Chinook and Sockeye salmon together as they ascended towards their spawning grounds. For hundreds of years the local native tribes had harvested fish from this spot:

"They are here today – 10 or so men are balancing on the rocks, sometimes secured by a rope as they lean out over the torrent wielding massive nets or, more gruesomely, a single or double gaff on a long pole or a swinging rope. They are experts too, especially an older man who seems to hook a fish with each swing of his double gaff – those caught are swiftly dispatched with blows to the head."

The canyon was in a small reserve belonging to the Carrier Indians (so-called because of the tradition that a widow cremated her husband, then carried his ashes on her back for the rest of her life), and fishing was forbidden to all but the Indians themselves. We visited several native settlements in this area – Ksan Indian Village was a prosperous tourist reconstruction of a traditional village with gaudily painted longhouses and family totem poles at the entrances, but Kitwanga Indian Village was just a cluster of poverty-stricken cabins and weather-beaten totems. Our driver/guide poured out a stream of information about the history of the native tribes, who reached the Americas from central Asia 10,000 years ago and split into 3 main groups: Athabascans (including the Carriers, Klingits and Haida tribes of the Alaskan coast, plus the Apache and Navajo who headed south to fill the American plains), Inuit (who went north to the Arctic) and Aleuts (who settled the islands between North America and Russia, and had now almost died out). The Klingits and Haida were great traders, especially dealing in furs, and became rich enough to develop an advanced culture, though the arrival of white men seeking land led to their wholesale slaughter. Though Canada generally seemed to have been more sympathetic than America in their treatment of the tribes, it still seemed to me that in modern-day Canada they did not share the nation's comfortable lifestyle.

We joined the Cassiar Highway, driving ever closer to the highest ridges of the Coastal Mountains – which were now forming the border between Canada and the Alaskan 'pan-handle':

"The mountains tower far above the forest, awesome and aloof, filling every vista. Every gully is picked out in snow, every peak outlined against the now totally clear sunlit sky – filling both our windscreen and side windows with breath-taking views. Glaciers crumble over the cliffs towards us, down hillsides eroded by earlier glacial action and now padded out with thick vegetation, laced with skeins of fast-flowing melt water."

Leaving the Highway, we turned westwards, cutting through the mountains beneath innumerable glaciers – one peered across the top of a cliff, before exploding downhill in spectacular waterfalls ... another squeezed itself into an impossibly narrow gorge, transforming itself as it descended the gully, from sparkling white ice into a pile of old grey snow just yards from our road. Bear Glacier was almost close enough to touch – a corrugated tumble of blue and white ice, crumbling directly into a muddy terminal lake.

We camped at Stewart (declaiming itself 'Canada's most northerly ice-free port') and then ... walked to Alaska! Actually just a short stroll around the ridge to visit the tiny settlement of Hyder (pop.70), no more than a line of run-down shacks sprawled around a dirt road, with a small store and the Glacier Inn Bar, boasting a pool table, some plastic seats and walls covered with money (traditionally miners pinned money to the wall, marked with their name, so that if they emerged from the wilderness broke, they had enough to buy a beer). Hyder was totally isolated from the USA, their only access a floatplane which collected mail twice a week, so there were no border controls or formalities for us as we passed back and forth over the next day. On the American side, we picked our way up an ancient mine track alongside Salmon Glacier (a broad, cobbled 'street' of ice, striped lengthwise by dark lateral moraines) to reach Bowser Glacier:

"It's not such a pretty glacier, since its surface is mostly covered by dirt, but it is accessible on foot ... so off we go! Along 'beaches' of fine silt, breaking through the crust with monotonous regularity; over massive reddish boulders; across insecure piles of stone crumbling rapidly into scree. At one point I find bear prints (fortunately not fresh) set into the firm surface of a silt bed – otherwise we are totally alone. At the face of the glacier are two great caves filled with blue ice-filtered light, where torrents of glacial melt water pour from the roof. Up here there is no sound but the rush of water and wind – the only buildings nearby are abandoned mines; the only road is empty."

Back in Stewart, there was time to explore the town, watching fishing boats and tiny one-man tugboats bobbing behind great rafts of logs being floated downriver for processing. The town itself was pleasant, with simple but tidy houses and every kind of shop needed for everyday life – even a video and book library. My diary declares: *"I could live here!"*

After our brief foray into Alaska, it was back to Canada to continue northwards on the Cassiar Highway, though sadly the weather had changed; the mountains were garlanded with swirls of cloud and rain, revealing only occasional glimpses of rock or snow – but now the waterfalls were in full spate, cascades of brilliant white foam piercing even the gloom of our misted-up windows. We enjoyed only half an hour of driving on a sealed tarmac road, before the surface turned to gravel – within minutes the minibus windows were not only steamed up, but thick with mud, allowing no more than a blurry view of timber trucks hauling huge logs out of the north, through forested landscape interspersed with patches of brilliant red fireweed (a much more evocative name than our 'willow herb') wherever forest fires had cleared a space. At least we were not calling for photo stops, which was a relief to our drivers since they were clearly tense and concerned that the mud might cause us to slip into the deep ditches alongside the road. Our lunch-stop beside an unnamed lake brought one scenic highlight to the day:

"The lake is beautiful – a vast expanse of flat water, pitted only by the pattering raindrops, reaching off into distant and mist-wreathed forests. The water laps gently at my feet, and a loon warbles in the distance like a demented soprano – this surely must be the Sound of the Wild."

Our campsite for the night was named simply 'Mighty Moe's' – especially memorable because of Mighty Moe himself! He was a true eccentric, living his own lifestyle with no neighbours to object. His campsite was a jumbled junkyard of eclectic decorations – two cabins adorned with hub caps, hard hats, dolls and toys. There were few facilities – toilets were two smelly holes inside wooden sheds (or behind a bush), water came from the river ... but what a joy to wash amid total silence broken only by the rippling of the river and the cry of a loon flying by. We barely had time to erect our tents before Moe hustled us off to try some 'wilderness canoeing'. I had expected a bit of gentle paddling on the nearby lake, but Moe had other ideas – starting when he forcibly organised us into a major operation to load canoes on to his Jeep, hurling out orders to our bewildered group: *'we need 4 men to lift a canoe ... I SAID 4! ... and men only! Women stand BACK'.* Having loaded the canoes, we drove a few miles upriver for a brief lesson in paddling – with the threat that Moe would stone us if we held our paddles wrongly! I was paired with a strong fellow traveller:

"Rob and I are first to launch – though it takes a long time to work out which way to paddle to keep straight. In fact, we perform an elegant pirouette – so far off-line that it's easier to go right round and start again! Then we are off ... a series of lurches, spurts, swerves and corrections, with periods of tranquil drifting on the current followed by power surges through patches of disturbed water. A bald eagle settles on a tree to watch us pass; two beavers swim wild-eyed in terror across the river, then slap their tails as

a resounding call to 'dive, dive, dive'. No moose, no bear – but the satisfaction of surviving the journey without getting wet."

Next morning, however, we were treated to our first sight of a moose in the river nearby, wading at a stately pace across the current, deeper and deeper until only her head was visible, before wading out again on the far side without changing speed at all. Later, after many more miles of unbroken forest, we spotted our first bear as we entered Yukon territory:

"Suddenly shrieks of excitement echoing from front to rear of our minibus – 'Bear! Bear!' One small black bear has wandered out of the trees on to the verge but is totally shocked as the van in front of us roars past him – ears flat in terror, he whirls and lumbers back into the undergrowth. But we have seen our first bear."

Our first Yukon camp was located at the native settlement of Teslin, spending the evening in the village bar (where I tried my hand, unsuccessfully, at pool and darts), surrounded by very drunk Indians and a few rough, tough settlers – one of whom arrived at the pub on his horse. Teslin truly felt like a glimpse into outback Canadian life:

"Tonight's campsite is a foretaste of the Far North – we are greeted by swarms of huge mosquitoes which hang in front of our faces, gazing into our eyes to distract us while their cousins stab us from behind. Out with the mosquito hats and the Jungle Formula! But the cool light of the North is enchanting, casting a silver runner across the lake with ever-changing cloud formations."

We were reaching the area which experienced the madness of the Gold Rush in the last years of the 19th century. The first rich gold seam was found in 1896 and successful prospectors took their fortune south to Vancouver and Seattle; word spread like wildfire and by winter 1897 all the claims were staked. The prospectors poured into Skagway, where army engineers had earlier found a way through the almost impassable Coastal Mountains – White Pass, which is now the border between Canada and Alaska:

"The valley is filled with scattered glacial lakes and moraine boulders, a lumpy bumpy scene glistening with sunlit pools. We descend from the summit, our trail following a stream which cuts its way through rock and shale, leaping from one side of the water to the other (what a challenge to those early miners), then across a particularly deep ravine. Here the Gold Rush

prospectors' overworked packhorses frequently fell to their deaths, as if committing suicide to escape the unrelenting agony of being driven into impossible tasks in the depths of winter."

As numbers of 'stampeders' grew, they established another (even more difficult) route through the mountains – the Chilkoot Trail. In Skagway (now a major cruise port), I saw historic photos turned into postcards, showing a human chain of hopeful gold-seekers plodding up an almost vertical slope carrying on their backs one ton of supplies in 6 or 7 relays (checked at the summit of the trail by Mounties, to prevent anyone trying to reach the goldfields without at least a year's worth of supplies). I could barely imagine the frenetic scene back in those chaotic years, as I walked along Skagway's quiet main street (there was no cruise ship in town when we were there) – laid out in 1890s Wild-West style, with wooden arcaded sidewalks and brightly painted wooden facades. Now the shops were selling souvenirs and coffee instead of the essentials of Yukon mining life, and the Red Onion pub (once the site of a Gold Rush brothel) had become an over-priced bar for tourists.

The story of the Klondike Gold Rush continued through Whitehorse, capital and only city of the Yukon (a town of little interest except to provide us with supplies) ... passing Miles Canyon, site of former horrendous rapids (now tamed) which wrecked the makeshift boats of the 'stampeders' on 'white horses' of foaming water ... and 5-Finger Rapids, the terror of the sternwheeler ferries, which required extra steel cables to be attached to winches to haul them through, and expert navigation to avoid hitting the rocky shore.

We were still driving through mile after mile of forest, though it was becoming thinner and shorter – our guide told us that these trees were actually over 100 years old but were stunted by the latitude, lacking the hours of daylight needed to let them grow to maximum height within their lifetime. Instead of the frequent lakes studding the forest further south, now we were crossing swamps and marshland, dotted with white bog-cotton plants, while dwarf blue lupins joined the colourful fireweed beside the road. At last we reached (for me) the highlight of our Yukon journey, turning north on to the Dempster Highway: 300 miles of gravel track, reaching all the way to the Arctic Ocean. Our drivers stopped to let air out of the tyres to make them less susceptible to puncture, and dropped our speed to below 40mph – even less as we picked our way across North Fork Pass (4000 ft). All around us the landscape opened up and filled with clear Arctic light, backlighting the serrated summits before gradually the mountains receded, leaving us driving across a vast treeless undulating plain spattered with bogs and pools – our first sight of the tundra. We pushed on and on, into the grey half-light which passes for night at these latitudes in summer – our drivers determined to reach a particular camping spot despite their weariness. Finally, we arrived:

"Eagle Plains – sitting on the highest point of the ridge, catching every puff of wind to blow away the huge and persistent mosquitoes. What a site! I camp on the very edge of the ridge, hurrying to peg down my tent before it blows over. In front of me is a vast bowl of land, edged with ridge after ridge of barren hillsides – a vista which I could imagine stretching all the way to the Arctic Ocean. Probably much of this land has never been trodden by man! Clouds reach almost to the horizon, but not quite – as midnight approaches, the skyline is transformed into a glowing fiery rim which embraces the entire visible world."

The Dempster Highway snaked on through dense dwarf forest (only 2ft high), distant puffs of dust the only indicator that anyone else was travelling the road with us – all day we passed just two trucks and a few battered campervans. We stopped to celebrate as we crossed the Arctic Circle, swatting at the swarms of mosquitoes as if performing an Austrian Schuplattler dance (thank goodness for my mosquito hat!). Then on, across now treeless plains to the small community of Fort McPherson, inhabited by Dene Indians and Inuit, and burial place of the infamous Lost Patrol (four Mounties who became lost in the winter of 1910, dying within a few miles of safety). We traversed the complex channels of the Mackenzie Delta on a powerful ferry, needed to combat the strongly flowing river, before continuing north through more monotonous terrain of stunted forest and marsh. We were so used to bumping and jerking on the gravel track that it was a shock to suddenly glide on to a stretch of tarmac, heralding our approach to the town of Inuvik, only founded in 1975 as a base for oil exploration. It was provided with all the trappings of modern life – including the Igloo Church (built on top of a concrete saucer balanced on a gravel base, to prevent damage to the permafrost) … and a restaurant selling burgers made of muskox (very dry) or caribou (deliciously meaty).

The Dempster Highway finished here – but I had booked a flight in a tiny 9-seater plane to take me on to the village of Tuktoyaktuk, on the shores of the Arctic Ocean itself:

"My nose is glued to the window, my finger to the camera button – what a huge delta! The largest volume of water of any river in North America flows through here during spring melt, creating a vast expanse of channels and lakes – some lakes are totally cut off so their water is clear or covered with green weed, though the main channel is thick with mud. Below us, the patterns of lake and land, water and weed, tree and plain, are ever changing."

From the air, we could see ancient graves – laid on the permafrost in winter and weighted down with driftwood, so that when spring brought a thaw, the wood pressed the body ever deeper into the earth … and pingas, mounds of earth pushed up like pimples by ice which formed in winter from water seeping into the ground during the summer: the ice would crack the permafrost, allowing more water to seep in and more ice to form, increasing the height of the pinga each year. In Tuktoyaktuk, an enterprising local Inuit man gave us a 'town tour' – visiting the Anglican driftwood church and cruising up and down each of the few streets. The community had lived from hunting, fishing and trapping since the departure of the oilmen, so we saw a wolfskin drying on a porch, caribou horns bleaching on a garage roof, fish and Beluga whale meat (each family was permitted to take one per year) drying on racks by the beach. As our guide talked, it became obvious that, for him, the best time of year was winter: *'hunting is better then'*, he said, *'and communications are much easier when the river freezes over – we can drive the ice-road all the way back to Inuvik'*.

Our return from the Far North was blessed with glorious weather so all the views and vistas we had glimpsed before, were now clear and spectacular – and our drivers were relaxed and cheerful, glad to have navigated the Dempster Highway without incident. We were still very much in 'Gold Rush' country, since the Yukon was still producing gold and the roads around Dawson were lined with mounds of 'tailings' – the waste produced by miners. Most of the mining was now done by companies, rather than individuals, but these 'tailings' were still valuable since many had been sluiced by machine and therefore could still contain small traces of gold, just waiting to be extracted when a new method could be invented. Some entrepreneurs at Discovery Claim were offering pans of gravel (spiked with a few tiny flakes of gold) for tourists to try their hand at 'sluicing for gold' – I managed to slosh my panful around gently enough to leave just a very small amount of gold in the bottom – not much, but it was mine ... all mine ... to keep!

We spent a couple of nights in Dawson, recuperating from the rigours of the Far North (and washing huge loads in the local laundrette), but I found it a difficult town to understand – as if it could not quite decide whether to provide rough and ready services for miners, or whether to prettify itself for tourists (as Skagway had done). There were grand mansions ... tiny log cabins ... abandoned and collapsing homes ... newly painted hotels ... multi-storey blocks with neat gardens ... messy cabins surrounded by junk. We watched can-can dancers perform in Diamond Gertie's Casino, then drove up to Dome Mountain for a view over the goldmines of Bonanza Creek – though to my eyes they seemed to be just an ugly scar slashed through the green forest, as if a giant bear had clawed the land. Our driver/guide was trying hard to fill our evenings with entertainment, but for me it was Nature which provided the highlight of our first night in Dawson:

"I am roused by the distant song of wolves, rising and falling in concert, accompanied by occasional dog solos. The sound ceases, then recommences nearer to our campsite, ceases again, then at 3am swells to full volume – apparently in the woods right beside our camp. The voices rise and fall in rhythms as complex as any opera chorus ... then disappear as a band of late-night revellers lurches into camp."

A free day in Dawson left many of our group sleeping off their night-time excesses, but I discovered that the local Indian tribe was holding a 'potlatch' meeting on the site of their former village nearby, so made my way down to the river to find an Indian dinghy to take me there. I was not sure whether I would be intruding, but everyone (native and white Dawsonites) made me very welcome. The potlatch site looked like an English garden fete – a few stalls, a tent for children's face-painting, lots of people sitting on the grass and chatting ... though there was also a tent where an Elder was instructing a group of mixed white and native people about the Indian view of life. I had just decided that there was little here for tourists when a loudspeaker invited us into a big tent for 'storytelling':

"I'm surprised that it is a young and highly educated woman who tells the stories, but she is fantastic! Her face and body contort and expand as she conjures up the characters – the kids are agog and absorbed, and so are the adults. She tells of the origin of mosquitoes (the exploded body of 'cannibal woman'), then the tale of a blind man who kills his family when they are seized by greed (a tale with a clear moral message)."

The storyteller returned to Dawson on my boat and we got chatting – she was an anthropologist cataloguing the history of her people, and (despite her youth) had been authorised by the Elders as a traditional storyteller. We stopped to drink coffee together – a chance to learn more about her people, her job and her faith: a special moment for me.

Now it was 'North to Alaska' (in the words of the 1960s film tune) – dodging the potholes and roadworks on the Top of the World Highway to reach the border: the Canadian post looked deserted, but an American in a crisply starched white shirt gave us a grilling before stamping us into the country – making no concessions to the remoteness of the setting. We passed more messy gold mines and rusting machinery, and stopped in the tiny settlement of Chicken (supposedly the intention was to name it Ptarmigan, but no-one could spell it!) to eat blueberry pie amid swarms of mosquitoes, before joining a long traffic jam behind a line of silver 'airstream' caravans – like a string of cigar cases on wheels, or slugs slithering through the mud which now coated the road. Finally, we managed to pass them all and descended to the luxuriously sealed surface of the Alaska Highway, reaching the little town of Tok – the true gateway to Alaska, since every road entering the state passes through it.

We were heading for Fairbanks through monotonous landscape of forest with only occasional glimpses of snowy peaks, but at least it gave us a chance to catch up on the story of Alaska. In the mid-1700s the state was claimed by Russians who opened it up to fur traders (virtually wiping out the sea-otters and decimating the fur seals). When the fur began to run out, the Russians agreed to sell the state to America in 1867 – a decision they certainly lived to regret as gold then oil were discovered there. Finally, Alaska became the 49th state of the USA in 1959. The story of American

Alaska has been a tale of 'boom and bust' – first the Gold Rush at the end of the 19th century, then the Oil Rush of the 1960s. Thousands of settlers came to Alaska looking for work, only to be disappointed when the price of oil dropped and the industry shrank. In the mid-1970s the oilfields in the Arctic Ocean off Prudhoe Bay were developed, shipping their oil to market via an immense pipeline right across Alaska to ports on the Gulf of Alaska. We saw this pipeline several times as we drove around the state, slashing its way through the forest, oblivious to the land around it, raised on stilts so that the heated oil (to keep it flowing) did not melt the permafrost.

Alaska was not impressing me at all, especially after the pristine wilderness we had seen in the Yukon, and Fairbanks did not help. Just outside the town we stopped at a community named North Pole (so-called in the 1950s in an attempt to attract toy manufacturers):

"... now home to a huge, touristy shop selling Christmas items to busloads of tourists. This is not what I came to Alaska to find! Where is the wilderness and the frontier atmosphere? Why do I work for an industry which can ruin beauty just by being there? Horror of horrors! Fairbanks itself is just like any American city – all the usual fast food outlets, advertising hoardings and, oh dear, 'AlaskaLand' – a cross between a theme park with children's entertainments and an open-air museum, where souvenir shops fill the few rescued historic buildings of the original town."

I was thoroughly depressed as we left Fairbanks, heading south towards Denali National Park, but my mood swiftly improved as we started to spot wildlife by the roadside – including a mother moose and her calf, grazing right by the road. As we slammed on the brakes, they calmly strolled across the road behind our van, then continued grazing as we scrambled out and stood in a ring around them, cameras whirring and clicking. Only when we returned to our vehicle, did they move into the bush, lifting their legs high and delicately. Denali NP sits directly among the mountains of the Alaska Range, so now we were surrounded by impossibly sharp peaks (buzzed by sightseeing helicopters) and tumbling scree slopes falling away to the grey glacial torrent of the Nenana River, where rubber rafts were negotiating the white water far below us. This was the scenery I had expected, though it seemed so heavily exploited for tourism compared to the Yukon. Many of our group were going rafting on our first afternoon in Denali, but I decided instead to walk alone on one of the marked 'acclimatisation trails' just outside the Park:

"It's a well-prepared path but steep – every step is uphill, moving from tree-root to tree-root, then rock to rock, through low forests of beech and spruce, spangled with blue harebells and bright red berries. My 2 new 'bear-bells' jangle from the straps of my rucksack – I feel like a Swiss cow en route to the alm, but at least I will not dangerously surprise a bear (though the bells are driving away all the other wildlife too). The evocative wail of a train hooter draws my eye into the valley where an Alaska Express engine is drawing the silver and blue carriages of Princess Line Tours into Denali Station – a few hundred more tourists to fill the wilderness."

Next day we entered the National Park, its single road closed to all but the official Park buses. Our bus driver tried very hard to spot wildlife for us, stopping often for photos as we travelled towards the end of the road at the foot of Mount McKinley (highest peak in North America at 20,310ft – restored to its original native name of Denali in 2015). We frequently spotted caribou grazing on the grassy hillsides… a dark bundle trundling among the bushes turned out to be a porcupine, with yellowy tail quills and an inquisitive snuffly face … a fat Arctic squirrel scurried into the bushes while an equally fat marmot sat high on a knob of rock … distant white dots high above us were sometimes wild Dall sheep – and sometimes just rocks! What we were all hoping to see, however, were grizzly bears, and finally we were successful:

"We stop to look at a caribou on our left, but he is forgotten at the shout of 'bear to the right!' Close to the road are two very energetic bears, romping, running, batting each other with their paws – 2 almost full-grown cubs (2-3 years old). And now another larger bear appears, plodding towards them in a slow, stately manner – Mama! Yes, they are grizzlies, with a golden sheen to their coats and the distinctive hump on their backs. They love this high, open terrain – it is the smaller black bears which prefer to live in the forests."

As we neared the end of the road, our eyes turned to the spot where the (notoriously shy) Mount McKinley might be seen. It seemed that our only view would be mist and cloud, but as we descended from the bus at the Visitor Centre, a sunlit snowy slope burst from the cloud – the ranger confirmed that it was part of the mountain and as we watched over a period of half an hour, more and more appeared – an impossibly massive wall of snow soaring above the red and yellow scree on peaks which I had originally considered impressive: now they looked like no more than ruffles around McKinley's snow-white neck. We never saw the summit but were pleased that we had at least seen part of the mountain.

Rather than travel straight back to the Park entrance, two of us decided to disembark from the bus at Sable Pass, an area of open terrain full of bushes laden with berries – prime bear country, so our driver checked that we knew our 'bear code' before dropping us off. We waded across a fast-flowing stream to climb up the other side of the valley:

"The hillside is steep but very soft and springy, inches deep in heather and moss, planted with a bewildering array of wild flowers – it's like walking through an Alpine garden, hundreds of feet high. After the hard work comes the reward – we sit to eat our lunch, bathed in warm sunshine with the whole canyon laid out at our feet. We pick our way back down the hillside, most of it in a wild slide on the scree, using saplings, roots and hands to control our speed. A passing car warns us there are grizzlies ahead. We advance carefully and there are two big bears on the far side of the road, plunging their muzzles into berry bushes. As we watch, they surge uphill with lunges of their powerful hind legs before slithering down in an uncoordinated way – a point to remember: grizzlies find it easier to climb than descend a slope!"

With my mind full of the wonders of Denali NP, I was not looking forward to our next destination: Anchorage, capital and largest city of Alaska – in fact, I was prepared to hate it, as I had hated Fairbanks and Whitehorse. However, I was quite favourably impressed. Most of the city had been destroyed by a massive earthquake and tsunami in 1964 so nearly everything was new, but most had been designed with characterful or impressive architectural features – though the bright yellow Sunshine Mall was rather an eyeful! Everywhere in the town there were flowers – in hanging baskets or lurid flowerbeds of marigolds and ornamental cabbages. I particularly enjoyed the Earthquake Museum, where the seats in their film theatre were shaken to simulate the sensation of the earthquake, as I watched newsreels from that era. The seaplane harbour was impressive too, lines of aircraft parked at the water's edge and a continuous stream of floatplanes taking off and landing on the water beside the conventional land-based airport.

I was also not sure what awaited us as we continued our tour to the oil port of Valdez, but the journey took us through the most dramatic scenery we had seen in Alaska so far. We travelled parallel to the glacier-clad Chugach Mountains, descending into deep forested valleys then climbing again to vast open plains which felt like the top of the world, before turning into the heart of the mountains where glaciers spilled over the sides of the valley. We crossed Thompson Pass, which held the snowfall record for the whole of Alaska – 67 inches in one day in the winter of 1952/3:

"The top of the Pass is a jumble of knobbly rocks planted with moss and grass ... the road is lined with huge snow poles to help the snowploughs in their almost futile attempts to keep the road open through the winter. The seaward side of the Pass is less rocky, a garden of grass, bushes and brilliant fireweed. Ahead of us are still range after range of glacier-decked peaks, seemingly reaching all the way to the coast. Over these glaciers, the first Gold Rush miners struggled, with huge loss of life – only 300 got through, out of 5000 who attempted this route."

This scenery was the beauty of Valdez, a rough, tough frontier town, home to oilmen and fishermen – not tourists. The original town stood some miles away, but it collapsed into the sea during the 1964 earthquake, so was rebuilt on a more solid rock base. Its fortunes improved with the arrival of the oil pipeline and now the seashore was covered with oil storage tanks and jetties where the tankers could load. No-one in the town would talk to us about the infamous oil spill in 1989 from the tanker Exxon Valdez, though I could still see black lines around the coastline which I assumed were the last vestiges of the spilled oil.

"The town's glory is its location – the inlet is spectacular! From my tent site, I can see the ring of huge peaks scooped and hollowed out by glacial action, daubed with snow and ice. They rise direct from the water, dominating effortlessly the oil companies' efforts to conquer them with lines of storage tanks and installations. Without the oil paraphernalia, this inlet would be a world-beater – even with it, the view is superb!"

Boarding a small cruiser to explore the waters of the fjord, we were introduced to some enchanting sea-otters, which looked like pieces of driftwood at first – floating happily on their backs; feet up except for an occasional dip to power a movement; light golden heads raised to curiously watch us without any fear, whiffling their whiskers and peering with beady eyes in our direction. Around us, silvery salmon were leaping high into the air; bald eagles sat unmoving and imperious on the branches of dead trees by the waterside. Our cruise took us as far as the Columbia Glacier – up until 1982 it was a wall of ice running right across the bay, but then suddenly holes began to melt behind the moraines, the extra water speeding the glacier forward at 20 metres a day, to crumble into a massive jumble of icebergs which filled the entire bay.

Valdez was the last scenic highlight of Alaska for us – when we disembarked from our cruise, our drivers were waiting to hustle us away, determined to cover as much distance as possible back towards the Canadian border (it was almost midnight before we reached our campsite in the town of Tok). By the next night we were in the Indian settlement of Burwash Landing, shivering around a campfire in ever-chillier temperatures as night drew on. After seeking warmth for a while in the village bar, full of native people chatting animatedly, I snuggled deep into my well-insulated sleeping bag …

"… but I am still reading by torchlight when I am roused from my comfortable spot by a cry from outside – 'Get up! Northern Lights!' I shrug into a few clothes and rush out barefoot on to the damp grass. Overhead is a yellowish-cream streak across the sky, which swells as I watch, wafting and rippling across the heavens, then stretching into 5 fingers which seem to reach down to embrace our campsite. It fades away, and I quickly don more clothes, just in time to see another swelling of light on the horizon – again yellowish-cream but gradually turning to pale green with hints of red and purple around the edges. It ripples into pleats spread across the whole western horizon, then lifts one end to sway back and forth like an animal scenting the wind."

There was little to see in Burwash Landing itself, but it lay close to Kluane National Park, which embraces the Elias Mountains, so I chose to take a sightseeing flight over the trackless wilderness of the Park:

"All around us is the most incredible sight – a jumble of rocky peaks rises from vast snow-covered glaciers, feeding into each other like a huge river system. Great slabs of snow are plastered to the windward slopes, cracking

or sliding down to join the mass already compressing into ice below. In the distance, the pilot points out a massif soaring above the rest – this is Mount Logan, nearly 20,000ft high and highest in Canada. It floats ethereally on the horizon, bathed in sunshine. The clouds hanging around Lake Kluane have vanished and the whole scene sparkles in cloudless brilliance as we fly across the vast Malaspina Glacier, largest in the world. I am filled with images of splendour and can find few words to express it to the rest of the group, waiting back at camp. "

Finally, we headed back into the Alaskan Panhandle to the town of Haines, where we boarded a crowded ferry for the 4-night cruise along the Inside Passage back to Vancouver (last of the season, so filled with campervans fleeing the onset of winter). The ship passed through calm black water sparkling with salmon returning to their spawning grounds – and tiny fishing boats trapping them in purse-seine nets. We stopped in Sitka, accessible only by sea – a delightful town scattered still with wooden houses dating from Russian times … then (in the small hours of the morning) in Wrangell, where I was one of the few passengers to disembark to explore a pleasant town of clapboard houses with verandahs and gardens, and a painted Indian tribal house surrounded by totem poles. More totem poles of the native Klingit people were evident in Ketchikan, as well as houses and even streets built out on stilts jutting from sheer rock cliffs (like Creek Street, a flimsy boardwalk once laden with bordellos, now transformed into souvenir shops).

The Inside Passage cruise was enjoyable, but mostly it gave us a chance to relax and recuperate from our tour in Alaska and the Yukon, and to reflect on the scenic wonders we had seen – a precious taste of true wilderness!

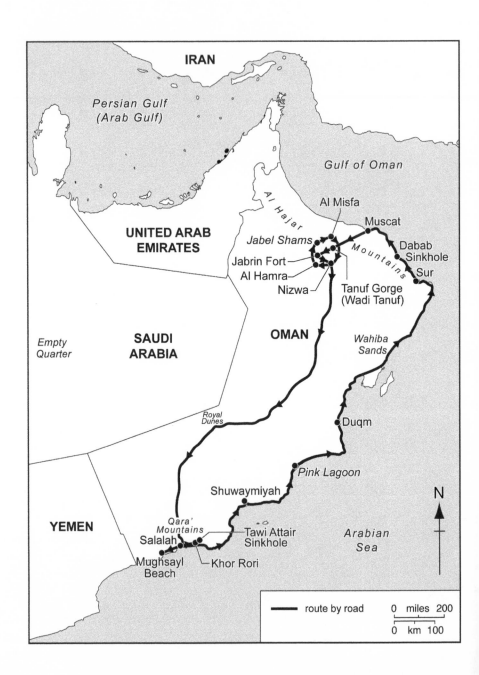

Oman (December 1998/ January 1999)

I HAD REALLY ENJOYED MY visit to Yemen a few years previously, so decided to book on a tour to neighbouring Oman, hoping to find an equally fascinating country. It certainly was an interesting visit, but I was amazed by the huge contrasts between two similarly located lands. Yemen was less than twice the size of Oman yet had a population in the 1990s of over 17 million, in contrast to Oman's 2 million (though that is increasing fast: by 2020 Oman's population has reached over 4 million). The standard of living in Oman was far higher – I saw little sign of the grinding poverty I had witnessed in the former South Yemen. Of course, Oman had vast wealth available from its sales of oil and gas, whereas Yemen was only just beginning to exploit possible reserves when I visited.

Yet equally important was Sultan Qaboos, ruler of Oman since 1970, who had done an amazing job of first defeating rebels and opposition (especially in Dhofar, where South Yemen had stirred up rebellion), then winning the support and loyalty of all parts of his diverse realm by launching major developments in education, health and infrastructure throughout the whole country. Before he took the throne, there were only 3 schools, 1 hospital and just 5km of sealed road in the entire land. Yet as we travelled around Oman, we saw innumerable examples of improvements to the people's lifestyle since he had taken control, bringing contentment and prosperity instead of Yemen's constant internal strife. He was even urging the nomadic Bedouin to settle, so that they could benefit from schools and health centres, and was encouraging a pride in Omani nationality (instead of tribal affiliations) symbolised by the national dress of sparkling white 'dishdasha' robe and pillbox 'kuma' hat (forbidden for foreigners to wear). It was not permitted to buy Omani citizenship (which carried an exemption from income tax), though work permits were easily obtainable, bringing large numbers of Indian and Pakistani workers to service everyday life and train Omanis in the skills needed by the modern world. Most remarkably, Sultan Qaboos had managed to achieve balanced relationships with his belligerent neighbours (Saudi Arabia, Iran and Iraq). An impressive leader, who ruled for 50 years until his death in January 2020. I hope the country can now continue on his well-planned path of peaceful development, in a region fraught with explosive tension.

Our visit started in the capital city Muscat, actually a cluster of 5 separate settlements squeezed between the ridges of the Hajar Mountains as they topple into the Indian Ocean in dramatic cliffs. One group of buildings comprised Old Muscat, hidden behind (reconstructed) walls and a gate which was closed to the outside world every night until 1970. Here we admired the exotic 'sugar palace' of the Sultan, an Arabian Nights vision of gold and blue columns with vast gates and a flower-decked avenue of fountains – though it was just one of many royal palaces and rarely used, since Sultan Qaboos did not like Muscat. Otherwise most of Muscat was modern: grand government buildings with car parks full of shiny new cars (we were told that anyone driving a dirty car was fined); bustling commercial districts with shops full of luxury goods; large elegant restaurants and cafes (all closed in daylight hours during our visit, since it was Ramadan). I was also fascinated by the city's roundabouts! Many of them featured imposing central sculptures: a replica of an ancient Omani trading ship, a traditional coffee jug and cups, a group of frolicking dolphins. The Grand Mosque which is now the highlight of Muscat sightseeing was no more than a mass of scaffolding when I visited, but I was impressed by the Zawawi Mosque (opened in 1985):

"... unusual because it has a women's area, though women usually pray at home. It also offers accommodation for the poor, with many villagers staying here when they come to visit the government offices nearby. It certainly is gorgeous with its gold mosaic dome, ornate minaret (adorned with a useful clock) and magnificent gold doors chased with fine patterns. The air is filled with the sound of splashing from tiled fountains, whilst water

runs silently through a formal maze of channels. As infidels, we are not permitted to pass through the doors, but the gardens of lush green lawns and exotic flowers are enchanting, surrounding a marble dining hall where rolled carpets await the arrival of guests."

We also called in at the Al Bustan hotel, at the time the top hotel in the Gulf (and reputedly best in the world), set amid arid rocks on a site where a village once stood – removed to a new location when the Sultan chose this spot for a landmark hotel:

"*A very gracious doorman receives us, chatting in both English and German. Inside, a vast atrium reaches up to a domed roof high above clusters of soft sofas, marble floors and a gently splashing marble fountain. In the lobby we find postcards and guidebooks for sale, and luxury toilets (yippee!), though the main attraction for us is a closed-off section of the restaurant, where non-Muslims are allowed to drink tea despite Ramadan restrictions.*"

Notwithstanding Oman's strict Islamic society, the country had attempted to make provision for non-Muslims visiting during the Ramadan fast: our hotels organised breakfast served in screened side-rooms so that we did not have to eat before daybreak; our guides took us to supermarkets where we could buy lunchtime picnics and then found out-of-the-way private corners where we could eat without causing offence. Outside major cities, our drivers sometimes took advantage of the Ramadan exemption which allows travellers to break their fast, though even then they usually only allowed themselves water (and cigarettes). We also tried to avoid sipping from our water bottles or nibbling snacks when there were local people around us – a basic courtesy to avoid upsetting our hosts. At 5.30pm the call of the muezzins released the population to eat and drink again, many already sitting on the terraces of restaurants waiting to order food, surrounded by the tempting smells of cooking – others sitting in parks or on beaches waiting to break open their food parcels and enjoy a picnic.

Leaving Muscat, we drove out into the Hajar Mountains, the road surrounded by jagged hills with their sides eroded into thousands of channels and their summits into dramatic stacks of rocks, passing occasional villages of small square crenellated houses where goats and chickens wandered the alleys. Turning into Tanuf Gorge, we followed an increasingly rough and stony track along the dry wadi until finally it was impossible to drive further and we had to continue on foot along a steep rocky trail:

"The path follows a narrow falaj (water-channel) among small terraces of palm and grain, to reach a tiny village of just 7 or 8 homes, perched precariously on a rock which dominates the valley. The young girls of the village gather to watch us scrambling up to meet them, bright as jewels in crimson and orange clothing edged with sparkling gold braid, and gold nose studs."

They were delighted to sit and chat with us in school English – one girl (Fatma) was curious to know if I was wearing trousers under my skirt ... and not shy to bend over to take a look!

Another mountain excursion took us along more stony, dusty tracks, winding up hairpin bends alongside vast slabs of grey-black stone, towards the summit of Jebel Shams, highest in the country at 2980m (though we were unable to reach the top, since it housed a radar post and military installation). However, we were able to reach a rock shelf from which we had a view over Oman's Grand Canyon – a deep and abrupt slash through the hillside, exposing layer after layer of cream or reddish stone liberally coated in yellow dust. Everywhere the sides of the valley were eroded into projecting ridges and shelves or cut back into semi-circular coves:

"Local villagers appear from nowhere: women in bright clothing and cheeky children, the women trying to sell firmly woven rugs while the children offer plaited wool bookmarks. But they are not pushy, and quickly settle down to chat among the rocks. Silence descends, broken only by the sound of the wind and the rustle of dry laurel leaves."

A violent history had left the mountains full of ancient fortresses, including Bahla Fort – swathed in scaffolding as it was being extensively restored on the orders of the Sultan (who was keen to preserve his country's Islamic history), and Jabrin Fort which was already fully restored. To my eyes, it looked over-restored, though that was only because the original stone had been coated with a new covering of cement. Once we entered the outer gate, we found ourselves in a courtyard dominated by a massive palace (built for the Imams who ruled the interior of the country until the 1960s, in opposition to the Sultan of Muscat), originally intended as a showy reception centre for visiting VIPs, and as a courthouse and prison:

"We are shown the prison where men had to stand in a pit looking through a slot in the wall to the chamber where the Imam was hearing their case, and the women's prison – a totally dark pit with niches in the wall where they could lie and sleep. In total contrast are the imposing, high-ceilinged, Persian-carpeted state rooms, with brightly painted wooden ceilings and shelves holding pots, dishes and racks of books. Everywhere there are spy-holes in the floors to watch for unauthorised movements, and beneath the floor of the meeting hall, a network of passageways where a group of bodyguards could hide."

Clearly, the Imam's hold over his lands was insecure!

Nearby was the city of Nizwa, once capital of the Imam's part of Oman, and now a bustling city which had benefited greatly from Sultan Qaboos' plans to improve its infrastructure. A few years before my visit, this had included a brand-new souk, enclosed within walls, with special buildings for fish, vegetables and local crafts. Most interesting of all, to me, was the livestock market:

"We arrive just before 8.30am and crowds of men have already gathered. Flocks of goats and sheep, and some cattle, are tethered around the arena. At precisely 8.30am the first vendor releases his goat and begins to parade it around the circuit, passing all the potential buyers. He is quickly followed by more sellers of goats and sheep, some dragging reluctant billy-goats, others cuddling tiny lambs. A hubbub of sound rises as each seller calls out the price he is asking, and goats and sheep bleat pitifully as they are dragged across to potential buyers who pinch their backs to check fatness and grope underneath to inspect udders."

Later in the day we visited Nizwa's Fort, another complex of well-restored buildings surrounding a massive circular tower – we climbed its steps to a precariously narrow walkway inside the parapets, for a view over the town. The rest of the building included luxurious sitting rooms above dark, echoing prisons and (most impressively for a 17th century building) two bathrooms, each with its own well to provide water for the bath, and an indoor toilet with a hole leading to a cess pit far below.

Another full-day excursion took us back into the mountains to visit two impressive villages: first Al-Hamra, which contained some of the oldest houses in Oman (up to 400 years old) – it had been a centre for religious women (we would call them nuns) who chose not to marry but instead to devote themselves to Islam. It was now partly abandoned:

"We are left free to explore the earthen or stone-slab alleyways squeezed between tall mud walls, punctured by gothic-style pointed windows. Some houses are in ruins, but most are clearly still in use – voices issue from dark rooms, flip-flop sandals lie at the base of flights of steps leading up from entry lobbies just visible through partially open doorways."

Most interesting of all, at the bottom of the village I discovered the main falaj (water channel), spanned in several places by bathhouses. One was occupied by bathing women, but I was able to peer into another – 3 separate cubicles, each with steps leading down to the falaj: an effective solution to the difficulty of maintaining hygiene in these remote regions. Even more impressive was the village of Al-Misfa, dramatically built of local reddish stone planted directly on top of a smooth rock beside a deep gorge, filled with date and banana plantations. Here we clambered down the steep steps which served as village streets, to find a delightful plunge pool created for the children out of the falaj system:

"Beyond this pool, a sign beside the falaj says 'Dear Visitors. No men beyond this point please' – of course, we females surge ahead, walking along the edge of the falaj channel towards a group of women who are busy washing and scrubbing their cooking pots. Two of the girls tell us they go to school and can speak a little English, though the older women are too shy to do more than smile. One follows me back up into the village, a huge tray of clean dishes balanced on her head, smiling her pleasure to be in my company."

Our drivers, understandably, hurried us away from these villages, keen to be back at the hotel in Nizwa in time to eat as soon as the Ramadan curfew was lifted. We also headed out to eat in a typical Omani-style restaurant – a challenge since our entire group of 19 was planning to eat together for the first time. Just finding transport was difficult – several taxi cars passed without stopping, but a minibus taxi pulled up across the street to unload his passengers (did they intend to get out there? Or were they ejected in favour of more lucrative clients?) and squeezed us in (4 sitting on bench seats intended for 3, with our escort leaning against the door). The same problem hit us at the restaurant – a series of separate family-sized rooms too small for all of us, though again we squeezed into one, sitting on the carpeted floor with our backs supported by cushions. However, the meal was a success – coffee and dates to start, then rice with shark, sheep or chicken meat, and sweet tea to finish. Only one of our group was disappointed: he ordered 'meat with grain cooked hot point pressure', which turned out to be a glutinous slab of something similar to suet pudding!

Now we turned southwards. The mountains of Oman run in a relatively narrow strip across the northern edge of the country, following the coastline of the Gulf of Oman, leaving the majority of the landscape as a vast, arid plain, featureless and stony, blending eventually into Arabia's infamous Empty Quarter:

"Gradually the last outriders of the Hajar Mountains disappear, and black gravel stretches out to the horizon on both sides. The road runs before us, straight as a die (though rather broken on the surface), a temptation to exceed the 120km speed limit – though our vehicle constantly warns the driver (Kabir) with an annoying beep when he exceeds the limit. A couple of spectacularly mangled car wrecks by the roadside remind us of the dangers – principally collision with camels, says Kabir."

Our drivers had to be careful of the camels especially – they told us that if one was hit by a vehicle, it was always the fault of the driver (even though camels seemed to wander freely back and forth across the road) and he would have to pay compensation of 500 rials (£1000). Otherwise, there was little to see on our long drive: in places red and white markers indicated the location of potential flash floods in case of rain; in other places we spotted the conical white mounds of a 'salt dome', where salt had worked its way up out of the ground; sometimes the whole surface of the land gleamed with a white crust of gypsum. A flame flaring into the sky indicated a gas field; a huge complex of towers and tanks heralded a major oil processing plant.

As the road drew closer to the Saudi border, we encountered sand-dunes, including the so-called 'royal dunes' where the Sultan camped (with his huge retinue of 500) during his annual 'meet the people' tours during winter months. Released from the confines of the cars for a short break, we raced towards the dunes:

"We set off to climb, each choosing a virgin face of rich reddish dune, breaking through the firm crust to soft warm sand which crumbles and

envelops our feet. I slip a foot backwards with each step, yet gain enough grip to push upwards again. Above me, the crust slips and trickles down, like the start of an avalanche, but the dry sand is not adhesive enough for the whole face of the dune to slide. Viewed from the summit, it is clear that this is just a small area of sand amid the vast gravel-covered plain – a mere outrider of the dunes of Rub' al Khali (the Empty Quarter)."

We were travelling in a convoy of five Landcruisers, four driven by Omani drivers (now abandoning their dishdashas in favour of jeans and t-shirts) and one by an Indian from Kerala (Kabir). How our Omanis rejoiced when they were able to show their expertise in desert driving, rescuing Kabir as his rear wheels bogged down in the sand, rocking the car from side to side as Walib handled the gears.

At intervals beside the road were small domed shelters, providing a patch of shade in which travellers could rest. Our lunch stop was in one of these shelters, a little larger than most, offering a footbath and toilet – and here we ate our Christmas lunch (yes, it was Christmas Day!) of dates, tangerines and biscuits. Then more monotonous miles of almost empty roads through arid landscape, only occasionally broken by thin lines of greenery where a wadi (valley) still retained a little hidden water:

"Finally, we bounce off the tarmac on to a gravel road, then on to the sands themselves, finishing up beneath a convenient thorn tree surrounded by low dunes. This will be our campsite for tonight – the kitchen perched on an array of rusted oil drums, the 'toilets' simply a walk behind the dunes with a shovel. A quick lesson in tent erection and we are organised, our tents scattered over a wide area and a blue tarpaulin spread on the sand as a lounge. Here we squat as the sun goes down, to distribute 'fun' Christmas gifts we have bought for each other – the strangest of all must surely be the toilet brush one fellow traveller receives!"

After a good night's sleep (sand makes a comfortable mattress, once the thorn twigs have been removed), next day brought more monotonous road, enlivened by another vehicle difficulty when Kabir (yes, our poor Indian driver again!) suffered a puncture – though it took no time for all five drivers to leap into action with a well-practised routine to change the wheel. Finally the featureless white plain was enlivened by clusters of rocks scattered like the tailings of a hundred mines, the road now forced to twist among them –

we had reached the low, rocky Jabal Qara Mountains which surround the southern city of Salalah, close to the Yemeni border. What a shock to the eye when the arid land around the road was transformed by thin yellow grass (nourished by the seasonal monsoon) where cattle were grazing alongside the more common camels. As we descended towards the coast again, we made a brief stop at a small mosque reputedly housing the Tomb of Job (though many other countries in the Middle East also claim association with the story of Job):

"We are allowed into the tomb to see the extra-long (as a sign of respect) grave of Nabi (Job), covered in green cloth and bathed in the scent of frankincense from burners at his feet. Outside is a trapdoor which one of our drivers (Adil) lifts, to show us the imprint of a large foot (with 5 toe-marks) in the rock on which the tomb is built – supposedly left by God himself when he brought water for Job to wash before prayer. We are suitably impressed, so Adil goes on to show us Job's prayer-hall next to the tomb – a square of mouldy concrete walls with a 'mihrab' prayer niche (clearly Adil is unaware that Mecca had no importance at the time when Job supposedly lived)."

Finally, we reached the coast, passing the urban sprawl of Salalah: a jumble of modern houses (some huge and luxurious – many Omanis had second homes in Salalah) and brand-new hotels, built to accommodate a burgeoning tourist industry. When we returned to the city in the evening, we found it buzzing with activity – a treasure trove of shops filled with bright clothing and incense, but in the heat of the day it was quiet. We drove on almost to the Yemeni border, stopping for picnic lunch on the beautiful white sands of Mughsayl Beach (sadly scarred by a line of rubbish at the high-water mark). On the hills behind the beaches grew short, scrubby frankincense trees, seeping beads of white sap when cut, which hardened over time into the brittle gum once worth its weight in gold (and still in demand today):

"The tree is unusual since its leaves grow straight out of the branches without any twigs. The leaves are bright green but curled tightly like young bracken. The bark on the trunk is peeling off in translucent flakes, while the upper branches are smooth and shiny."

Closer to the sea were groves of banana or coconut palms and papaya trees – all along the beaches were stalls selling their fruits. A group of uniformed riders galloped along the sands on magnificent horses from the royal stud in Salalah. Wading birds fed peacefully in pools just inland from the coast or dodged the waves on the beaches – an idyllic glimpse of the Indian Ocean coastline.

A full day's tour took us northwards from Salalah, turning on to a gravel track into the village of Khawr Rawri – all that remains of the ancient city of Sumhuram which was once one of the richest towns in the world, at the heart of the frankincense trade. The entrance to the harbour where ships loaded their precious cargo, was still clear to see – a broad gash in the seaside cliffs leading to a basin filled with sparkling water (though access to the sea was now blocked by a sandbank). The excavations of the historic city were less impressive, just a few walls of neatly cut cream sandstone marking a jumble of surprisingly small rooms. There was no sign of any recent archaeological digging – apparently the Sultan was wary of exposing pre-Islamic relics. As the heat of the day increased, we headed for the nearby beach where a crescent of clean white sand stretched around the mouth of the river which once gave access to Sumhuram's port:

"A confusion of water swirls at the point where the strongly flowing river forces its warm weedy water into the sea surf. Inland, a small grey heron hovers over the river from beneath a shady overhang of rock; a large white spoonbill sifts busily through the water; a group of flamingoes feed peacefully in a quiet corner of the lagoon. On the beach, large ghost crabs scuttle frantically across the sand; hermit crabs nestle into their temporary seashell homes – I pick one up by accident as I collect souvenirs: an amazingly large crab for such a small shell, who plunges into the wet sand as soon as I put him down again, dragging his home behind him."

Our group splashed merrily in the water while our drivers (except lonely Kabir) retired to the shade of a cave above the beach. An Omani man in a gleaming dishdasha patrolled the beach, chatting to us – 'just passing the time', Kabir told us (though with a look that implied 'and watching the women').

We continued alongside the shore, past tiny fishing ports where innumerable small boats were pulled up on the beach while others hustled back and forth across the waves using powerful outboard motors. Part-way through the afternoon, our British escort Mark informed us that he wanted to seek out a 'special place' which he had failed to find on previous tours. On his instructions, our drivers turned back into the mountains behind the coast – where were we going? We stopped beside some cattle pens, in the middle of nowhere, and picked our way on foot across a boulder field of eroded limestone rocks. Suddenly the ground dropped away – a huge hole opened up at our feet, its sides still hung with stalactites: the Tawi Attair Sinkhole, over 100m wide and 200m deep, the remains of a collapsed underground cavern:

"I pick my way down to a ledge of rock, but the view over the edge is worryingly precipitous. I still can't see the bottom, but I can see the remains of an old iron bridge which is perched precariously on a ledge above the abyss, with a tiny track running down the cliff beside it. A rickety wooden trolley hangs from a single wire running over the chasm – access for (very daring) cavers perhaps? I feel vertiginous just sitting here on a solid rock, but Mark has noted the line of the path for his next group – I think I am glad that he is not leading US into the depths of the sinkhole!"

It was time to return to Muscat, but this time following the Indian Ocean coastline instead of using the highway through the desert. No hotels on this route, so we were to camp along the way – which meant a last visit to Salalah's bustling souk for supplies:

"The people are very different from those in Nizwa – heavy, very black African faces are mixed with fine-featured Arabs. Old men squat under a tree at the edge of the souk, their heads swathed in tasselled turbans – some have unwound the turban to sit bareheaded, using the cloth to wrap around back and bent knees (to support them as they sit?). African-looking women squat over their piles of fruit and vegetables, dressed in brilliantly coloured clothing and mostly unveiled – proudly displaying the gold rings which dangle from pierced nose-tips."

Fully stocked up, we headed off on the 'dancing road' (as our driver Talib named it) – no smooth tarmac now, but a gravel surface which set our vehicles (and our teeth) rattling. The drivers were on top form – they had used the travellers' Ramadan exemption and taken breakfast with us that morning and were now excited to be travelling off-road. At first the route was fairly well-travelled, regularly enveloping us in clouds of dust from passing vehicles as we drove close by large oilfields with tall derricks and smaller ones accessing the oil by 'nodding donkey' pumps. There also seemed to be frequent military camps – apparently the Sultan's strategy was to make enduring international friendships by being so strong that no-one wanted Oman as an enemy. We encountered few permanent settlements, but often saw Bedouin camps – a few tents, a few corrugated iron sheds and clusters of camels.

We made a brief stop in a desolate ramshackle village called Shaleem, where I was amused to notice two camels snacking on the same piece of cardboard from a rubbish bin, nibbling towards each other from either end:

"Then up drives a madly cheerful man in the most ancient and battered pick-up I have ever seen, gesticulating that he wants us to photograph him with his four little girls. They arrange themselves shyly while he wraps his turban correctly to create the best image. He has come back specially for this, having noticed our arrival as he passed us in the opposite direction on the edge of the village!"

Finally, we reached a basin beneath impressive 300m cliffs of sparkling white limestone, surrounded by eroded ridges of stone resembling waves of the sea which once lapped at the foot of the cliffs. The road had now disappeared entirely, and we were driving across sand still wet from a previous rain shower, revving the engines to keep up speed and avoid getting stuck. Mark ordered a sudden turn, and we arrived in a hidden valley beneath a horseshoe of crumbling sandstone strata – our campsite, secure from prying eyes and sheltered from the sea breezes. Once the tents were erected, I was free to wander off along the beach, crunching on a solid layer of ancient seashells bleached by the sun over the centuries. Nearby lay the village of Shuwaymiyah, no more than a cluster of simple concrete huts but we were made very welcome:

"As soon as we arrive, local ladies come running from their homes, dragging reluctant children with them and hastily adjusting the masks or cloths over their faces. They carry armfuls of basketware and immediately the scene descends into delighted chaos, some members of the group plunging into the shopping while others jostle into position for photographs. Kabir leaps into action, relaying bids and attempting to bargain on our behalf – eventually holding up each item and calling its price as loudly as the women themselves!"

I still have a beautifully made basket bought from these ladies, and a finely polished shell she gave me as an extra gift.

The 'road' degenerated more and more as we continued northwards, little more than a rough track, deeply cut by runnels caused by recent rains. Still we encountered tiny hamlets of concrete huts and animal pens – presumably signs of the Sultan's settlement of Bedouin people, still living in their family encampments but now in permanent homes instead of tents? At one point we even passed a camel trotting along, attached by a lead to a vehicle – a racing camel in training (Talib told us that the Bedouin raced their camels at least once a month). There was little other traffic now – in fact we had to make an unscheduled stop when we met a pick-up truck halted by a flat tyre (he had no spare), who had been stuck by the side of the track since the previous night. With the generous camaraderie necessary to survive in these remote places, our drivers donated one of their spare tyres and helped to change the wheel (arranging for the other driver to replace the tyre in the near future).

Picnic lunch was taken beside the waters of Khawr Gawri Lagoon, watching browsing flamingoes, then we stopped at the Pink Lagoon – its waters an unhealthy metallic red colour (caused by algae in the extra-salty water). I waded in to see if the water would stain my feet (which it didn't), but Mark still insisted that I clean my feet in sand in case the algae were dangerous. Continuing close to the sea, we passed ever more frequent Bedouin communities (living from fishing as well as animal-herding), with permanent plywood huts (available for use by any nomadic family as they passed) or modern colourful tents, including brightly striped tents topped with a crescent moon – travelling mosques, standing out in the distance like circus tents:

"Tonight's camp is just a sand dune away from another long, empty, white beach – there's time for a relaxed paddle in the surf before dinner, seeking attractive shells. Tonight, we build a fire of driftwood in the heart of our campsite. The waves crash on to the shore, flashing with bursts of phosphorescence, rippling like lightning across the surface of the ocean."

Next day we continued along the gravel plains just inland from the sea, spotting occasional small groups of elegant (and rare) wild gazelles. At one point we turned into the fishing village of Ras Duqm, to replenish our supplies:

"The beach is bustling with activity as fishing boats are pulled from the sea, hitched to a tow-truck and hauled unceremoniously on to the sand.

Offshore, where two currents meet in a swirl of surf, small dark-skinned boys in sarongs are patrolling with hooks on long poles, suddenly darting into the water to catch brilliantly coloured cuttle fish. They dangle proudly from the hook as the boys bring them ashore, dropping them on the wet sand to the accompaniment of an irate gush of ink from the doomed fish."

Otherwise, all our stops were simply among the dunes and low sandstone cliffs – wherever we could find a few shady trees where our drivers could rest, and a beach where we could paddle or even swim. Another beach-side campsite brought a moment of drama, when Mark was stung by something which popped out of the sand – very painful and frightening (in such a remote location) but fortunately with no serious consequences. After four blissful nights wild-camping among the dunes, we began to find larger communities again, like the small town of Hayy – clearly geared up to provide essential services to vehicles emerging from the 'wilderness': garages offering fuel, 'Oil Chang' and 'Puncher' (a tyre being repaired beside the fuel station gave me an insight into the meaning of that last service!).

We were approaching Wahiba Sands, close enough to Muscat and Nizwa to offer an accessible 'desert experience' to the populations of those cities. Our drivers stopped to let air out of their tyres to give better traction, then launched on to the sands:

"Our drivers whoop with glee – it's time for some 'dune-bashing' along a broad swathe of sand ploughed up by innumerable vehicles between rocky outcrops. Engines revving, 4-wheel-drive engaged, we swoop down each dune and hurl ourselves at the next slope, each driver choosing his own route with no attempt to hold formation."

After an hour of adrenalin-pumping action, we continued our journey on a gravel track via the dusty concrete town of Khuwaymah (full of auto-repair shops, where we re-inflated the tyres). None of our drivers had any difficulties driving through the Wahiba Sands, but as we turned off the gravel tracks in search of another beach-side camp, it was the turn of our Omani drivers to get into difficulties. First it was Walid who needed towing out of a sand-hole, then Adil sank up to his wheels – Kabir roared forward to help, only to get stuck himself:

"It's all out to help. First Kabir's car – with us rocking and pushing, Nasser handling the gears, and he's safely back on to the gravel. Now

Walid – a bit of digging, then more mighty heaving ... and he's out. Finally, Adil – we're all gasping for air and pouring with sweat by now. Thank goodness this did not happen at midday! A bit more digging and a lot of pushing, and he's free too. Mark decides to give up on this campsite and move on to a firmer beach instead."

One more idyllic night: paddling, shell-hunting, watching the sun set in a blaze of swirling red clouds, to be replaced by a full moon illuminating our camp with cool clear light. Next morning, even a pod of dolphins frolicking out to sea, chasing fish which leaped out of the water in their efforts to escape. These wild-camps beside the sea have provided some of my most treasured memories of Oman. However, we had to return to 'civilisation' – the gravel track was transformed into a smooth sealed road as we travelled back through the mountains to the northern coast and the historic port of Sur. Its harbour was dotted with traditional fishing dhows (called sambuks), and fascinating waterside shipyards where sambuks were being scraped and calked or even newly constructed ... as quickly as possible, since tradition said that a woman who steps over the keel will give birth, but at the cost of a sailor's life. So the men were trying to build up from the keel before the women could get there! We took a small ferry across to the old village of Ayja, wandering along dirt alleyways between haphazardly placed houses:

"All is quiet, though the voices of women and children ring from inside homes, hidden behind huge wooden doors carved in elaborate patterns and studded with brass knobs (Zanzibar-style – Oman once ruled the island of Zanzibar). Occasionally a door opens and a gaudily dressed woman with headcovering, but no mask, emerges – one with a tray of greenery for the small flock of goats browsing nearby. A few black-faced children call out, but most ignore us – unlike the Bedouin settlements, there is no excitement to meet strangers here."

The return to Muscat led us along the northern coast on a heavily used gravel road, soon due to be transformed by tarmac. This coast was totally different from the white sandy beaches we had been seeing further south. The mountain ridges ran directly to the seashore, falling on to the beach in massive yellow cliffs, slashed in places by deep ravines which ran straight across the coastal plain into the sea, like fjords. The ravines were cool and dark, green with trees and often full of flood water (signs warned that the roads were 'liable to washout'), crossed by concrete causeways to prevent vehicles from bogging down. Everywhere the parking areas were packed with Landcruisers, bringing Muscat's citizens on daytrips out of the city. One especially popular sight was the sinkhole of Dibab, nowhere near as deep as the one at Salalah, and totally 'tamed' for the tourists with a protective fence around the top and concrete steps to the bottom. If we had not spent the past week exploring the remote attractions of southern Oman, I would have been entranced by this scenery – but now it was just a mildly interesting way of ending the tour.

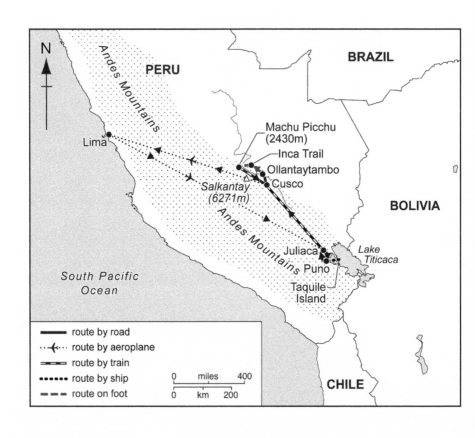

Peru (December 1999/ January 2000)

WITH THE NEW MILLENNIUM APPROACHING, I started to plan a way to celebrate its arrival in my own way. The media was full of hype about all the events which would celebrate the event – my only thought was to get as far as possible from all the fuss! The first plan was to enter the new century whilst sitting around a campfire in the middle of the Namibian desert, but then the flights which would have taken me to Africa were cancelled amid fears that the New Millennium would cause planes to fall out of the sky (I never did quite understand why). Instead my tour operator offered a range of other trips, including one to Peru. I had considered this trip before but was not sure whether I would physically manage to trek into Machu Picchu – and I did not want to arrive at this unique location by any other means than on foot. Now here was the opportunity, unexpectedly presented to me – I took a deep breath ... and made the booking.

Sixteen hours of flying, squashed into narrow Economy Class seats, brought me to Lima – the west coast of South America is just so far away! What a surprise to find a city perched on top of crumbling earth cliffs, high above Pacific waves kept so chilly by the Humboldt Current (coming straight from Antarctica) that the city is often bathed in sea-fog yet rarely receives any rain. Lima itself was a strange mixture of historic palaces, modern luxury villas, run-down facades adorned with crumbling balconies and colourful slums creeping up the hillsides. Our city guide told us that the city centre was largely abandoned by wealthy people in the 1970's, but was now beginning to be restored by an energetic new mayor, determined to bring back the grandeur of the 18th and 19th centuries. Everywhere there were people – crowds of shoppers at the Christmas market in Plaza Mayor; knots of friends standing chatting on street corners; children playing with spinning tops on strips of greenery in the middle of roads; young people weaving among the cars in traffic jams, offering all kinds of goods for sale. Highlight of our city tour was to be a visit to the Gold Museum, once the private collection of a rich Peruvian, determined to preserve as much pre-Inca treasure as possible before it was all sold abroad and lost to the nation. I found it a disappointing jumble of riches (including 23,000 gold items and 45,000 weapons) displayed higgledy-piggledy without any attempt at interpretation – and just one year after my visit, the Peruvian Consumer Defence Institute declared much of the collection to be fake, anyway!

History throughout Peru is categorised into three time periods: Pre-Inca – when the country (in fact most of the northern Andes) was occupied by a wide range of different tribes, with different skills and cultures … Inca – from the 15th century, one of these tribes dominated and organised all the others, establishing communications by fast-moving runners, and developing productive agriculture (with terracing, irrigation and storehouses) which kept an ever-growing empire fed … Spanish Occupation – in the 16th century, a few well-armed Spanish soldiers arrived, swiftly defeating the Inca (whose empire was built on peaceful development and therefore had few defences). They were followed by wave after wave of European settlers who established an 'upper class' which relegated the remnants of the native tribes to life as peasants or manual workers.

From Lima we flew southwards, high into the Andes to Juliaca where the tiny airport gave us a lively welcome with a Peruvian pan-pipe band (unexpectedly, the only one I saw in the country) and enthusiastic ladies trying to sell us alpaca cardigans or gloves, while outside the streets of the town were bustling. There were crowded stalls selling Christmas baubles; bicycle rickshaws cruising the streets; ladies wearing distinctive tall-crowned bowler hats … and our first llama, lying in the road like a fluffy pillow. It made an exciting introduction to our days on the Altiplano – the second largest area of high-plateau in the world, with an average height of 3600m. Our destination was even higher: Puno (at 3780m), right on the shores of Lake Titicaca:

"We crawl into town through stall after stall of markets thronged with local shoppers, many of the women wearing very full skirts and bowler hats, their loads tied on their backs in shawls. The coach drops us a few yards from our hotel, yet even walking that short distance makes us dizzy, with pounding hearts. Once in the lobby, we sit quietly, drinking the slightly glutinous green coca tea we are offered to help us cope with the altitude."

Still groggy and nauseous from altitude, our next day was designed to be relaxing – a cruise on Lake Titicaca:

"At first, we traverse a narrow channel between knobbly rocky hills, through layers of greenery floating on the surface, alive with wading birds, moorhens and herons. A few fishing boats pass us, rowed standing up (in Venetian style). Then we are out into the main lake, now sparkling in the sunshine ... and there are our first floating reed islands topped with clusters of reed huts (some newly built and gleaming gold in colour), with reed boats rearing their animal head prows above the rushes."

We were keen to stop to explore immediately, but our guide was determined to keep going to the far southern end of the lake so that we were first group of the day to reach Taquile Island. He was considerate enough of our physical state, too, to land us at the back of the island so that we could climb a moderately sloping track to the village on the island's summit, instead of attacking the 540 steps from the usual jetty:

"All is quiet ... there are few people about yet and the only sounds are the buzzing of insects and the song of birds. The air is richly scented by herbs along the stone-flagged path as we approach the village, where we start to see people working the fields with mattocks. They are wearing brilliantly coloured costumes – the men with 'sleeping cap' bonnets, white shirts and black trousers; the women in full green skirts and huge head-covering shawls weighted with bright pompoms. In the village square, clusters of ladies from the neighbouring peninsula have gathered to sell fish and vegetables to the islanders, wearing their own distinctive costume with spectacular flat hats adorned with pompoms. It is good to see that their costumes are everyday dress, not just for the tourists."

We arrived in the village early enough to watch as local people brought their handicrafts to the co-operative store, all carefully inspected by the village elders and noted into a ledger before being set out on the shelves for sale to the tourists – an impressive system which ensured a fair price for everyone. We explored the island in peace, descending the stone staircase just as a boat disgorged a stream of local people struggling uphill with huge loads of goods ... and a few tourists laden with weighty rucksacks who were eyeing the steps in dismay.

As they arrived, we left – returning now to visit the floating Uros Islands, originally established by local Indians fleeing the arrival of Spanish colonisers in the 17th century, cutting sheaves of the abundant lakeside reeds and laying them on top of each other to make a firm base on which to build village homes, also of reed. The first island we visited was exceptionally firm – it was already 20 years old, repeatedly refreshed with new layers of reed bundles until the island had become so deep that it had grounded on the lake bottom. However, the second island was only a few months old – the inhabitants had fallen out with the residents of their former village (not surprising when you consider that up to 5 families were living permanently in one claustrophobic space, not often travelling even to the lakeshore) and had decided to establish a new community. This island rippled gently with the swell, especially when a motorboat passed in the vicinity – as if on board ship, I needed sea-legs to walk across the island to visit one of the homes: furnished only with a bed of reeds and an oven in a separate reed hut, for safety's sake.

One more memorable experience awaited us back in Puno – as it was Christmas Eve, we were taken out to a local restaurant to sample the local delicacy ... deep-fried guinea pig!

"It comes complete with head and big protruding teeth, splayed on its back amid a plate of salad and roast potatoes. It is a fine white meat, without any strong flavour (yes ... it tastes like chicken, as all these 'strange' dishes seem to do), but requires a lot of effort to strip the small amount of flesh from the bones – perhaps not really worth the time?"

Later I visited homes in the countryside where guinea pigs were kept in a small enclosure on the beaten-earth floor of the house – treated as pets for most of the time, but always providing a source of food when times were hard. High in the mountains, in the depths of an Andean winter, there is no room for sentimentality!

Christmas Day, and we were moving again, out across the broad expanses of yellowing grass which make up the Altiplano – passing small clusters of cattle or sheep, tethered by one leg and watched over by a scruffy child, and isolated mud-brick huts or animal enclosures ... all bathed in a clear, desolate light beneath dark, rain-heavy clouds. We made a stop to visit the pre-Inca graveyard of Sillustani, a cluster of impressive funerary towers – some built in roughly jumbled stone, others with expertly cut blocks more reminiscent of the Incas' style. Then back to Juliaca to join a train taking us across the Altiplano to Cusco. It was amazing to us that such a train would be running on Christmas Day, yet we were 'spoiled rotten' by the smiling train crew (wearing Santa hats) who constantly brought us trays of hot drinks, chocolates and other delicacies (as well as a 'special' Christmas lunch of omelette ... you can't have everything!). The train rattled and rolled constantly, with sections almost like riding a bucking bronco – we could barely get our drinks to our mouths, yet the crew carried them from carriage to carriage without a spill.

We squeezed out of Juliaca, almost scraping against trackside stalls selling everything from haircuts to coca leaves, then climbed steadily through rolling barren grassland and tiny desolate villages – in some of the villages we made a stop, though each was so brief that anyone boarding had to leap aboard instantly or fall by the wayside. Eventually we reached the highest point of our journey at La Raya (4300m), no more than a few tumbledown huts sheltering shepherds and sheep, and a platform encrusted with icy snow:

"We are crossing a marshy valley edged by rolling grassy hills which are topped with snow-spattered rocks and the occasional glacier. Sheepdogs bound alongside the train as we crawl uphill, enveloped in black smoke from the struggling engine. Large herds of alpaca, mixed with sheep and horses, are minded by women whose already colourful dress is enhanced by lurid plastic sheets worn as ponchos against the increasingly heavy rain – a few herdswomen take shelter in tiny thatched huts, their entrances so low that they must enter on hands and knees."

As we descended the far side of the Pass, the landscape quickly softened into fields green with crops and villages of more substantial houses and gardens. In one village my eyes were drawn to a cluster of cars parked by the roadside, and a field ringed by colourfully dressed spectators ... was it a football game? Looking more closely, I could see that groups of brilliantly costumed youngsters were dotted around the field and one group was dancing a very energetic circular dance involving much kicking and stamping – a folkloric festival to celebrate Christmas? Further downhill, the communities grew larger – now dogs were running from every village we passed, usually followed by little boys; at every stop, merchants were gathering outside the train windows to thrust alpaca hats and bootees towards us. Finally, we drew into Cusco, dismayed at first to see its river filled with litter and detritus, washed down from the Altiplano by heavy rain – though an evening stroll in the city transformed my initial impressions:

"This is a grand monumental city with beautifully illuminated churches – the main square is lit by romantic lanterns and decorated with a Christmas tree which flashes its lights energetically. Smiling restaurant boys are attempting to entice us into their establishments, and I accept an offer to sit on a balcony overlooking the square, sipping a beer."

In the end, I loved Cusco – spending over 9 hours exploring on my own, with the aid of my guidebook, and also touring with a guide when we returned from our trek. Many of the monuments dated from Spanish times, including churches crowded with worshippers who were admiring impressive Nativity scenes – in the cathedral a life-size Holy Family dominated a miniature village of animals and other figures; in the Compania de Jesus, the nativity was more in proportion, but included a platoon of soldiers on their way to the Stable; in El Triunfo, many of the women had brought their own 'infant Jesus' to church (a little doll in a basket or on a tray), and the processional statue of Mary stood ready for a parade later in the day. Some of the streets were lined with closed-looking mansions, with windows hiding behind shutters and massive doors barred to the street – but peering through one of those doorways, I was enchanted to discover a 16th century palace, now converted into a hotel, with courtyards lined with arcades and balconies overlooking hidden gardens. Behind the ornate Santa Clara archway, I found lines of market stalls selling a huge variety of fruits, including fragrant wild strawberries, and tradesmen offering to sharpen a knife or repair a bicycle. In nearby San Francisco Square, crowds of people were roaring with laughter as entertainers told funny stories to the accompaniment of rolling eyes and bouncing knees. Boxing Day in Cusco was not a day to rest at home!

Of course, the most impressive sights of Cusco were the Inca remains:

perfectly cut and fitted stones from the Inca Roca temple, set into the foundations of the Spanish archbishop's palace (the Spanish delighted in asserting themselves by building on top of former Inca sanctuaries) ... the Dominican monastery built above the Incas' most important temple, dedicated to the Sun God – the Inca walls were only discovered when an earthquake in 1950 tore the city apart; the Spanish-built structure fell down, revealing Inca walls totally undamaged by the quake ... and Qenko temple, just outside the town:

"I don't expect too much, since this site merits only 1 star in my guidebook, but I find it amazing ... what stonemasons the Inca were! It is basically one huge boulder with a labyrinth of natural cracks – the Inca masons added steps, benches, a massive altar and various niches, all in the heart of the rock. Priests alone would have been allowed inside the boulder, to sacrifice llamas and read their entrails. The surface of the rock is pitted and eroded into thousands of holes and cracks, enhanced in places with tiny, high steps leading to the summit where two stone 'hitching posts' stand – perhaps to anchor the Sun? With no written language, the Inca left no explanations of their religion; interpretation of all Inca sites is a matter of debate."

I also climbed up to the massive Sacsahuaman (pronounced 'sexy woman') Fortress, though I was surprised how little there was to see – our guide later said that it would have been 80% larger, but the Spanish took many of its stones to build their city, leaving just a large parade ground ringed by huge zig-zag walls and a few relics of gateways and towers.

Our local guide (proud of her Quechua ancestry, descendants of the Inca) explained the Inca mastery of stone: walls which leaned inward for stability when shaken by earthquake; stone blocks which were not square but trapezoid to better support each other; blocks cut with either concave or convex surfaces which clasped the stones tightly together without mortar (Inca stonework was locked in place horizontally instead of vertically, with virtually no foundations). What a contrast between Spanish walls built with thick mortar (which crumbled when the earth shook) and Inca walls which could move with the earth and yet still stand. Our guide talked of how the Spanish destroyed the essence of the Inca people when they burned the body of their last 'Inca' (emperor), instead of allowing his spirit to migrate from his mummy to the next 'Inca'. Their morale sank so low that they were unwilling to acknowledge their origins, to eat traditional food or even to speak their own language – only in the 1970's did the Quechua people once again start taking pride in their heritage. We were approached by a native family group asking if we would like them to make a sacrifice on our behalf to Pachamama (the earth mother) – they belonged to one of the families considered to have a hereditary special link to the gods. Quechua religion was complicated, our guide explained – they were devoutly Catholic, yet blended their Catholicism with ancient cults, worshipping Christ in the form of Vilcabamba (their top god) and Mary as Pachamama. Even during the Mass, they sang songs in praise of both the gods of nature and also Jesus.

The highlight of the entire tour was the 4-day Inca Trail trek, which started with a bumpy bus ride packed in alongside our baggage and a crew of tough-looking escorts, passing through rolling fertile farmlands before plunging down a series of hairpin bends into the Urubamba Valley (the Sacred Valley) to Ollantaytambo village. It bustled with Inca Trail activity: the main square was heaving with salesmen (trying to sell sunhats, rain ponchos and wooden trekking poles) and women wearing hats that looked like a shallow basket, made of felt and decorated with safety pins – I looked into one of these hats, to find the woman was keeping her coca leaves inside! The roads were blocked by a crowd of porters waiting for their groups, some wearing orange ponchos and flat woven hats, others dressed in red-patterned ponchos and bright knitted caps. The latter were our porters, all farmers from the tiny village of Misiminai (near Ollantaytambo, but inaccessible to vehicles) who earned extra income as porters during the trekking season. At our first campsite we were formally introduced to them, learning that they ranged in age from 16-50 years old, and would carry up to 45kg weight each … and also that some of them were practising the tradition of 'indefinite trial marriage'.

There was a pause in the village while all our baggage was transferred from the bus into a battered pick-up which hurtled off down the track, with our porters piled on top of the load. Meanwhile we had a few minutes to explore the village, an Inca site in its own right:

"Huge, neat terraces lead up to a ruined fortress; other roofless structures cling to the cliffs – once Inca storage houses. No time to climb up

there, but the village itself is fascinating. Alleyways run out of the main square, all neatly cobbled, some with stone channels of fast-flowing mountain water running through the middle. Most of the buildings rise from foundations of massive Inca stones, though imposing gateways now lead only to muddy yards where ducks and geese roam free."

A short drive now, along a narrow, muddy single-track road to Chilca, past herds of goats and cows guarded by cheery children waving to us as we passed ... then the trek began. I was nervous whether I would have enough stamina and strength, but the first section was easy – like a stroll through a botanic garden. Our Peruvian guide (Alvaro) stopped again and again to point out interesting plants – biting off the tip of a 'gravus' leaf to extract a strong thread once used to make rope; squashing a cochineal bug between his fingers to show us the red dye; giving us samples of leaves whose peppery taste was used to flavour local 'chicha' beer. The red and yellow carriages of the Machu Picchu train startled us with loud hooting as it sped past, laden with excited tourists. Then, across the river, we spotted a hubbub of buses and trucks ... big gangs of porters were running over a suspension bridge and powering up a rocky path ahead of us. Only now was the real trek beginning!

No more gentle introductions – now the route took us steeply up a narrow track enclosed by high hedges and walls, the sweat pouring off us in the midday sun. A lunch stop provided a short respite – and an introduction to our luxurious camping style, with a dining table and chairs (no perching on rocks or walls, as in Nepal). Then we slithered into a deep gorge, only to have to plod up the other side towards our overnight stop near Llachtapachta Inca site. However, it was an early camp since we had been obliged to start out earlier than normal: the Inca Trail was to be closed for the New Year period, to anyone who had not started out by midday. So we had plenty of time to explore this first Inca site – a vast array of terraces which provided food for Machu Picchu and (above the terraces) lines of houses, stores and a few defensive towers:

"First a scramble up terrace after terrace, all now unused, until we reach the residential part of the site. Roofs were thatched, so are long gone, but the walls stand firm – each group of tiny homes clustered around a central courtyard, each home containing just a row of alcoves and no fireplace (presumably cooking was done outside in the courtyard?). Then downhill to a *circular temple – once again it is clear how the Inca venerated the rocks: this tiny structure is perched on top of a huge boulder, the tip of which projects into the sacred area to form an altar."*

The campsite was idyllic, looking back down the valley towards the imposing mountains which enclose the Urubamba Valley – and as we admired the view, a condor soared high above the crags around us.

Our guide had promised that the next day would start with a flat section to a village, followed by a steep section – I had yet to learn what Andean 'flat' and 'steep' mean! We plodded steadily up the side of the valley, walking on muddy paths beneath lush trees till finally we reached the upper reaches of the stream and a tiny hamlet. Now it was a steep climb uphill, playing 'put and take' all the way with our porters – they moved faster than us, but stopped more often to rest their loads on well-used and conveniently positioned flat rocks by the track (I did not realise at first that these resting spots were part of the carefully designed Inca trails). Feeling I had managed the 'steep' section well, I joined the rest of the group sitting in the shade of a little house by the trail – sampling a little of the 'chicha' (maize beer) which the porters were quaffing from huge mugs:

"Oh dear! This was the village our guide had mentioned – now the steep part was to commence! It's into bottom gear now, at first very hard because the path is cut into steps which are each higher than my normal stride. But soon I'm back to a steady pace on a steep dirt and rock trail – I can switch off and plod on, at approximately the same speed as the porters. It's HOT now, so I'm walking from shade spot to shade spot, stopping to write this beside a stone irrigation channel: fresh cool green shade, with the gurgle and splash of water – bliss!"

The sight of our dining tent and table across the valley encouraged me onward, though I tried not to look beyond, to where a few laden porters were already toiling upwards towards the Pass at the top of the valley. No doubt that was where our afternoon's trekking would take us! In fact, the afternoon's walk was more pleasant than I had expected, since we entered the cloud forest (at 3000m) where twisted trees hung with lichen and Spanish moss, provided shade from the burning sun:

"It's a botanic walk again! We pass beneath dangling showers of pink and white 'Macha Macha' bells – an odd flower, hard as plastic yet so

sensitive that it drops to reveal its stamen at the slightest touch. A glorious fuschia tree makes a violent splash of red by the track, and the branches of an ancient Queuna tree are glowing with the red leaves of hundreds of bromeliads. Another Queuna has a peeling trunk, gleaming salmon pink beneath the bark. Winding between the big trees are sinuous lichen-hung branches of rhododendron – what a sight this path must be when they are in bloom! The path is littered with huge striped hairy caterpillars, falling from the trees and waving their heads in confusion as to which way to go next."

Only the last part of the day's climb is recorded in my diary as 'HARD' – we emerged from the cloud forest to ascend high Inca steps, squeezed between rocks and bushes so there was no way around them (how long were the legs of those Inca runners?). But the campsite made up for the difficulty – placed on the edge of a terrace at 3800m (12,500ft), above the tree line so there was nothing to block the view of peaks, cliffs and wide, open sky.

It was becoming evident that I was the least fit of our group (perhaps the oldest too?), so next day I started ahead of everyone else, hoping to reach the summit of the Pass alongside them. The route was painfully steep, partly on a muddy track, partly a stone path and partly steps … but what a delight to encounter so much birdlife along the way – fat wrens, reddish thrushes and jewel-coloured humming birds darting from side to side of the path, drinking from tiny red flowers on the bushes nearby. The speediest members of the group steamed past me, followed by the 'tent porters' (each day, our guides were sending the fastest porters, lightly laden only with our tents, to grab the best spots in the next campsite – the advantages of experience!), but I was pleased to reach the summit of the Warmiwanusca Pass (4200m/ 14,000ft) in the middle of the group. I was less pleased to hear that we had another Pass to conquer … before lunch!

"The path is amazing! At first a flight of very steep stone steps, then alternating paved path and shallower steps. We are in a valley which seems totally remote and shut off from the world – the only sounds are the very faint and distant rush of water, the chirrups of occasional birds and the hum of insects. The silence is so deep that it quickly swallows up the footsteps and chatter of walkers passing me as I sit to write. And yet, through this remote valley runs a perfectly made 'motorway' – the original Inca pathway (though

regularly maintained for trekkers), complete with frequent raised benches for porters to rest their loads."

A combination of slow walking and stops to record impressions in my diary, meant that I was last to the lunch stop – but still arrived before the food was served. The fastest members of the group had been early enough to visit another small Inca site nearby, but most had simply waited around for their food on a dusty shadeless terrace; I did not regret my leisurely pace! The rest of the day took us through a marshy area, where water dripped from the rocks and dribbled between the stones of the path, while rustic wooden bridges took us across the main branches of the stream. Amid this morass was another official campsite, and porters from one of the other groups were setting up tents on whatever dry hillocks they could find – but our porters had been told to continue on … and on… Across another gentle pass where the stone path was built out on to a man-made embankment beside sheer rock cliffs – again the work of Inca engineers, who had even added 'laybys' reaching out into the abyss, originally used for communication by flashing mirrors or blowing conch shells. At one point, it was impossible to build alongside the cliff, so those engineers had enlarged a crack in a boulder and cut steps down through its heart (the so-called 'Inca Tunnel').

In a blur of rain-laden cloud, with thunder rolling in the nearby mountains, we reached our campsite, located on soft wet peat where our crew had laid armfuls of reeds in an attempt to make a solid base for the tents. Why had we pushed on so hard to reach this miserable spot? However, as evening drew on, the choice was justified – we had glimpses of spectacular mountain scenery all around us. Early next morning we rose to find the cloud had rolled away and the whole view was revealed – range after range of snow-capped mountains. Close to us was the massive conical block of Salkantay (6271m), divided from its twin Umantay by a deep gorge. A jumble of dark peaks reached towards an ethereal strip of snow gleaming on the glaciers of Pumasillo, while further east was a great open space filled with fluffy white cloud – the dank wet Selva jungle, part of the Amazonian rainforest:

"As we watch, the sunlight creeps across the dark ridges, transforming them to soft green and russet, highlighting each ridge with shadow. The cloud sinks first from the summit of Pumasillo, leaving the tiniest snow-cone

peeping through, then peels right back from Salkantay, allowing the sun to sparkle on every snowy ridge and rock. Finally, the light reaches the peaks to the south, thickly forested slopes culminating in the glaciers and snow of the 'mountain of sacred tears', Mount Veronica (5750m)."

Our crew assumed that, for our last breakfast, we would not want to lose the view – so they erected no tent and we regaled ourselves on pancakes and jam, while gazing in awe at this glorious Andean spectacle. By the time we were packed up and leaving, the cloud had ascended from the jungle to hide the mountains – the other groups climbing from their campsites would not experience this sight. How privileged we were!

This was the last time we would see our porters – they were going to speed through to the town of Aguas Calientes, dropping their loads and boarding the train back to their homes immediately. So there was a ceremony to complete before they departed. We had all donated gifts (torches, pens, T-shirts, trainers and, most popular, tiny radios – all acquired before the trek) and these were divided by raffle, accompanied by formal thanks. Then we were off, not following the route used by Hiram Bingham when he discovered Machu Picchu in 1911, but instead taking an ancient Inca route only re-discovered in the 1980s:

"Wow! This is an amazing path! Solid rocks are cut into steps, steep slopes are paved with massive blocks smooth enough to run across. One huge boulder is cut into 32 shallow steps, carved from the living rock. We descend into the sound-absorbing jungle of bamboo and moss-clad trees, hearing only the tinkle of running water ... plus heavy footsteps and gasping breath! Then comes the distant whistle of the Machu Picchu train and the faint whirr of helicopter blades – we are emerging from the remote Andean valleys back to the realm of mass tourism."

We had more Inca sites to visit at the start of the day, including Winaywayma (translated as 'live forever' or perhaps 'the fountain of youth'). Once more there were abundant terraces and storehouses, the keys to Inca agricultural success ... and a circular temple crowned the site, from which rock-cut channels descended the slope carrying water to 16 miniature stone baths, used probably only for ceremonial purposes. But our minds were now fixed firmly on our goal, following an easy stone path until suddenly we were faced with an almost vertical flight of extremely high steps. I climbed (on hands and knees) up to an Inca wall, then along a steep path, higher and higher till I spotted Alvaro waiting patiently (in his poncho, since it was drizzling with rain). Welcome to the Gate of the Sun! At last, I had reached the Inca entrance to the sacred city of Machu Picchu – and there it was, nestled in a hollow within a rocky ridge, a blur of grey walls speckled with the brilliantly coloured clothing of tourists … much larger than I had expected, after seeing so many other small Inca sites during the trek, with terraces of buildings reaching far down into the valley.

As the day drew to a close and the rain increased, we hustled only through the edge of the site – saving our explorations till the next day. We jumped on board one of the tourist buses, swooping back and forth down the tight hairpins of the access road to the valley below:

"A couple of children in Inca-style tunics wave as we pass (on their way home after a day posing as photo models, no doubt) – but one is determined to turn one last profit. He shouts 'Goodbye' loudly, then runs down the pedestrian short-cut in time to shout again as we emerge from our hairpin ... then again ... and again. He accompanies us all the way to the valley, giving us at least ten 'Goodbyes', then leaps aboard the bus to circulate with his donation bag – he makes a good sum!"

Overnight was spent in a hostel in Aguas Calientes, a jumble of shacks and half-built houses, every ground floor filled with a restaurant or bar, every two-storey building offering 'rooms with hot water'. Most remarkable of all, the railway line ran right through the heart of the town, converted into a road lined with market stalls which were all cleared whenever a train was due. Further up the street lay the Hot Baths, after which the town was named:

"A quick wash with soap at the overflow pipes from the pool, then into the main bath (avoiding the very hot and the icy cold tubs!) – relaxingly warm, thick green water over a gravel bed. The barman, stripped to the waist to show off his rippling muscles, prepares cold beers and Pisco Sour cocktails to be served in the pool, where we bob about chatting, drinking, laughing ..."

The last day of the Millennium started early for us, so that we could catch the first bus back up to Machu Picchu (at 6am) – the site was closing early so that the President could visit on this special day, and we wanted maximum time for our sightseeing. Alvaro was passionate and excited to be here on the last day of the 20th century – his explanations of the site were laced with wonder, speaking of 'the harmony of man and nature' and 'the site of peace' (strangely, the white water of the Urubamba River calms as it passes Machu Picchu, churning again into rapids once the city is left behind):

"It is certainly an amazing site! From this terrace we can gaze out at the Upper Town (marked by the circular Temple of the Sun) and the Lower Town, with its jumble of walls, doors and windows. Above it all, lie the main temples, dominated in turn by the four holy peaks and the ranges of mountains which ring the city."

The tour was confusing … there was no certainty about the purpose of any of the structures here, as in all Inca sites, and Alvaro spent much of his time dispelling the theories of Hiram Bingham and replacing them with other interpretations of the site. I listened with half an ear but was more impressed by the dramatic location of this sacred city – fully revealed by a perfect day of sunshine. We climbed through narrow passageways between massive stone walls which covered the hillside above the deep chasm of the Urubamba River, looping right around the site. Passing a shady courtyard around an unusually shaped rock, supposedly the Temple of Pachamama (Mother Earth), I was attracted by the pounding rhythm of a drum – inside the courtyard, a family of New Age Americans were pressing their foreheads and palms to the sacred rock, humming loudly in worship:

"One more temple to see – the Temple of the Condor (called the 'Prisons' by Hiram Bingham). A lot of what Alvaro has said, seems spurious to me, but here I can see his point. A triangular rock is carved with a beak and a huge collar, while two neighbouring rocks have been enhanced with stones to resemble the wings of a condor in flight. Behind the two wings are man-sized niches where royal mummies could be brought out for their regular 'sun-bath'."

Left to explore on my own, I decided to ascend the sacred peak of Huayna Picchu (overlooking the city). The first part of the climb was familiar – descending then ascending again on a path cut into rock steps, in many places barely wide enough for two people to pass, in other places so steep that I had to grab for the hawser rope provided to help visitors. The path led to the 'photographic summit' – an original Inca signalling terrace with a spectacular view over the ruined city below. The climb from here to the jumble of rocks forming the actual summit, was more challenging:

"We have to pass another Inca tunnel, this time a tight squeeze into a low narrow cave from which the only exit is a set of steps cut from the rock. To pass through, I have to take off my backpack and hat and push them ahead of me. Some visitors are already panicking here, and even more panic as they have to step from rock to rock on the vertiginous summit. Then the descent (a one-way system to avoid a traffic jam in the cave) starts with a slither down a rock slide (with no barrier to prevent you continuing over the edge), followed by a steep stairway hanging over the precipice ... a slow journey, dodging past tourists who are shaking in terror: were they not warned by their guides?"

We returned to Cusco on the afternoon train, after waiting around in cafes where televisions were tracking the Millennium celebrations around the world. Our own celebration came back in Cusco, where we had booked (very expensive) tickets for the extravaganza at Sacsahuayan Fortress, seated with the richest Peruvians in the grandstands while behind us 'ordinary' Peruvians perched all over the illuminated rocks. Every time I looked around, there seemed to be more and more of them, like a scene from the horror film 'The Birds':

"At last it starts: a bit of Quechua chanting, then a very impressive scene as 400 runners carrying flaming torches, spread themselves over terrace after terrace, each level progressively illuminated as they arrive. A confusing bit of jumping around and shouting (supposedly 'defending against the weather') is followed by a huge mock battle on the plaza below us. Finally, a church parade files across the back of the plaza while a wild pagan dance whirls across the front (the 'fusion of two religions'). As midnight arrives there is much embracing and well-wishing, and a thousand costumed dancers from all over Peru surge on to the plaza, joined by the audience. We slink away to our beds!"

In the end, I greeted the new millennium in a very different way than I had originally intended, amid crowds of strangers instead of isolated in a desert. Yet the whole experience of the Inca Trail and the mysterious sacred city of Machu Picchu (hidden so deeply in the mountains that the Spanish never found it) gave me a memorable start to the 21st century.

Acknowledgements

OVER THE YEARS, SO MANY fellow-travellers had asked whether I was planning to use my diaries to write a book, and my answer was always 'perhaps one day' – but that day would never have come without the enforced leisure time provided by the Covid lockdown in 2020. Even that was not enough to convince me it was time to write my book, so my greatest thanks must go to my friend Mary Kerslake for nagging and harassing me until I finally got it started!

Thanks also to many other friends, especially Jan Bates and Gill Weghofer, who gave up their time to critically study my writings and offer invaluable advice … and to my friends Gloria and Colin McBean for helping me to master the internet skills needed to tell the world that my book was finally on its way.

I am hugely grateful to Mirador Publishing, and especially my editor Sarah, for patiently guiding me through the intricacies of publishing with unceasing encouragement and enthusiasm.

Many thanks are due to Cath d'Alton for producing clear and informative maps, again with incredible patience as I struggled to explain exactly what I wanted.

Most of all, my eternal thanks are due to my God, who created this wonderful world we live in, and has allowed me to see so much of it – Praise Him!

Lightning Source UK Ltd.
Milton Keynes UK
UKHW010044191220
375516UK00001B/12